China - America Relations: Review and Analysis
(Volume 1)

Editor-in-Chief: Ni Feng

Paths International Ltd

社会科学文献出版社
SOCIAL SCIENCES ACADEMIC PRESS (CHINA)

China-America Relations: Review and Analysis

Acknowledgements

We sincerely appreciate the input of Social Sciences Academic Press's president Xie Shouguang and Zhou Li, Li Yanling, Zhao Shixiong, Feng Xuan, Lu Bei at Social Sciences Academic Press served as editors and support staff. They have done much work in arranging the preparation of the English version.

We also sincerely appreciate the hard work of translators Jiang Hang and Lu Michelle Yin, as well as the final proof-readers, Leila Kandret and Eric Levy. Without their diligent work this English version would not exist.

Finally, we especially appreciate the financial support in the publication of this book from China Book International, supported by the General Administration of Press and Publication and the Information Office of the State Council of China.

December, 2011

CONTENTS

List of Contributors

Ni Feng, the vice-director, researcher and doctoral supervisor of the Institute of American Studies, Chinese Academy of Social Sciences, and the vice-director and secretary general of the Chinese Association for American Studies

Wang Jisi, professor of the School of International Studies, Beijing University

Cheng Chunhua, engaged in post-doctoral research at the School of International Studies, Beijing University.

Huang Ping, researcher of the Chinese Academy of Social Sciences and director of the Institute of American Studies, Chinese Academy of Social Sciences.

He Xingqiang, the doctoral candidate of the Department of America, Graduate School of the Chinese Academy of Social Sciences.

Wang Wei, research assistant of the Institute of American Studies, Chinese Academy of Social Sciences and doctor.

Zhou Jing, research assistant of the Institute of American Studies, Chinese Academy of Social Sciences and doctor.

Chen Baosen, the honorary academician of the Chinese Academy of Social Sciences and the researcher of the Institute of American Studies.

Yuan Peng, director and researcher of the Institute of American Studies, China Institute of Contemporary International Relations.

Wang Honggang, assistant director of the Institute of American Studies, China Institute of Contemporary International Relations.

Wang Rongjun, the Master of History, vice researcher of the Institute of American Studies, China Institute of Contemporary International Relations.

He Xingqiang, the Doctor of International Politics, the vice researcher of the Institute of American Studies, China Institute of Contemporary International Relations, mainly engaged in the studies on the domestic politics of America with interest groups and Congress as the main body, America's policies on trade with China and China-U. S. relations

The United States Under President Barack Obama

Ni Feng

Barack Obama was sworn in as the 44th President of the United States in front of the Lincoln Memorial in Washington D. C. on January 20, 2009. Approximately two million people from every corner of the United States flooded to the capital to witness this historic inauguration. According to Thomas L. Friedman, the well-known critic of The New York Times, "Nearly 233 years after our founding, 144 years after the close of our Civil War and 46 years after Martin Luther King Jr.'s 'I Have a Dream' speech, this crazy quilt of immigrants called Americans finally elected a black man, Barack Hussein Obama, as president."[1] As stated in an editorial by a Japanese media, "Obama's father was a black man raised in the Muslim faith, his mother is a white woman from Kansas, while he grew up in Hawaii. You cannot find a president combining so many nations, cultures and experiences in United States history."[2] Meanwhile, a similar question was raised in everyone's mind: whether Obama, who had already created history, could write another new history. His inauguration only ended the era of George W. Bush but did not start the new era yet.

I. Background of the United States Under Obama

Obama was elected the President of the United States at a significant time, when the only super power of the world encountered unprecedented challenges after the Cold War and was faced with a key choice.

Firstly, the United States was experiencing the most serious economic crisis since the Great Depression of the 1920's. The credit crisis caused by sub prime mortgage defaults spread rapidly. Bear Stearns was the first famous investment bank affected by the declining market. As the 5th largest investment bank of U. S., it was purchased by J. P. Morgan Chase on March 16, 2008. The two mortgage associations, including Fannie Mae and Freddie

---

1 [US] Thomas Friedman, "Radicals of the White House," *New York Times*, Jan. 21 2009.

2 "An Era Moving from Split to Dialogue," *Tokyo News* of Japan, Jan. 22, 2009.

Mac, were mired in difficulties and taken over by the U. S. government on September 7, 2008. Lehman Brothers, the 4th largest investment bank in the U. S. with a 158-year-history, appropriately known as "a cat with 19 lives" for its survival from a variety of tribulations. However, it was caught in the credit crisis, suffered the plummeting share prices, and thus had to file for bankruptcy on September 15, 2008. On the same day, the 3rd largest U. S. investment bank of the 94-year-old Merrill Lynch was sold to Bank of America for a total price of 44 billion USD, 29 USD for each share. On September 16, the American Federal Reserve Committee (Fed) authorized Federal Reserve Bank of New York to provide an emergency loan of 85 billion USD to America International Group (AIG), the insurance tycoon facing bankruptcy. Consequently, the U. S. government held about 80% of AIG shares. On September 21, Fed approved Goldman Sachs and Morgan Stanley to transform from investment banks to bank holding companies to protect the two banks from the Wall Street crisis. The bankruptcy, sale or transformation of the top five U. S. investment banks in succession ended the business mode of independent investment banks that Wall Street was once very proud.

Affected by the bankruptcy of investment banks, the U. S. stock market saw a significant decline. In 2008, Dow Jones Industrial Average (DJIA) dropped by 4488, down 33.8%, while the share prices of blue chips fell by more than 65%. Investors suffered a total loss of 7 trillion USD, equal to the whole profits in the previous six years, which was the most serious loss ever experienced since 1931. The crisis led to a significant decline of net family assets in the United States. As shown in statistics from the Federal Reserve Committee, the net family assets of the U. S. in 2008, with a decline by 18%, regressed to the level of 2004. The rate of decline in the 4th quarter of 2008 was at a record high of a half-century. By the end of 2008, the net assets of U. S. families decreased to 51.48 trillion USD, 11.2 trillion lower than 2007. The crisis also rapidly spread to production and consumption. Owing to credit constrictions, sluggish economy and flagging confidence of consumers, the domestic automobile sales dropped by 32% in October 2008, slumping into the bottom of monthly sales in recent 17 years with a sales volume of only 838,000. In this month, General Motors sold 169,000 automobiles with a decline of 45%, while Ford sold 132,000, dropping by 30%, and Chrysler sold 95,000, with a decline of 35%. The cash flow of the three major auto manufacturers in the U. S. faced constant danger, exerting the threat of bankruptcy over companies. The real estate market also shrank under the influence of the economic crisis. According to the statistics of U. S. Real Estate Tracking Company in August 2008, a record 820,000 houses were reclaimed, far more than the 224,000 houses by the end of 2006. As many as 1.2 million houses were reclaimed by banks by the end of

2008, accounting for 1/3 of the total number of houses for sale. About 1.9 million people lost their houses in 2009. According to the Fed, the unemployment rate reached 8.1% in February 2009, a record high of the past 25 years, and more than 4 million employment opportunities had fallen away since the beginning of the financial crisis.

Secondly, the U. S. became entangled in two wars. The unilateralism and militaristic policies of the George W. Bush administration not only greatly damaged the power of the United States, but also tarnished their international image. At the beginning of the 21st century, al-Qaeda terrorists under the leadership of Osama bin Laden launched a brutal attack against the United States, resulting in heavy casualties and loss of property. On the morning of September 11, 2001, four passenger jets were hijacked in a coordinated suicide attack and intentionally crashed into the Twin Towers of the World Trade Center in New York City and the Pentagon in Arlington, Virginia. Americans realized unprecedented unity to confront the attack, raising the approval rating of the George W. Bush administration to as high as 90%. All governments and their people showed great sympathy to the United States. Under these circumstances, the U. S. launched the War in Afghanistan with the authorization of UN, and rapidly overthrew the Taliban government that gave shelter to al-Qaeda. However, soon after the end of the War in Afghanistan, neo-conservatives shifted the political mobilization capacity obtained from the September 11th attacks to fight terrorism and regain power. The government adopted a foreign policy featuring unilateralism and a plan of "striking first," placing the U. S. beyond the international community, putting forward the concept of "axis of evil" and bypassed UN and forced to start the Iraq War despite the common objections of other countries, attempting to create a "new Roman Empire" of eternal hegemony. The U. S. saw unprecedented isolation during the Iraq War. World opinion strongly condemned the U. S. was strongly and was expressly opposed by most countries. Now it appears that the Iraq War was one of the most serious strategic errors in United States history, bringing even more profound effects to the U. S. and world politics than the September 11th attacks and led tocatastrophic consequences similar to that from the Vietnam War. The "hard power" and "soft power" of the U. S. was largely consumed by the war. The six-year war resulted in more than 4,000 deaths and 30,000 injuries of US military and a military expenditure of more than 740 billion USD, as well as various hidden costs, such as the interest on the loan for the war, investment loss, medical care expenses for injuries and accrued fees owing to the rising price of petroleum. According to the report of the Joint Economic Committee of the Senate and the House of Representatives, the United States had spent 1.3 trillion USD on the Iraq War from 2003 to 2008, equal to an expense of 16.5 thousand USD for each American family of four.

The misinformation provided by George W. Bush's advisors stated that Saddam Hussein and Osama Bin Laden were collaborating to produce nuclear weapons, thereby instigating the United States' declaration of war on Iraq. It was only after the war was it revealed that there were in fact no nuclear weapons being produced in Iraq. In addition to the Iraq War, the world was shocked by the abuse of Iraqi detainees at the Abu Ghraib prison by a small group of U. S. soldiers in 2004, which aroused deep public indignation. Although the soldiers involved were dishonorably discharged, their inappropriate actions hindered the world's view of the United States. Moreover, U. S. image was seriously damaged by U. S. politicians and the George W. Bush administration slandering Islam, turning a blind eye to Israel's organized military attack on the Palestine Liberation Organization (PLO), rejecting the Kyoto Protocol and insisting on unilateralism in Doha, Qatar round of trade talks of (World Trade Organization) WTO and some other issues.

Thirdly, the social cohesion of the U. S. saw a decline and a division into two opposing extremes, the striking expression of which was the increasingly fierce party politics. As shown in a study of Brookings Institution, about 40% congressmen politically stood the middle ground, but the figure dropped below 10% in recent years. In the Brookings Institution President Talbot's view, "in recent decades, the gerrymandering of congressional districts has tended to congregate liberals and conservatives, thus segregating them from each other, which turns the boundaries between districts into ideological battle lines. Polarization and the dysfunctions it causes at the federal level are reflected in the country at large. The electoral map of the USA is increasingly a patchwork of red and blue states and, within those states, red and blue counties. The purple is fading."[3] Another famous American scholar Fareed Zakaria also concerned that U. S. politics were dominated by money, special interests, emotional media and groups launching an ideological attack, which led to vicious debates on insignificant issues without going to the heart of the matter. Comprises cannot be reached and actions can hardly be adopted in such a state. The process was once highly efficient, but now falters. It provides a stage for party struggle instead of solving problems. In the previous three decades, the expanding special interests, large scale lobbying campaign and growing election expenses revealed the increasingly fierce party struggle of U. S. politics, thus resulting in the low operation efficiency."[4] He also pointed out that the party system of the U. S. actually encourages politicians to stick to their own

3 Talbott, Strobe. The Angels of Our Nature: Restoring Unity of Purpose and Civility of Discourse in America—The Challenge to Think Tanks and Universities, available at http://www.brookings.edu/speeches/2011/0207_civility_talbott.aspx?sc_lang=en.

4 Fareed Zakaria, *The Post-American World*, (US: China Citic Press, July 2009), 1st edition, P 204-205.

ideas or even stand back on its ground, and declaring to never surrender to the enemy, which facilitates them raising funds but causes catastrophic effect on the governance of the country."[5]

Fourthly, the U. S. was also challenged in terms of ideas and international system. Americans welcomed the end of the Cold War and the disintegration of the Soviet Union. As pointed out by a British economist, "Ironically, in the post-Cold War era, another Utopian ideology rose after the collapse of communism. A market fundamentalism has become the guiding theory in western countries, especially in Britain and the U. S."[6] As the U. S. regards itself as the model of global economy, it has continued to promote most countries to reduce government interference in finance and industry sector in the past 20 years. However, the global financial turmoil was mainly a result of the United States' excessively lax credit without the intervention of the government, which damaged the real estate market. Therefore, huge non-performing assets were generated on Wall Street, damaging the global financial system and leaving rooms for ubiquitous unlawful practices and corruption. The famous economist Alfred Stieglitz commented on this situation with the following, "The world envied our economy once. We told them you should transfer the power to the market if you wanted to be like us. But now, no one respects this model any longer after this crisis and they question our reputation. Everyone feels that is was us who brought about their sufferings."[7] In addition, the intervention of the U. S. government in the market after the financial crisis further prejudiced the prestige of the U. S. to sow the seed of laissez-faire capitalism.

While the U. S. stretched its influence to every corner of the world under the banner of "anti-terrorism," the world pattern was experiencing a profound change, "the rise of the rest" as described by Zakaria. According to the opening chapter of his famous work *The Post-American World*, "Look around. The tallest building in the world is now in Taipei, and it will soon be overtaken by one being built in Dubai. The world's richest man is Mexican, and its largest publicly traded corporation is Chinese. The world's biggest plane is built in Russia and Ukraine (sic), its leading refinery is under construction in India, and its largest factories are all in China. By many measures, London is becoming the leading financial center, and the United Arab Emirates is home to the most richly endowed investment fund. Once quintessentially American icons have been appropriated by

---

5 Ibid.

6 [UK] John Gray, "Crash Moments in the Power Decline of US," *The Observor*, Sept. 28 2008.

7 [US] Anthony Faiola, "The End to US-Style Capitalism?," *The Washington Post*, Oct. 10 2008.

foreigners. The world's largest Ferris wheel is in Singapore. Its number one caChina is not in Las Vegas but in Macao, which has also overtaken Vegas in annual gambling revenues. The biggest movie industry, in terms of both movies made and tickets sold, is Bollywood, not Hollywood. Even shopping, America's greatest sporting activity, has gone global. Of the top ten malls in the world, only one is in the United States; the world's biggest is in Beijing. Such lists are arbitrary, but it is striking that only ten years ago, America was at the top in many, if not most, of these categories. For the first time ever, we are witnessing genuinely global growth. This is creating an international system in which countries in all parts of the world are no longer objects or observers but players in their own right. It is the birth of a truly global order. At the politico-military level, we remain in a single superpower world. But in every other dimension—industrial, financial, educational, social, cultural—the distribution of power is shifting, moving away from American dominance. That does not mean we are entering an anti-American world. But we are moving into a post-American world, one defined and directed from many places and by many people."[8]

Henry Kissinger, another famous U.S, strategist, also agreed that the current international system was experiencing "the biggest change in 400 years." It referred to four trends: the rise of mass emerging powers; the overall decline of the Western countries; the eastward movement of world power; and outbreaks of numerous global issues.

In conclusion, U. S. President Obama encountered an unprecedented situation that no president had ever met. As stated in Obama's inaugural speech, "Our challenges may be new"[9] and "that we are in the midst of crisis is now well understood."[10] He also promised "The instruments with which we meet them may be new."[11] He said, "Today I say to you that the challenges we face are real. They are serious and they are many. They will not be met easily or in a short span of time. But know this America: They will be met."[12]

II. Internal and External Policies of Obama

In the presidential election of 2008, the political newcomer Barack Obama came out with the slogan of "Change" and "Yes, We Can!" in a country full of challenges and widespread discontent, and aroused the political enthusiasm of voters, especially young

---

8 [US] Fareed Zakaria, *The Post-American World*, (US: China Citic Press, July 2009), 1st edition, PX-XIII.

9 *President Barack Obama's Inangural Address,*http://www.whitehouse.gov/blog/inaugural-address/

10 Ibid.

11 Ibid.

12 Ibid.

voters, with his charisma and innovative election tactics. After having defeated the strong opponent Hillary Clinton in the primary election of the Democratic Party and won a major victory over John McCain, the candidate of the Republican Party, in the final vote, Obama successfully rotated the ruling party and became the host of the White House at a crucial time in U. S. history. However, the question remained on how he would lead Americans to stand behind their country make hard choices and protect the U. S. from the storm of war and recession.

1. Obama's Governing Principle and Style

Barack Obama is on the left wing of the Democratic Party. One of the most essential differences between the Democratic and Republican Parties lies in the role of the government in social and economic policies, i.e. the battle between the "big government" and "small government," which is also the main difference between "conservatism" and "liberalism." The Republican Party places great emphasis on individual liberty, opposes government intervention in social and individual liberty and advocates to lower tax and social welfare and cut public expenses. The Democrats pay more attention to human rights and social equity, stand for strengthening the protection of rights and interests of women, oppose racial discrimination, advocate to expand the power of the government to actively solve social and economic issues, increase public input, raise taxes and social welfare and facilitate social equity. In terms of foreign policies, the Republican Party stresses American interests and carries out unilateralism, while the Democratic Party attaches more importance to the value of human rights and social equity as well as international cooperation.

Conservatism has dominated the political ideas of the U. S. since the election of Ronald Reagan in 1981. Because of this, left wing Democrats must scrupulously abide by basic principles of the Democratic Party. Obama would continue in a development direction very different from the previous 30 years. He did not label his own policy program as an "ism," but he covered the best of different schools of thought, from Post-Keynesian to New Growth theory, in his brain trust. They had already started to draw up the economic program of the "left wing," including increasing taxes of the rich, reducing taxes for the middle class, enhancing the welfare for the lower class and creating jobs by vigorously supporting the emerging green energy enterprises.

Meanwhile, Obama also challenged the free-market dogma of Republicans. In his view, practices had denied the "old and discredited philosophy" that the free market, where everyone relies on himself, enables some people to become prosperous and will later benefit others.

Obama expressly stated in his inaugural speech that he would implement a "grand plan" as Roosevelt did in his "New Deal." The government would ambitiously construct roads, bridges, power grids, digital highways, solar energy applications, wind energy and soil resources, and reform the medical treatment and education. "Government can do, and must do."[13]

Regarding the relationship between the market and government, Obama said that "Nor is the question before us whether the market is a force for good or ill. Its power to generate wealth and expand freedom is unmatched. But this crisis has reminded us that without a watchful eye, the market can spin out of control. The nation cannot prosper long when it favors only the prosperous. The success of our economy has always depended not just on the size of our gross domestic product, but on the reach of our prosperity, on the ability to extend opportunity to every willing heart - not out of charity, but because it is the surest route to our common good."[14]

Within two years of the Obama administration, many major policies and decisions have abided by the basic policy logic of the Democratic Party adopted since Roosevelt's New Deal. To cope with the economic crisis, Obama carried out government intervention on a large scale and strengthened government supervision, including the fiscal stimulus plan of 787.2 billion USD put forward once he took the office of President, known as "Obama New Deal," and the comprehensive financial regulatory reform program officially announced in June 2009. In terms of social policies, he attempted to complete the unfinished tasks of the "Great Society" plan of President Johnson. The health care reform plan, the greatest social welfare system reform in several decades, was finally signed on March 2010. The plan will enable some 30 million people to obtain medical insurance and raise the coverage of U. S. medical insurance coverage from 85% to 95%, only one step away from 100%. The government will also subsidize the low-income population. For the competitiveness promotion of the country, he advocated to increase input on infrastructures and research and development of high technology and develop a high-speed railway system and new energy technology, like the construction of inter-state highway and "Apollo mission" in 1950s and 1960s. He even sought the support to this action by using the slogan "our generation's Sputnik moment"[15] in various occasions. At the same time, he proposed the "Plan for Doubling U. S. Exports in Five Years" to the federal government in 2010 and

---

13 Ibid.

14 Ibid.

15 Author note: the former Soviet Union launched the first artifical earth satellite in 1957. Greatly shocked by the satellite, Americans considered US to be defeated by the Soviet Union and called the moment as "Sputnik Moment." Since then, US government had increased the input in education and technology. It established lead again against the Soviet Union and had developed numerous new technologies, industries and jobs.

employed many kinds of government measures to enlarge the export of the U. S. These policies can be considered to be the contemporary version of "Roosevelt New Deal."

As a pragmatist, Obama also timely adjusted policies based on new situations and attempted to reach a compromise with various political forces. Obama vigorously promoted non-partisan politics. In the Democratic National Convention in July 2004, Obama had made a famous speech named "Audacity of Hope," focusing on eliminating partisan and race resentment and realizing the dream of "one America." He said, "There is not a U. S. of liberalism or U. S. of conservatism. There's the United States of America."[16] He won overnight fame with this speech and was successfully elected as the United States Senator. During the presidential election in 2008, he made commitments, saying he would change the way of Washington, realize the "new politics" beyond the ideology based on multi-party cooperation, "usher in the post-partisan era" and create an "effective government."

Although he is a Democrat, his idol is Lincoln, a Republican. The theme of his inauguration ceremony, "New Birth of Freedom," can be traced back to the Gettysburg Address of Lincoln in 1863. He followed the footprints of Lincoln in the inauguration ceremony as well as in the President's tour. He incorporated the government of the old Washington D. C. where Lincoln pardoned black salves in 1862 and the Ford Theater where Lincoln was murdered in 1865 in this tour, seemingly to bridge divergences of parties.

Despite being on the left wing of the Democratic Party, he established a strong administration team, with moderate Democrats and technologists as the main body, having appointed Hillary Clinton as Secretary of State, his primary competitor in the campaign for Democratic Party presidential candidate and Robert Gates, the moderate Republican U. S. Secretary of Defense. Since his inauguration, he appealed for the end of partisan war almost at every occasion. In his first Congressional Address, he called on "everyone to get beyond partisan barrier." According to his first *State of the Union Address*, "We have to recognize that we face more than a deficit of dollars right now. We face a deficit of trust."[17] He called on the Democratic and Republican Party to end the dispute over beliefs and to jointly find a way out of current difficulties. He also indicated his open mind to constructive suggestions of the Republican Party, his willingness to maintain the

---

16 Barack Obama, *2004 Democratic National Convention Keynote Address*, available at http://www.americanrhetoric.com/speeches/convention2004/barackobama2004dnc.htm.

17 President Barack Obama State of Union Address 2010, available at http://www.nowpublic.com/world/president-obama-state-union-address-2010-full-text-2564747.html

communication between both parties by regular meetings of the President and leaders of both parties and his hope to promote the reform and legislation upon the cooperation between two parties.

With regard to the major difference of both parties, i.e. the dispute between the "big government" and "small government," Obama expressed in this way, "Our problem lies in the efficiency of government instead of the big or small government." As reflected these political ideas, Obama's public policies regarded the government efficiency as the focus instead of the ideology. The main direction of public policies of Congress under the control of the Obama administration and Democratic Party in the next four years would be to change the political direction of the U. S. and execute liberal internal and external policies. However, they would come to a compromise with conservatives if necessary so as to legislate for key issues.

The most important bazsis for Obama to carry out the "reform" was his high popularity obtained in the election of 2008 and the obvious advantage of Democratic Party over the Republican Party in the Congress and the Senate, respectively reaching 57:41 and 256:179.

2. Obama's Economic Policies

Among Obama's domestic and foreign policies, the most crucial and emergent problem is how to cope with the most serious economic crisis since the Great Depression and rejuvenate the economy, as the economy is the "source of U. S. power."

We can surely find similarities in the measures respectively adopted by George W. Bush and the Obama administration to cope with the financial crisis. For example, both administrations had proposed the financial stability plan and fiscal stimulus package. However, we will discover, through detailed studies, that the two governments had different understandings of the crisis. In George W. Bush's opinion, the economic crisis was a periodic crisis instead of a structural crisis, so the government only needed to employ a short-term and across-the-board tax cut and economic stimulus package. However, Obama regarded the long-term economic structural imbalance as the cause of the economic crisis. Therefore, in addition to the measures to stimulate the economic growth in the short term, Obama also increased input on measures to stimulate long-term economic growth. As the main feature, the Obama administration's economic policies integrated fiscal and tax, monetary, financial, trade and industrial policies, attempted to rebuild the basis for the economic growth of the U. S. and gave consideration to "equity" at the same time. The specific plans mainly included increasing the input on public expenditure, such as innovation, science and technology, infrastructure, education and green industry as well as the input on the new energy and climate change.

With long-term planning and consideration, Obama's economic policies attached more importance to an extensive and sustained economic recovery. As described in the new edition of *National Security Strategy Report* by the Obama government, "We must build a stronger foundation for economic growth. That foundation must include access to a complete and competitive education for every American; a transformation of the way that we produce and use energy, so that we reduce our dependence on fossil fuels and lead the world in creating new jobs and industry; access to quality, affordable health care so our people, businesses, and government are not constrained by rising costs; and the responsible management of our Federal budget so that we balance our priorities and are not burdened by debt. To succeed, we must also ensure that America stays on the cutting edge of the science and innovation that supports our prosperity, defense, and international technological leadership."[18]

Obama's short-term policies mainly aimed to help the U. S. economy get out from the recession as soon as possible. The following measures were applied:

On February 10, 2009, Timothy Geithner, the U. S. Secretary of Treasury, declared the new round of comprehensive financial rescue plans in Washington. Under the name of "Financial Stability Plan," it would improve the transparency and accountability of the rescue of the banking sector by the government. To be specific, the government and the private sector would jointly establish an investment fund to help banks clean up non-performing assets, conditionally invest for banks that need extra help and promote the liquidity of the credit market. Geithner named it the Financial Stability Plan (FSP) to distinguish it from the Bush administration. He promised that the government would provide a maximum of 2 trillion USD to receive the non-performing assets of 500 billion USD to 1 trillion banks in trouble, and meanwhile expand the new loan support program of the Federal Reserve to 1 trillion USD, so as to provide finance to revive the credit market, solve the troubled assets of the banking sector and thus to stabilize the financial market.

On February 13, 2009, the Senate and the House approved Obama's economic stimulus plan, named the *American Recovery and Reinvestment Act*, which was signed by Obama on February 17. As the largest economic stimulus plan after the World War II, it amounted to a total of 787.2 billion USD. One third of the plan, i.e. 288 billion USD, would be put into personal and corporate tax cuts. According to the details of the plan, the

---

18 *National Security Strategy*.available at http://www.whitehouse.gov/sites/default/files/rss_viewer/national_security_strategy.pdf

focus of whole tax cut plan would be the tax cut of 250 billion USD for individuals and families, and 95% of U. S. families would receive tax relief.145 billion USD would be put into long-term investment, including road and bridge construction, the development of new energies, the infrastructures of the broadband network, medical insurance and internet technology investment etc. 144 billion USD would be invested in financial aid to state governments to avoid large-scale redundancy, especially the unemployment of teachers and nurses. 82 billion USD would be used to help the unemployed, especially the poor unemployed.

On March 18, 2009, the Federal Reserve announced that it would purchase the long-term national debt of 300 billion USD and the institutional debt of 850 billion USD (mainly referring to the mortgage bonds guaranteed by "Fannie Mae and Freddie Mac"), which symbolized a new stage of the quantitative accommodative monetary policy.

The "Cash for Clunkers" program, started since July 1, 2009, provided a subsidy for each car owner of U. S. to encourage them to replace the old car of high-energy consumption with the new car of low energy consumption. As shown in the statistics from the U. S. Department of Transportation, approximately 700 thousand cars were sold under this program, with a total refund of 2.87 billion USD.

On March 18, 2010, President Obama officially signed the *Act on Hiring Incentives to Restore Employment* (HIRE), a job-creation package of 18 billion USD, which would provide a tax preference of 13 billion USD to private enterprises to improve the employment situation in 2010.

On March 26, 2010, the U. S. government released the mortgage default prevention plan valued at 14 billion USD, intending to incorporate unemployed owners or owners whose house price was lower than the mortgage value in the federal housing plan, to reduce their pressure on repayment and lower the foreclosure rate. The 14 billion USD needed in this plan was derived from the 75 billion USD "owner stability fund." The new plan would give homeowners with a home value of 3 million to 4 million USD the opportunity to revise or reduce the mortgage before 2012, in order to stabilize the housing market.

Three employment promotion policies were adopted in the new fiscal year of 2010. 30 billion USD was employed to the tax deduction for companies taking on new staff. In 2010, the company could obtain a corresponding tax reduction by employing a new staff member, while the amount of relief would depend on the work position. For example, an enterprise that has newly hired an employee with an annual wage of 60,000 USD could get a tax deduction of 4,000 USD. About 150 billion USD was contributed to ease the pressure on the finance of state governments. According to the plan, the federal government would provide financial support to state governments to prevent them from reducing important social service (such as education, medical care and unemployment security) and increasing taxes, so as to increase or maintain jobs. 30 billion USD would be used to finance small banks. The government would provide funds to small banks and community banks in order to back banks to release loans to small and medium-sized enterprises.

Obama attempted to establish a brand new foundation to promote the sustainable economic development of the U. S. as shown in long-term policies, which included:

Strengthening financial regulation. In June 2009, the Obama government published the *Financial Regulatory Reform: A New Foundation*, as a prelude to the greatest financial regulatory reform of the U. S. since 1932. Its core was to largely increase the authority of the Federal Reserve Committee. The institution would be responsible for supervising the systematic risk over the U. S. financial sector, mainly for large financial institutions and financial market as well as all non-bank financial institutions of the same scale and complexity with the above. In addition, the institution would also be responsible for the supervision over the executive pay of these companies and the trade system of financial market. Moreover, the new Consumer Financial Protection Agency (CFPA) would be established according to this plan, which would be endowed with authority over the current regulatory institutions. It also suggested to improve the financial regulatory level. The plan was approved by Congress on May 20, 2010. It could be regarded as a milestone in the financial and economic history, as it was the most comprehensive and strict financial regulatory reform act since the Glass Steagall Act enacted in 1933 after the Great Depression.

New Energy Strategy. According to the Obama government, new industries may emerge upon the long-term investment in renewable energy sources, and will create more jobs and revive economic vitality. Based on the strategy, he would improve the current power grid system, incorporate solar energy, wind energy and geothermal energy in an integrated power system of the U. S. to maximize the service efficiency of the national power grid and develop energy-saving vehicles. He also planned to transfer the capital of petroleum import to the development of solar energy, wind energy and geothermal energy, thus reducing their dependence on petroleum. In this respect, Obama planned to invest 150 billion USD to studies on new energies, provide tax preference for relevant enterprises and create five million jobs in the next 10 years. According to the plan, one million locally produced, rechargeable hybrid cars should be put into use by 2015; 10% electric energy in the U. S. should be derived from renewable energy sources by 2012; and the greenhouse gas emissions should be lowered by 80% compared to 1990 by the end of 2050 based on the "Total Control and Carbon Emissions Trading." The energy system of the U. S. would see a revolutionary change if the plan succeeds. Then it will further change the production and life style of the whole of America, playing an equal role as the internet technology industrial revolution in history.

Plan for doubling U. S. exports. In Obama's opinion, the U. S. shall learn an important lesson from this financial crisis: strategic transformation is necessary for the U. S. macro economic policies, including turning the previous dependence on consumption to export growth and get back to the real economy. In January 2010, Obama proposed the "Plan for Doubling U. S. Exports" in his State of Union Address, aiming to double the total export of goods and service in the next five years, drive the economic growth and create two million employment opportunities. Obama signed an executive order in March 2010 and established the "Export Promotion Cabinet," made up by more than 10 members from relevant departments, including U. S. Treasury Secretary, Agriculture Secretary, Commerce Secretary, Labor Secretary, Energy Secretary, Transportation Secretary, Director of the Office of Budget and Management, President's economic policy adviser, National Security Review Commission and the governor of U. S. Export-Import Bank. On September 16, 2010, the "Export Promotion Cabinet" announced a plan of "National Export Initiative," which proposed to enhance the trade financing of the Export-Import Bank, including the new trade loan of 2 billion USD each year exclusively for small and medium-sized enterprises. Obama also proposed to reform the export control system of the U. S. to achieve two goals simultaneously: controlling the export of core technologies of the U. S. to ensure national security and promoting the international competitiveness of key industries of the U. S.

3. Obama's Social Policies

Compared to the Republican Party, Democrats are more representative of interests of middle and lower classes and more focused on equality and justice, so their social policies reflect the interest demands of middle and lower classes. This was fully demonstrated by Obama's medical care reform and immigration reform plan.

The most attractive and controversial among Obama's social policies was the medical care reform. Nearly every president from the Democratic Party after Roosevelt attempted to make breakthroughs in this issue but failed. In the most recent case, Bill Clinton proposed the medical care reform package in 1993-1994 and appointed Hillary Clinton as the person in charge of the reform, but the plan was strongly opposed by conservatives and failed before being carrying out. Due to this plan, the Democratic Party slipped into the minority in the mid-term Congress election in 1994. President Clinton faced many difficulties after his plan failed.

However, bad old practices in the medical care issue of the U.S take a long time to fix. According to the U. S. Census Bureau, approximately 46 million people in the United States do not have medical insurance, with a proportion ranking the first among developed countries. The medical expenses of the U. S. amount to 16% of GDP and per capita expenses rank the first in the world, while several indicators, including the average life expectancy and infant mortality, are all behind many developed countries. This situation was challenged by all western countries. Obama posed the sharp question of how to solve this problem in the election and placed the medical insurance reform as one of his important election programs.

Obama made a speech on June 6, 2009, stating that the U. S. was confronted with urgent challenges and was crying out for medical care system reform, so the Congress prepared to introduce the discussion on the health reform act.

In July 2009, Obama formally submitted the medical care reform program to Congress. According to the plan, he suggested to cover uninsured people in medical care insurance, regulate the upper limit of premium growth and require to maintain the medical care rights and benefits of people leaving and changing their jobs. His medical care reform program was estimated to last for more than 10 years and involve 900 billion USD. With the aim to lower the insurance cost and increase the health quality of the masses, the plan incorporated a government insurance plan and encouraged people to make a two-way choice to participate in the cooperative medical insurance. The plan involved an expenditure cut of medical insurance and a tax increase of insurance companies. It was the first plan to stipulate that all Americans should purchase medical insurance, otherwise they would be imposed a fine of at least 695 USD. The employer would be imposed a fine of 2,000 USD annually for each person if he/she failed to provide payable insurance. Insurance companies could not reject applicants for insurance based on pre-existing conditions. Minor children could be covered by the policies of their parents.

The program led to controversy in the Congress and in the U. S. Opponents feared that the government would take over the medical care industry based on the medical care reform, led the U. S. in the way of "high tax and high welfare" and prejudiced the economic competitiveness of the U. S. and the motive for individual industriousness. Obama had made great efforts and compromises, and ultimately the medical insurance act named as the *Patient Protection and Affordable Care Act* was passed by the House of Representatives with a slight advantage on March 21, 2010 and was officially signed by

Obama two days later. This law will be gradually implemented in the next four years to continue to enlarge the coverage of the national insurance, make people healthier and feel more economically safe, and reduce the long-term national debt by raising the operation efficiency. According to the estimation of the Office of Budget of the Congress, the act would incorporate 30 million uninsured Americans under the insurance, while the government would bear a medical care cost of 938 billion USD and reduce a national debt of 138 billion USD in the next 10 years.

Another focus of Obama's social policies lay in the reform of the immigration policy. Obama proposed the immigration reform plan during his presidential election. In his view, the great improvements of the border management laid the solid foundation for the immigration reform. He promised that he would improve the immigration policy of the U. S. once he was elected President. Therefore, he constantly promoted the "DREAM" act after his installation. The "DREAM" act (Development, Relief and Education for Alien Minors) was jointly put forward by Democratic Senator Dick Durbin and Republican Senator Dick Lugar in 2001. It stipulated qualifications for illegal immigrants to obtain a legal identity, entry into the U. S. under 16 years of age, continuous residence for at least five years, senior high school degree or the same education level, study in universities of the U. S. or two-year military service and without criminal record. He hoped to help children brought to the U. S. by their parents as illegal immigrants through this act. They often had a life of hardship after graduation from senior high school, since they did not have legal identities in the U. S. As it was unrealistic to repatriate them back to their original places, an appropriate policy was adopted to legalize their identities and overcome any potential social problem.

On July 1, 2010, Obama made a speech exclusively on immigration reform, where he reaffirmed the determination of the government to promote immigration reform and explained that it was the foundation of the U. S. to provide immigrants with freedom, equal rights and development opportunities. However, the immigration reform was postponed several times since the medical insurance reform required great efforts from Obama administration. The "DREAM" act was approved by the House of Representatives under the control of the Democratic Party in December 2010, with 216 yes-votes and 198 no-votes. Eight Republican representatives voted for the bill (including three Cuban Republicans) and 38 Democrats voted against. However, the act was not passed by the Senate. Obama expressed his disappointment but restated his determination to upholding this act.

4. Obama's Foreign Policies

The consistent strategic goal of the U. S. has been to maintain a leadership role as the only superpower of the world, since the end of the Cold War and the disintegration of the Soviet Union. Despite different methods, measures and focuses of the hegemonic policies of the U. S. in different periods due to the rotation of ruling parties, strength fluctuation and changes of the external world, the general objective remained unchanged, that is to maintain power, including the Obama administration.

Compared to the "peace dividend" at the beginning of Clinton's term and the rising strength of the U. S. when George W. Bush took office, Obama was faced with more complicated and difficult internal and external circumstances, including two wars, an economic crisis and the massive rise of emerging great powers. The biggest challenge in the foreign policies under the Obama administration was the contradiction between the high cost to maintain their hegemonic status and the relative strength decline.

Obama was primarily required to have a clear understanding over the U. S. and the international environment, which was the basis to carry out appropriate policies. In fact, it was exactly the Bush administration's misunderstanding over the situation after 9/11 attacks that dragged the U. S. in difficulties. When George W. Bush started the Iraq War, he miscalculated the U. S.'s strength, especially their military strength, which led to heavy debts, casualties of soldiers and damages to the strength of the country. The new government assessed the situation better, compared to the George W. Bush administration.

Regarding external threats, Obama said, "Yet these wars, and our global efforts to successfully counter violent extremism, are only one element of our strategic environment and cannot define America's engagement with the world. Terrorism is one of many threats that are more consequential in a global age. The gravest danger to the American people and global security continues to come from weapons of mass destruction, particularly nuclear weapons. The space and cyberspace capabilities that power our daily lives and military operations are vulnerable to disruption and attack. Dependence upon fossil fuels constrains our options and pollutes our environment. Climate change and pandemic disease threaten the security of regions and the health and safety of the American people. Failing states breed conflict and endanger regional and global security. Global criminal networks foment insecurity abroad and bring people and goods across our own borders that threaten our people."[19]

Regarding the strength of the U. S. itself, Obama thought that "Yet even as we have

19 *National Security Strategy*, available at http://www.whitehouse.gov/sites/default/files/rss_viewer/national_security_strategy.pdf

maintained our military advantage, our competitiveness has been set back in recent years. We are recovering from underinvestment in the areas that are central to America's strength. We have not adequately advanced priorities like education, energy, science and technology, and health care—all of which are essential to U. S. competitiveness, long-term prosperity, and strength. Years of rising fiscal and trade deficits will also necessitate hard choices in the years ahead."[20]

According to the Obama administration's view on the international power pattern, though "the United States remains the world's preeminent power,"[21] "we must recognize that no one nation—no matter how powerful—can meet global challenges alone."[22] Currently, "a growing number of state and non-state bodies exhibit consequential influence. This changing distribution of power indicates evolution to a 'multi-nodal' world."[23] "The European Union has deepened its integration. Russia has reemerged in the international arena as a strong voice. China and India—the world's two most populous nations—are becoming more engaged globally. From Latin America to Africa to the Pacific, new and emerging powers hold out opportunities for partnership, even as a handful of states endanger regional and global security by flouting international norms."[24]

Obama proposed foreign strategies completely different to George W. Bush based on current challenges and different understanding of circumstances. The basic characteristics of Obama's foreign strategies included: promoting its own strength and taking advantage of external strengths; defense in whole and offense in part; moderating the position and adopting smart tactics; and increasing inventory and cultivating growth.

(1) Proposing the concept of "smart power" and regarding it as the philosophy of foreign strategies of the U. S. The core was to create a comprehensive strategy integrated with political, economic, diplomatic, military, law and cultural resources and measures based on the combination of soft and hard power, thus to cover the shortage of the hard power and realize the goal of U. S. foreign strategies.

(2) Transferring the focus of the Bush administration on military security, centered on

---

20 Ibid.

21 *National Military Strategy 2011*, available at http://www.jcs.mil/content/files/2011-02/020811084800_2011_NMS_-_08_FEB_2011.pdf

22 *National Security Strategy*, available at http://www.whitehouse.gov/sites/default/files/rss_viewer/national_security_strategy.pdf

23 *National Military Strategy 2011*, available at http://www.jcs.mil/content/files/2011-02/020811084800_2011_NMS_-_08_FEB_2011.pdf

24 *National Security Strategy*, available at http://www.whitehouse.gov/sites/default/files/rss_viewer/national_security_strategy.pdf

anti-terrorism and non-proliferation, to economic security emphasizing to maintain global financial stability and facilitate the economic recovery. The U. S. advocated stabilizing global finance, facilitating the economic recovery and opening up greater international market through the G-20 Summit and other international mechanisms.

(3) Emphasizing coordination with global powers and attempting to establish "new multi-partnership." It contained two major tasks, one was to give full play to leading role of the U. S. in developed countries and maintain the dominated position of the west in the world by enhancing multilateral cooperation mechanisms including G-20, despite the significant decline of the strength of the U. S.; and the other one was to adopt cooperation, exploitation, disunion and diversion for emerging powers, such as China, India, Russia and Brazil, to prevent them from standing opposite against the west.

(4) Setting the nuclear non-proliferation and prevention of nuclear terrorism as the primary goal of national security and isolating Iran and North Korea, which intended to develop nuclear weapons. Under the moral banner of a "nuclear-free world," Obama convened the Global Nuclear Security Summit and signed the *Anti-Ballistic Missile Treaty* (ABM Treaty) with Russia again. The Obama administration had successively released the *US Quadrennial Defense Review* (QDR), *Nuclear Posture Review* (NPR) and *National Security Strategy* in 2010, comprehensively outlining the direction of security strategy adjustment.

(5) Determining to solve the problems of the Iraq War and Afghan War left over by the Bush administration. Obama successively formulated the plans to withdraw all troops from Iraq and Afghanistan. However, it could not ensure the stability of Iraq after withdrawal. Unlike Iraq, the security conditions in Afghanistan and Pakistan were obviously worsening now that other countries of NATO had no desire to continue fighting and the nuclear weapons of Pakistan would cause a great deal of destruction. Though the U. S. declared its ultimate goal to withdraw from Afghanistan, it stated that it would firstly clean up Al Qaeda groups and the Taliban. The Afghanistan and Pakistan problem had become the biggest and most urgent burden in the global anti-terrorism of the Obama administration.

(6) Mitigating the conflicts with the Islamic world. The U. S. would no longer place "Islamist militants" as the main opponents, nor mention "anti-terrorist war" or "preemptive strategy." The hostility of more than a billion Muslims against the U. S. was a huge potential threat to U. S. security. Bush's policy, linking terrorism with Islam, increased the contradictions between Islamic countries and the U. S. Obama had unveiled a series of policies and made adjustments to show the "goodwill" gesture toward the Islamic world

and isolate terrorism and extremist forces. In September 2010, the direct Palestine and Israel talk restarted in Washington after nearly two years of inaction. Obama also increased aid to Islamic countries.

(7) In terms of non-traditional security, the U. S. listed the climate change and development of new energies as the dominant theme, put forward various initiatives and plans and attempted to obtain leadership.

(8) Emphasizing the construction of international mechanisms, multilateral diplomacy and public diplomacy. Having inherited the diplomatic tradition of Democratic administrations, the Obama administration featured idealism, but it did not regard the promotion of democracy and human rights in all countries as one of diplomatic key points as Clinton did.

(9) Strengthening its strategic influence in the Asia-Pacific region, called the "return to Asia." Along with the rapid growth of China's strength, expanding Asian economy and constant development of regional cooperation, the strategic importance of the western Pacific and the Indian Ocean is increasing. The U. S. would strengthen its influence in Asia-Pacific region as a long-term strategy.

(10) Strengthening China-U. S. cooperation by coping with the financial crisis, climate change and Afghanistan and Pakistan problem together based on the stable China-U. S. relations. At the same time, U. S. maintained policies with China to embrace dual characters, utilization and prevention. Along with the rapid growth of the strength of China and the relative decline of U. S. power, the U. S. regarded China as the biggest "uncertainty" of the future world, tended to be alert against China and had employed pertinent strategies and military deployment.

The development track of foreign strategies of the U. S. in more than two years under Obama administration can be summarized as follows: In 2009, the foreign policies focused on management of the financial crisis and improvements of the U. S.'s image that was damaged during the Bush administration, with "making good affinity with others" and "listening to others" as the basic measures. In 2010, the government transferred its attention to the rise of emerging powers. In 2011, the turbulence of the Middle East became the focus of the foreign policies of the Obama administration. Obama was always seeking the balance between stability and changes to maintain the vested interests of the U. S. in this area and also comply with the rapid changes of the situation, so as to continue to play a leading role in this area.

III. Obama Changed the United States or the United States Changed Obama

Burdened with a thousand hopes, Barack Obama became the first black U. S. Presidentunder his anthem of "reform" at a very difficult time in U. S. history. That is why so many Americans gathered at the National Mall in Washington, D. C. He spared no effort to carry out an assignment in his two-year term. On January 3 of 2011, the Columbia Broadcasting System (CBS) published the statistics of Obama's activities related to state affairs since his installation. In approximately two years, he made 883 speeches, statements and remarks, attended 69 news conferences and press availabilities, attended 40 town hall meetings, went on 111 domestic business trips, spanning 176 days, and inspected 38 states; made 16 trips to foreign countries, visiting 25 countries, spanning 70 days; traveled by Air Force One 328 times and traveled by Marine One 386 times; signed 329 bills; held 12 cabinet meetings, accepted 254 interviews; and met with 61 foreign leaders in 2010, with only 45 days of no appearances.[25] As shown by the data, Obama was really cautious and conscientious and made every effort to do a good job, though he was widely criticized for his slow management of oil spill in the Gulf of Mexico in April 2010.

The performance of the President is often judged by the number of approved bills in Congress. In only two years, Obama has signed 329 acts, including 10 bills that were promoted by him and may have great impact on the development of the country, including *Patient Protection and Affordable Care Act, American Recovery and Reinvestment Act, Financial Regulatory Reform Act, Act on Hiring Incentives to Restore Employment, Extending Unemployment Relief Act, Loan Fund for Small Enterprises Act, Extending Tax Cuts Bill*, abolishing the policy of "Don't Ask, Don't Tell" for homosexuals serving in the army and the *New Strategic Arms Reduction Treaty* between the U. S. and Russia. Even for another Democratic President, Bill Clinton, who held the office for eight years and made remarkable achievements, no act under his administration could compare to the above acts.

Seen from the two sets of statistics, the Obama administration has worked hard, made significant achievements and realized substantial reforms. However, a considerable gap can be discovered between the efforts and achievements of the government and the current situation of the U. S. and perceptions of Americans.

Economically, Obama has placed the response to the economic crisis at the forefront

---

25 Knoller, Mark. Obama's 2010: By the Number, available at http://www.cbsnews.com/8301-503544_162-20026885-503544.html.

since his inauguration. He has proposed the largest economic stimulus plan in U. S. history and carried out policies to maintain the sustainable economic growth and avoid the regeneration of crisis in finance, medical care, clean energy and education sectors. In addition, the Obama administration strengthened the trade protection and reduced the debt pressure by dollar depreciation. Though these measures have attained the expected effect in terms of prevention of economic decline and recovery of confidence in the domestic market, the slow economic recovery did not spur employment, but, on the contrary, the unemployment rate continued to rise and remained high. When Obama took office, the unemployment rate of the U. S. was 7.6%. The rate rose to 10.2% by October 2009, maintained as high as 10% for three months and kept between 9.6 and 9.9% throughout the entirety of 2010. The unemployment rate only saw a limited decline since the beginning of 2011 and remained above 9%, which meant that some 15 million people were still seeking jobs. Analysts pointed out that the real unemployment rate might be higher. According to statistics from the U. S. Department of Labor, only 81.2% of adults ranging from 25 to 54 years old had jobs in certain forms, while the rate was about 90% before the economic crisis. The Department of Labor also admitted that about 7% among the 81.2% could not find full-time jobs, much higher than the previous two years. It meant that one out of four Americans of working-age could not find a full-time job, and one out of five could not find a part-time job. The middle class was greatly hit by this situation, while Obama put all burdens on the shoulder of the middle class, but spared no effort to rescue financial institutions of Wall Street, saving the economy at the brink of collapse and promoting the medical care reform. The life of the middle class worsened due to the "vicious circle" of unemployment, house auctions and no access to loans.

Meanwhile, the U. S. economy also faced significant uncertainty, mainly represented by the slow economic growth, huge financial deficit and monstrous government debt. The economic growth of the U. S. was 0.1% and 2.9% respectively in 2009 and 2010. The 1.29 trillion USD financial deficit in 2010 ranked the second in U. S. history. In May 2011, the national debt of the U. S. broke the upper limit of 1.429 billion USD as set by the Congress. U. S. economy was at the most unstable period within the past 25 years, according to a study by the Rockefeller Foundation, and would perceivably get worse. The recovery in the first two years of Obama's time in office was considered to be the result of the government input and the stimulus from the entire world. The real test begins now.[26]

Although he struggled with the financial crisis, Obama had better performance in

---

26 Hacker, Jacob S. Rehm, Philipp. Schlesinger, Mark. Standing on Shaky Ground—Americans' Experiences with Economic Insecurity (December 2010), available at http://news.yahoo.com/s/yblog_thelookout/report-finds-widespread-economic-insecurity

diplomacy. He started to improve the damaged image of the United States since his inauguration, replacing the unilateralism of the Bush administration with multilateralism and partnership diplomacy, replacing the hard strength diplomacy with the smart power diplomacy, replacing the militarism with peaceful diplomacy and employed the climate diplomacy. Regarding practices, Obama pushed to replace isolation and confrontation with contact and dialogues, replace the dictatorial manner with negotiation and cooperation and replace giving out orders with listening and study. The feature could be reflected in the relations between the United States and its allies, relations between the U. S. and the Islamic world and the relations between the U. S. and emerging powers, as well as solutions to important issues. For example, in withdrawing from Iraq, anti-terrorism in Afghanistan and Pakistan, restoration of peace process of Palestine and Israel, Iran nuclear and North Korea nuclear issues, Obama stressed to solve problems through multilateral dialogues, restarting negotiations on disarmament and arms control and putting forward the long-term goal of a nuclear-free world. All these measures have helped Obama reach the following achievements: (1) The international image of the U. S. improved, represented by the 2009 Nobel Peace Prize won by Obama. (2) The U. S. won a favorable external environment to cope with the financial crisis based on the success of the G-20 Summit. (3) The U. S. started to get out from the mire of Iraq War through their withdrawal. (4) Achievements have been made by the adjustments of anti-terrorism strategies, including the U. S. Army's elimination of Osama bin Laden. (5) Relations between the U. S. and Russia improved. Both parties signed the new treaty on the reduction of nuclear weapons.

However, some structural challenges in the United States' foreign policies have not been well eased. Firstly, the future of the nuclear proliferation, the premiere threat in the Obama administration's views, was not bright. The North Korea and Iran nuclear issues were getting worse, while the U. S. was in more serious contradiction against the two countries. Secondly, the troop increase in Afghanistan changed the Afghanistan issue to "Obama's War," and the U. S. faced a dilemma since it could not win the victory or easily withdraw all troops. More and more Americans realized that it was a mistake for Obama to upgrade the Afghan War. Thirdly, the peace process of Palestine and Israel was obstructed as soon as it started. As Obama did not stop Israel from expanding residential areas, more and more people worldwide realized the peace process could stretch on for a long time. Fourthly, contradictions between the interests and political principles in diplomatic policies intensified. The U. S. showed drastically different attitudes towards Libya and the Bahrain and Saudi Arabia issue. Fifthly, the complexity of the world made it more difficult for the U. S. to maintain power. Currently, the U. S. had to put forth great efforts in the Middle East to cope with the sudden uproar, however, it had to speed up the strategic "eastward movement" to respond to the rise of emerging powers. Its strength could no longer match its ambitions.

Obama consistently advocated to reform politics and realize the joint governance of two parties, in order to enhance social cohesion. Nearly in every important occasion, he called on Democrats and Republicans to stop the dispute over their beliefs and make joint efforts to solve the current difficulties of the world. He evidence of his open mindedness was also revealed through his constructive suggestions of the Republican Party, his willingness to maintain communication between both parties by regular meetings of the President and leaders of both parties and his hopes to promote the reform and legislation upon the cooperation between the two parties.[27] However, the party politics was contrarily intensified during Obama's term in office. Democratic and Republican representatives only voted based on partisan for almost all major acts, demonstrated by zero "yes-votes" from Republican Representatives and three "yes-votes" from Republican senators for the economic stimulus program with a total value of 787 billion USD. The bill was approved only owing to the significant edge of the Democratic Party in the House and the Senate, but nothing to do with party cooperation. The party conflict reached a climax over the medical insurance bill, as one part of Obama's "New Deal." Though Obama and the Democrats had compromised on some key questions, no Republican had voted for the bill in both the House and the Senate, which was rarely seen in history. As commented by a media, "The approval of medical insurance bill in the House was even more meaningful than the victory won by the flesh and blood of Macarthur and his subordinators in the World War II, for Obama."[28] Obama had done all he could to contribute the approval of the bill even though the House and the Senate were under the control of Democrats.

Even so, Republicans challenged the bill by legal proceedings after the bill was approved. In December 2010, the Virginia federal court announced that the provisions of the medical care reform bill to force citizens to purchase medical care insurance violated the Constitution. Republicans, who had obtained the dominance of the House after the mid-term election, swore to cease the medical insurance bill, which meant that the achievements made by the medical care reform in the previous two years might be subverted. Soon after the generation of the new Congress in 2011, the two parties fought on the budget of the fiscal year of 2012, nearly leading to the end of government.

More seriously, the political "polarization" was intensified both among the political elite

---

27 President Barack Obama State of Union Address 2010, http://www.nowpublic.com/world/president-obama-state-union-address-2010-full-text-2564747.html

28 Jiang Lin, "Will Obama 'Return as a King'," *Guangzhou Daily*, Jan. 1 2011.

and in the grassroots level. Shortly after Obama's inauguration, a political movement named the "Tea Party" set themselves against Obama's economic and social policies, which spread nationwide. On April 15, 2009, the Tax Day in the U. S., more than a million people in different places participated the mass demonstration to oppose high taxes, high expenditure and the medical insurance reform and pushed to reduce the size of the government. They held a banner of "Tax Enough Already," "TEA" for short, which referred to the Tea Party Campaign organized by people in colonial America to fight against the high tax policy employed by the British government. Since Obama's installation, most gatherings and demonstrations were launched by the Tea Party, not because of immigration or racial problems. On April 15, a Tea Party protest broke out in several hundred cities across the U. S. More than a thousand demonstrators gathered outside Obama's office, carrying placards of "Do Not Reward the Wrong Behavior!" and "Stop Big Government!" The campaign reached its climax in the "Million People" gathering in Washington on August 28, 2010. Tea Party members were often classified as fellow travelers of Republicans, though they opposed this opinion. However, same as conservatives Republicans, they generally oppose the concept of "big government" and considered it to be impossible to solve difficult problems by strict legislation. The Tea Party campaign, as it were, was a conservative grassroots movement.

All these revealed the widening split of the U. S. society. On one hand, Americans generally believed that the U. S. was going "in a wrong direction"; on the other hand, they could not reach a consensus on what is the "right direction." Obama could not change the reality, although he has constantly called for unity. An American scholar was anxious about the situation and wrote, "The political system of the U. S. seems to have lost the ability to create a broad coalition and solve complicated problems."

Regarding the restoration of the power and status of the U. S., it was demanding to evaluate Obama's performance only based on the first two years. However, Obama himself constantly warned Americans that we "never accept second place" and "this is our generation's Sputnik Moment" while the discussion of the decline of the U. S. was heated. It demonstrated the anxiety of Americans, which was even intensified by the reports and estimations of various authoritative institutions. In January of 2011, Eurasia Group issued a report and warned that the biggest risk in the world in 2011 was "G-0," because it was the first time that no country or alliance was equipped with both political will and economic capability to carry out its global goal since WWII.[29] On April 18 2011, Standard & Poors

---

29 Bremmer, Ian. Gordon, David. The G-20 is 2011's Biggest Political Risk, available at http://blogs.hbr.org/cs/2011/01/the_g-20_is_2011s_biggest_political_risk.html

(S&P), the rating organization of the U. S., lowered the credit rating of the national debt of the U. S. from "stable" to "negative" for the first time in 70 years, having greatly embarrassed the U. S. government. It meant that the U. S. might be kicked out from the top rating of AAA, the highest credit rating assigned by S&P, in the next two years of 1 in 3 chance. In the report, S&P pointed out that the main reasons for the change in credit rating were the huge financial deficit and no clear solution to the deficit. According to S&P, "We believe there is a material risk that U. S. policymakers might not reach an agreement on how to address medium and long-term budgetary challenges by 2013; if an agreement is not reached and meaningful implementation is not begun by then, this would in our view render the U. S. fiscal profile meaningfully weaker than that of peer 'AAA' sovereigns."[30] As reported by U. S. media on April 26, International Monetary Fund (IMF) predicted in a recent report that the GDP of China would grow from 11.2 trillion USD to 19 trillion USD by 2016 based on the calculation of purchasing-power parities (PPP), while the GDP of the U. S. would increase from 15.2 trillion USD to 18.8 trillion USD by 2016. According to the report, the U. S. proportion in the total global production would drop to 17.7%, the bottom in modern times, but in comparison, China would grow to 18%.[31] Though it was only an estimation, the prospect of the U. S. was not so optimistic in many people's opinions, despite its strong power and great influence.

Corresponding to the unsatisfactory conditions of the Obama administration, the approval rate of Obama has been trending down in more than two years. He had once obtained an approval rate as high as 74% at his inauguration, and 67% Americans predicted him to be an excellent president. However, as shown by the poll result, the approval rate saw a linear decline, dropping to only 53%, while 44% were not dissatisfied with him. More than half of Americans recognized Obama's diplomacy and anti-terrorism policies, but also more than 50% of Americans resented the domestic medical care reform and his plan to revive the economy. Americans' passion to the reform and creation of a new history had cooled down, and started to review the performance of Obama in an objective manner. As displayed by the result of Gallup poll in November 2009, 48% of voters supported the Republican Party, and the approval rate of the Democratic Party dropped to 44%.

The approval rate of Obama continued to decline in 2010. According to a poll result published by the *Wall Street Journal* and National Broadcasting Company (NBC), the

---

30 'AAA/A-1+' Rating On United States of America Affirmed; Outlook Revised To Negative ,http://www.standardandpoors.com/ratings/articles/en/us/?assetID=1245302886884

31 Alex Newman, IMF: Chinese Economy To Surpass U. S. By 2016, available at http://thenewamerican.com/economy/economics-mainmenu-44/7263-imf-chinese-economy-to-surpass-us-by-2016

approval rate of Obama dropped from 53% in January to 48% in July. The poll result, published by the Quinnipiac University Polling Institute, indicated that the approval rate of Obama was only 44%. Obama accepted an important examination in the mid-term election of the Congress on November 2, 2010. Democrats under the leadership of Obama suffered a bitter defeat, and the Republicans had won 63 parliamentary seats among the 435 congressmen in the reelection of the House of Representatives, reaching a peak since 1948. Republicans gained the control of the House with a predominance of 242 to 193. In the reelection of the Senate, Republicans gained six seats, narrowing the gap with Democrats from 41: 47 to 47: 51. Therefore, Obama lost the most important predominance to carry out "reform." He would face the "divided government" similar to the situation that Clinton encountered after the mid-term election in 1994.

The embarrassment resulted from several causes. Firstly, Obama was elected president in the face of a large-scale financial crisis. He could not solve the leftover problems of the previous government in a short amount of time. However, he had carried the expectations of Americans and the world, who even believed that Obama had a solution to all problems. High expectations were derived from Obama's superior tactics and rich and special experiences and their negative feelings towards the Bush administration. However, these could not help Obama solve all difficulties the United States faced. Obama seemed to have a clear understanding on this at his inauguration. For example, he expressed in his inaugural speech that problems "cannot be overcome in a short time."

Secondly, Obama moved to the White House with a long "task list" in hand, covering economic rescue, medical care reform, financial regulation, climate change, nuclear-free world, partnership, Iraq withdrawal and troop increase in Afghanistan. Though Obama had to cope with major issues, including the economic crisis, many tasks on this list were added by the President himself. He was soon proved to be so ambitious that the Congress and administration could no afford to address every task on his list. An alarming vicious circle revealed in the Obama administration when the President firstly announced an ambitious goal, then the administration could not realize the goal after a period of bustle and finally the President lowered the standard to win a nominal victory.

Thirdly, Obama's reform method did not match the reality of U. S. society. Obama vigorously promoted the medical care reform for interests of the masses and the development of the U. S., but it aroused great dispute and anxiety under the background of high budget deficits. As shown in the poll conducted before the mid-term election, the economy was the matter of prime importance in American voters' eyes, even more important than sum of medical care reform, anti-terrorism, illegal immigrants and Iraq War and Afghan War.

Fourthly, a fairly strange political structure existed in the United States under the leadership of Obama. The President on the left wing led an administration team on the mid and left wing to govern the country of "right wing." The gap between the idea and interest demand would necessarily lead to the wrong understanding and intricate policies. Intense contradictions and conflicts would be incurred by irreconcilable problems.

Joe Wilson, an American political scientist, reached a conclusion from the experiences of the U. S. engaged in the League of Nations that the passionate reformers should know that they were losing all their rights when they were leading masses. This conclusion could also apply to Obama. Actually, Obama began to change the reality, owing to the political change after the mid-term election. Firstly, he had put more efforts toward the economy and attempted to resolve the high unemployment rate, which was the key to his renewal of termin office. Secondly, he seemed to care more about the policy demands of Republicans, exerting efforts to reduce the high financial deficits and easing down on government regulation. Thirdly, he gave every effort to maintain his legislative achievements, but gave up the towering ambition and promoted legislation with smaller dispute. Fourthly, he socialized with Republicans in more patient way to reconcile the social split between the two parties. Fifthly, he attempted to rebuild the confidence of the U. S. as the leader of the world through "smarter" methods in this complicated world. It looks like an impossible task to solve all these problems. The answer to the question of how Obama will deal with the situation can only be found in his future actions.

The United States in Chinese Scholars' View

Wang Jisi and Cheng Chunhua

The international financial crisis broke out in 2008. Since then, the media and Internet have been overwhelmed by comments and predictions on the "U. S. decline." Political leaders, strategists, columnists, critics and scholars of all countries have always discussed and argued about the rise and fall of the U. S., while more people held the pessimistic view. Most comments were given based on political stands, emotions and preference on ideologies, or in the case of group benefits or policy objectives. It is not so much an academic thesis as a political topic that when the United States, the only super power of the world, will fall from the top.

Wang Jisi[32] published an academic thesis, *Lonely at the Top – Study on the Status of the United States in the World after the Cold War*[33], in 1997. Directed against the "Idea of American Declining," the thesis pointed out that the U. S. was still ahead of the world, rather than falling behind it. The major challenge to its strength lay in its internal cohesion. Other western developed countries saw a decline compared to emerging developing countries, and the U. S. was too isolated to lead the world. Now, it seems that the basic argument of the thesis is valid.

This article will try to reassess the status of the U. S. in the world from an external academic perspective based on the development and changes over ten years, especially after the international financial crisis in 2008. Different from the above-mentioned thesis, this article will no longer employ many figures or information, but focus on the analysis of internal conditions and international circumstances of the United States, since data, literary sources and other material can be easily found on the internet, but the ability of analysis and integration is in demand. Owing to the rapid communication of information and the idea infiltration, the subjective cognizance of influential people and institutions may affect the predictions of relevant organizations and countries for the future and further influence

---

32 A professor of the School of International Studies of Beijing University and famous scholar of American studies. (Translator's note)

33 *American Studies*, 3rd issue of 1997, P 7-34.

the decisions of interest groups and governments, which plays a more important role in the future development of the U. S. than its own strength. For example, if a potential hostile country of the U. S. makes a strategic decision that the U. S. has declined or will decline, it will attempt to challenge the U. S. and thus weaken its strength and status. However, it's another story whether the challenge will prejudice itself or both countries will sink together. In view of this, the article will focus on the integration and evaluation of the current views on the fluctuation and the status of the U. S. at the macroscopic level, so as to update the conclusion of the above-mentioned thesis.

I. Political Motivations and Policy Implications of Views of the Rise and Fall of the U. S.

Now, let's divide the views of the rise and fall of the U. S. into the "Idea of Thriving" and "Idea of Decline" for simplicity. This will make it easy to see the political motivations and policy implications of the two opposite ideas.

The "Idea of Thriving" believes that the U. S. is not declining but will remain to be the strongest country the world. Therefore, problems such as how the U. S. will utilize its power and dominance and how to improve the "style of leadership" of the U. S. to gain world popularity will be discussed.

Representatives of the "Idea of Thriving" include Joseph Nye, a professor at John F. Kennedy School of Government in Harvard University, Robert Kagan, a senior researcher at the Brookings Institution, Zaki Laidi, the researcher of the Center of European Studies in Paris Institute of Political Studies, Hillary Clinton, the U. S. Secretary of State, Robert Gates, the U. S. Secretary of Defense, Leslie Gelb, the honorary chairman of the Council on Foreign Relations, Michael Mandelbaum, a professor at Johns Hopkins University, Philip Stephens, the columnist of the *Financial Times* in the United Kingdom, Victor Thomas, the head of the Royal Institute for International Affairs, Joseph Joffe, the publisher and chief editor of the German magazine *Times* and Li Guangyao, the former senior minister of Singapore, etc.

Most people that agree with the "Idea of Thriving" are governors of the U. S. or intellectuals related to the political mainstream in the U. S. or pro-American politicians or critics outside the U. S. Of course, some of them are common people without clear political objectives. "Theorists of Thriving" with political emotions generally identify with American values, wish to preserve the strong power of the U. S., advocate enough confidence over the U. S. and emphasize the weaknesses and uncertainties of other powers, especially challengers against the U. S.[34]

As one of representatives of "Theorists of Thriving," Joseph Nye, a professor at John F. Kennedy School of Government at Harvard University and former high official of the U. S., has called upon his own opinion in his works and in different occasions. In Nye's view, it is too early to jump to the conclusion on the long-term effect of the 2008 financial crisis on the U. S.'s strength. Despite the financial crisis, the U. S. economy is rated as the second most competitive in the world (second only to Switzerland) by the World Economic Forum based on its flexible labor market, high education level, stable politics and innovation stimulus. The U. S. will remain the forerunner in biotechnology, nanotechnology, second-generation internet and some other areas. Obama has successfully changed the image of the U. S., making it easier for people to accept the leadership of the U. S. compared to the end of the Bush administration. The U. S. leading the world seems a better choice than the cooperation among powerful countries. According to him, China may surpass the U. S. in future decades but it will face many insurmountable problems in its development.[35] Stephen Walter, another professor at the John F. Kennedy School of Government, has also analyzed the status of the U. S. In his opinion, the best understanding of the status of the U. S. in the world is that the U. S. dominates the whole world and has established its leadership in nearly every important aspect. The U. S. is featured with the largest economy, an overwhelming military dominance, leadership in key international systems and profound cultural and ideological influence. Moreover, these advantages are even enlarged by its favorable geopolitics. The open mind of the U. S. society to immigrants and innovation allows better adaptability to new situations.[36] Robert Gates, the U. S. Secretary of Defense, stated that it was a mistake to regard the U. S. as a declining country solely due to the financial crisis.[37]

The Singapore politician, Li Guangyao, had once energetically advocated the "Asian values" and criticized the values and diplomatic policies of the U. S. However, he emphasized in his speech made in his visit to the U. S. in November 2009 that "the U. S. will remain the only super power in the next 20 to 30 years," and China would only play its

---

34 One of representative works of the "Idea of Thriving" written by non-Americans is the *Überpower: The Imperial Temptation of America,* by Josef Joffe (Germany), New York: W. W. Norton, 2006.

35 Joseph S. Nye, Jr., "The Future of American Power: Dominance and Decline in Perspective," *Foreign Affairs*, November/December 2010.

36 Stephen M. Walt, *Taming American Power: The Global Response to U. S. Primacy*, New York: W. W. Norton, 2005.

37 Elisabeth Bumiller, "U. S. Will Counter Chinese Arms Buildup," January 8, 2011, http://www.nytimes.com/2011/01/09/world/asia/09military.html.

global influence 20 years later, because China was not ready or willing to assume the same obligations in handling the international system as the U. S. He also indicated that "the U. S. is still the largest economy and the 'final market'. USD will continue to be the principal international reserve currency, though euros, Chinese RMB, Japanese yens and other currencies will finally become the reserve currencies." In the same speech, he clarified that he emphasized the dominance of the U. S. in the hope that the U. S. could balance against China. He said, "No matter whatever challenges the U. S. meet, it has to maintain its superiority in the Pacific in consideration of the core interests of the U. S. Its influence would be significantly reduced without its dominance in this area."[38]

In comparison with the "Idea of Thriving," people considering that the U. S. has declined or will decline are of more complicated identities and motivations. Firstly, not only foreigners but also many Americans have bad-mouthed the U. S. for several decades. Foreign "Theorists of Decline" often quoted the materials and opinions of Americans as their basic arguments. Samuel Huntington, a professor of Political Science of Harvard University, published an article in the quarterly magazine *Diplomacy* more than 20 years ago, where he pointed out that the "Idea of American Declining" had lasted for a long time ever since 1950s.[39] The "Idea of Decline" has a history over 50 years, while relative theorists have spun for two or three generations. At the beginning of the 1950's, some people thought that the U. S. could no longer show off its military strength after the Korean War. When the Soviet Union launched the first artificial satellite, Sputnik, in 1957, people exclaimed that space technology and even the whole technology field of the U. S. had been surpassed by the Soviet Union. As the Vietnam War was the Waterloo for the U. S., in some people's view, the withdrawal of troops from South Vietnam in 1975 symbolized the loss of political and military influence and moral prestige of the U. S. In the 1970's, the U. S. experienced a deepening economic crisis and an oil crisis, and the Bretton Woods system with the USD as the center collapsed, seemingly leading to the decline of the dominance of the U. S. economy. The swift and violent strategic expansion of the Soviet Union in the middle and late 1970's forced the U. S. to be on the defensive, so the prediction of "the Soviet Union would surpass the U. S." became influential. In the 1980's when Japan and the West Germany emerged as economic powers and the European integration was strengthened, some people asserted that the world economy was developing

38 Li Guangyao, "Full Text of Li Guangyao's Speech: the World Order Will Be Rebalanced," website of Sing apore Lianhe Zaobao, November 5 2009, http://www.zaobao.com/special/singapore/pages4/sg_cn091105c.shtml.

39 Samuel P. Huntington, "The U. S. – Decline or Renewal", *Foreign Affairs*, Winter 1988/89.

into "three tops" and Japan would replace the U. S. as the economic superpower at the end of the 20th century or the beginning of the 21st century. The U. S. asked allies, including Japan, for financial assistance in the Gulf War, the first large-scale war after the Cold War, which demonstrated, in some people's opinion, its incapacity to lead the world economy. The September 11th attacks in 2001 seriously shocked the U. S. and the argument of U. S. decline became popular again. In 2003, the U. S. was politically isolated since its launch of the Iraq War in defiance of strong opposition by the international community and even damaging their relationship with France and Germany, illustrating the serious fall of the soft power and hegemony of the U. S. The "Idea of Decline" in economic and financial areas was again aroused by the international financial crisis. As counted, the "Idea of Decline" has appeared almost a dozen times in over five decades.

The first category of "Theorists of Decline" refers to radicals or left-wing thinkers of the U. S. The "Idea of Decline" reflects the standpoint and ideology tendency of theorists. They will never abandon their habits of thinking to criticize the U. S. since they will not change their political stand. According to the *Living in the Post-American Age* by Immanuel Wallerstein, a sociologist at Yale University, "the U. S. had led the world for 25 years after World War II. Its influence started to decline later, but it employed appropriate measures to put off the decline. Then neo-conservatives took office and attempted to rebuild the leadership of the U. S., which contrarily facilitated the fall. Now we are living in a post-American age."[40] Wallerstein always compared the current situation to the U. S. right after the end of WWII, when U. S. economy accounted for more than half of the total industrial output value of the world. As early as in 1980s, Wallerstein declared the tendency of decline of the capitalist world system and the ruin of the global economy of neoliberalism. In 2002, he also pointed out that "the U. S. had obtained the hegemony after the War, while it meanwhile laid the way to the destruction of the hegemony. Four symbols revealed in the process, including the Vietnam War, 1968 Revolution (Civil Rights Movement, U. S., Wallerstein's note), the fall of the Berlin Wall in 1989 and the terrorist attack on the U. S. in September 2011. The four symbolic events led the U. S. to the current situation, a superpower without real power, a leader without obedience and respect and a country going with the tide in the global chaos without control."[41] Another left-wing thinker of the United States, Noam Chomsky, summarized the role of the U. S. in the world

---

40 Immanuel Wallerstein, *Living in the Post-American Age*, January 8 2008, http://www.chinaelections.org/newsinfo.asp?newsid=121255.

41 Immanuel Wallerstein, *The Decline of American Power*, Social Sciences Academic Press, 2007; Immanuel Wallerstein, "The Eagle Has Crash Landed," *Foreign Policies*, US, Issue July/August, 2002.

pattern in his book *Hegemony or Survival.* According to him, the U. S. was committing itself to establishing an empire-style unipolar hegemony so as to control the world. In terms of the global war on terror launched by the U. S. after the September 11th attacks, Chomsky was mainly concerned about America ignoring the basic right to subsistence of countries under attack and making use of the fear of the American pubic, because In fact, the so-called "terrorists" only hate American policies, but not the country itself.[42] Chalmers Johnson, a professor at the University of California at San Diego and an expert on Asia, was another representative.[43]

The second type of the "Idea of Decline" was more like to impel the U. S. to greater effort. As a country never lacking awareness of unexpected development, 47% Americans considered China to be the top economy\ic power in the future two decades, comparing to only 35% believing in the U. S., according to an investigation made by Gallup in February 2011.[44] Thomas Friedman, a columnist for the *New York Times*, is one of the representatives of this school of thought. Friedman had written several articles in recent years to present his anxiety over the lack of sense of direction and competitiveness of the U. S., especially whether the government could adjust the energy policies to cope with the climate change. Since a huge obstruction in the development lies in the struggle between the Democratic and Republican Party, he appealed for the establishment of a third party to avoid following the old road of ancient Rome to ruin.[45] He also pointed out that China was the economic partner as well as the competitor of the U. S. He hoped that Americans could regard the rise of China as the Soviet Untion's launch of the first artificial satellite in 1957, when the U. S. was challenged, but spurred on, by the strength of the Soviet Union and realized the development of education, infrastructure and technology.[46]

Another "Theorist of Decline" is Fareed Zakaria, an American critic, who appeals to the government to be alert and facilitate development. In his book, *The Post-American World,* he pointed out that structural power has transferred three times in the previous 500

---

42 Noam Chomsky, "*Hegemony or Survival: America's Quest for Global Dominance,*" Shanghai Translation Publishing House, 2006, P 2-10. Chomsky is a linguistics and philosophy professor of MIT. He accepted interviews by media worldwide when any major incident happened in international politics and strictly criticized diplomatic policies of US government.

43 Chalmers Johnson, *Sorrows of Empire: Militarism, Secrecy, And the End of the Republic*, Shanghai People's Publishing House, 2005.

44 Lydia Saad, "China Surges in Americans' Views of Top World Economy", February 14, 2011, http://www.gallup.com/poll/146099/china-surges-americans-views-top-world-economy.aspx.

45 Thomas Friedman, "Third Party Rising", *New York Times*, October 3, 2010.

46 Wang Jisi, "Background for the U. S. to Exaggerate China's Strength," *Orient Morning Post*, March 24 2010.

years, the rise of the Western world, the emergence of the U. S., and currently, the emerging powers, such as China and India, that are rebuilding the world. Compared to the past, the U. S. has not really declined, but has seen a relative fall of international status. The best response of the U. S. is to maintain political and economic openness and tolerance. He vigorously blamed the Bush administration for prejudicing the image of the country by launching the Iraq War. Now he has great expectations for the Obama administration and gives counsel to them. In fact, at one time, Obama always carried the book with him.[47]

Since the end of the Cold War, Zbigniew Brzezinski, the strategist and former Assistant to the President for National Security Affairs, has emphasized in his several works that the U. S. should awaken its moral consciousness, rebuild the domestic political consensus and comprehensively develop the economy. Only through finding solutions to various issues, including the heavy debt, deterioration of infrastructures, urban blight and polarization of rich and poor and fundamental reform, can save the U. S. from a more serious crisis and incapacity to play a leading role in the world.[48] Another strategist and former Assistant to the President for National Security Affairs, Brent Scowcroft, also pointed out that the U. S. became conservative and complacent after the Cold War and even became fearful after the September 11th attacks, while this loss of optimism will give birth to potential risks for the country.[49] Samuel P. Huntington, a professor of Harvard University, attributed the possibility of the decline to the national identity crisis brought by the large number of new immigrants in his last book, *Who Are We*.[50]

The view of Dominique Moisi, the Senior Consultant of the French Institute of International Relations, draws a great deal of attention among the foreign critics that hold to the "Idea of Decline." He agreed with the basic conclusion of *The Post-American World* by Zakaria, but he also criticized the "culture of fear" spreading among Americans, making Americans more anxious and introverted, therefore losing its pursuit of democracy, freedom, openness and tolerance which had once brought great brilliance to the U. S. Similar with Zakaria, Moisi wished a new outlook for the U. S. under the Obama administration.[51]

---

47 Fareed Zakaria, *The Post-American World*, China Citic Press, 2009.

48 Zbigniew Brzezinski, "How to Stay Friends With China," *New York Times*, January 2 2011. http://news.xinhuanet.com/world/2011-01/04/c_12942649.htm.

49 Zbigniew Brzezinski and Brent Scowcroft, *The Great Game: Challenges of Global Political Awakening*, Xinhua Publishing House, 2009, P 187-189.

50 Samuel P. Huntington, *Who Are We: The Challenges to America's National Identity*, New York: Simon & Schuster, 2005.

51 Dominique Moisi, *The Geopolitics of Emotion: How Cultures of Fear, Humiliation, And Hope Are Reshaping The World*, Xinhua Publishing House, 2010, P 125-132.

To be specific, the theorists of the second category of "Idea of Decline" may not reach the conclusion that the U. S. will necessarily decline, but point out that the country may fall without the inhibition of certain negative phenomena, unfavorable policies and a downward trend. They are distinguished from critics who wish to study this issue in a more external perspective without strong emotions. For example, Paul Kennedy, a historian at Yale University, had deduced the long-term development tendency of decline of the U. S. according to the law of historical development in his work *The Rise and Fall of the Great Powers*. As revealed in an article of the *Wall Street Journal* on December 21, 2009, the U. S. has become a country displaying the deficits of capitalism from a good example.[52] America was once the model for other countries, but now has already lost this status to a great extent. In the view of Richard Haas, the Chairman of U. S. Council on Foreign Relations, the U. S. has already lost its role as a dominant economic power, the power is distributing and the world will come into an age without polar points.[53] As Charles Kupchan wrote in *The End of the American Era: U. S. Foreign Policy and the Geopolitics of the Twenty-First Century*, the end of the Cold War was not the final victory for the U. S., but the start of the decline of its global leadership and people would witness the end of the American Era instead of the history.[54] Kennedy and Kupchan are typical theorists of the third kind of "Idea of Decline."

The fourth type of "Idea of Decline" is popular in countries that hope for the decline of the U. S. or countries in conflict with America, such as Russia, Venezuela and Iran, as well as among radicals and left-wing thinkers of many countries. As early as July 2008 when the international financial crisis just broke out, Russian President Dmitry Medvedev indicated that "owing to the serious decline, the U. S. is now no longer the center of world economy and cannot lead or interfere in the economic development of other countries." In November 2007, the Venezuelan President Hugo Chavez told reporters during his visit to Iran that "the U. S. is on its way to decline, with the dollar weakness as the symbol of the loss of dominance over the world. Venezuela will fight together with Iran against American

---

52 Mark Whitehouse, "Beacon of capitalism," December 22, 2009, http://online.wsj.com/article/SB126135856019499555.html.

53 Richard N. Haass, "The Age of Nonpolarity", *Foreign Affairs*, May/June 2008, http://www.foreignaffairs.com/articles/63397/richard-n-haass/the-age-of-nonpolarity. Quote from Liu Weidong, "Impact of the Financial Crisis to the International Status of America," *Ideological and Theoretical Education Guide*, 5th issue 2010, http://www.wyzxsx.com/Article/finance/201008/175841.html.

54 Charles Kupchan, *The End of the American Era: U. S. Foreign Policy and the Geopolitics of the Twenty-first Century*, Shanghai People's Publishing House, 2004, P 28-38.

imperialism."[55] In December 2009, Iran's president Mahmoud Ahmadinejad asserted that "the U. S. is on the decline. The world needs a new order based on Islamic revolutionary value, which can only be guaranteed by Iranians."[56] Therefore, we can predict that Theorists of Declinethey will never change their mind no matter what changes occur in the world situation, because it is their political belief and demand.

Here it is necessary to analyze Chinese opinions on the rise and fall of America. As one of politicians who reached the conclusion of the "inevitable decline of the U. S.," Mao Zedong gave his famous opinion that "U. S. imperialism is a paper tiger" in 1945, so China, under his leadership, insisted on that "the East Wind prevails over the West Wind," "the enemy is getting worse and worse, while we are becoming better and better," and "we are living in an age when the imperialism is stepping towards total collapse and the socialism going to an all-around victory." The "West Wind," "enemy" and "imperialism" mainly referred to the U. S. As the China-U. S. relations improved in 1970's, Chinese leaders once felt concern over whether the U. S. could resist against the strategic expansion of the Soviet Union. They only made a new judgment until the obvious decline of the Soviet Union after the death of Brezhnev.

After the end of the Cold War, though China was anxious about the "unipolar world," the multipolarity was considered to be an irreversible direction of the world. The multipolarity can only be realized based on the decline of the international status of America. Despite no official statement on the rise and fall of America in China, the direction of the public opinions has favored the "Idea of Decline" for more than six decades. The "Idea of Thriving" boosts the enemy and lowers our morale, which cannot be accepted politically. Therefore, the official statement was "multipolar was developing despite twists and turns" when the U. S. stood firmly on its leading role. The statement would be "multipolar was developing rapidly" when America was encountered with major setback. Examples can be found everywhere from media and publications tending to "badmouth" the U. S. instead of "thinking highly" of it.[57]

Comments that "praise" or "badmouth" the U. S. based on clear political motivations

---

55 Global Online, *Chavez Visited Iran, Indicating that America Is Declining*, November 21 2007, http://news.163.com/07/1121/08/3TQEPG1F0001121M.html.

56 Huanqiu.com: *Ahmadinejad Predicted the Defeat of the U. S. and Stated Only Iran Could Ensure the New World Order*, December 24, 2009, http://world.huanqiu.com/roll/2009-12/669280.html.

57 For Example, Joseph Nye's works, *Bound to Lead: The Changing Nature of American Power* and *The Paradox of American Power: Why the World's Only Superpower Can't Go It Alone;* Nina Hachigian and Mona Sutphen's works, *The Next American Century: How the U. S. can Thrive as Other Powers Rise.*

are meaningless to academic research. We shall attach more importance to the long-term research based on cool-headed observation, especially the arguments on the domestic development and changes of America, since internal factors instead of external factors decide the rise and fall of a country.

II. Three New Topics in the Current Argument on the Rise and Fall of the U. S.

The recent global argument on the rise and fall of America was brought about by three factors. Firstly, the U. S. was greatly shocked by the financial crisis in 2008, so the U. S. strength based on economy saw an uncertain prospect in the middle and long term. Secondly, the Iraq War launched by the Bush administration in 2003 seriously damaged the image of America. Many critics, including Joseph Nye, who created the concept of "soft power," showed great concern about the decline of the soft power incurred by unilateralism. The Obama administration lifted their hopes by strategic adjustment. The third factor was the rapid growth of emerging powers, especially China, contributing to the "transfer of world power" and challenging the leadership of America.

1. Economy, Innovation and Competitiveness

Those who dispute the rise and fall of America have their eyes on the economic trend of America in the globalization. According to the "Idea of Decline," the decline of the status of the U. S. led by the long-term economic recession is mainly featured by its falling proportion in the global economy, its serious debt deficit, insolvency of the government, economic recession and economical virtualization. Right after WWII, American economy once accounted for nearly half of the world, which has dropped to 25% in recent years. The financial deficit of the federal government amounted to 1.42 trillion USD, making up approximately 10.8% of GDP, the highest among developed countries. The total deficit of America in future 10 years was estimated to be 7.2 trillion USD.[58] In economist John Williams's opinion, the federal government of the U. S. is completely bankrupt.[59] According to Claude Smadja, the former Director-General of World Economic Forum

58 According to IMF, American financial deficit will account for 10.8% of its GDP by 2011, ranking the first among major economies. IMF urges the U. S. to reduce the financial deficit. "Weak Basis for American Plan on Deficit Reduction," *Wall Street Journal*, February 15 2011, http://cn.wsj.com/gb/20110215/hrd104158.asp.

59 Gao Jian, "Total Debt of American Government Exceeds Global GDP," *China Security News*, February 18, 2009, http://finance.people.com.cn/GB/8215/134583/135009/150129/9001894.html.

(WEF) and president of Switzerland Smadja Strategic Consulting Company and Clyde Prestowitz, the head of the American Economic Strategy Institute, the age of globalization equal to Americanization has ended, and the market economy and the contract of the political democracy has been forgotten.[60] As predicted by the economist Jacques Attalicwho served as the advisor to French President Francois Mitterand, the American Empire dominating the world now will be finally defeated in 2035 owing to the serious ecological crisis.[61] Simon Johnson, the economist from Massachusetts Institute of Technology (MIT), indicated that the financial crisis brought about a perpetual strike to the U. S. and caused a loss of superiority.[62]

On the contrary, the "Idea of Thriving" believes that the financial crisis does not speed up the decline of America but facilitates its progress. Kara Nolov thought that the global edge of the U. S. included the broad market, rich people, control over the world finance and ability to print USD, while the bond of the U. S. Treasury remained attractive after the financial crisis broke out.[63] American scholars Francis Fukuyama and Joseph Nye wrote articles in Germany's publication, *Times*, on January 8, 2009 respectively under the name of "What the United States Will Be" and "No Longer Do It Alone," pointing out that no lethal blow is incurred by the crisis on the American system. The U. S. is still the strongest country in the world, and its leadership plays an important role in the world.[64]

The opinion that the U. S. economy will finally recover from the crisis is hidden in some aspects of the "Idea of Decline." According to Gideon Rahman, the critic of international affairs of UK *Financial Times*, despite severe damages to American economy, the U. S. still possesses the largest economy and most top universities and large companies of the world, lead the global technological revolution and attract large amount of talented immigrants for the American dream. It will revive the economy and maintain its superiority

---

60 "Globalization Revolution," *Newsweek*, January 09, 2010, http://www.newsweek.com/2010/01/09/globalization-revolution.html.

61 "Predictions of French Scholars: The U. S. will Decline, And Drinking Water Will Lead to Wars," *Global Times*, April 15 2009, http://www.chinanews.com/gj/ywdd2/news/2009/04-15/1647648.shtml.

62 Reuters, "Gloomy economists predict US's decline," January 10, 2011, http://www.ft.com/cms/s/0/a1cfa9e8-66e8-11dd-808f-0000779fd18c.html#ixzz1B6ysU7jK.

63 Michael Cox, "Too Early to Determine the Decline of the West," 40th Issue of *International and StrategicStudies Report of Beijing University*, November 29 2009. See the original text at Michael Cox, "To lead the world? Not any Longer", *H-Diplo Roundtable Reviews*, Vol. X, No 9 (2009), http://www.h-net.org/~diplo/roundtables/PDF/Roundtable-X-9.pdf.

64 Liu Weidong, "Impact of the Financial Crisis to the International Status of America," *Ideological and Theoretical Education Guide*, 5th issue 2010, http://www.wyzxsx.com/Article/finance/201008/175841.html.

in military and technologies.[65] In French critic Nicholas Baverez's view, the U. S. is the only developed country with an active population. The estimated population growth of 100 million by 2050 from now, the reviving investment and deposit, the global network promoted by American government, social flexibility and awareness of innovation can enhance the transformation of the economic development method.[66]

USD hegemony is the focus of the debate of the rise and fall of America, as well as the "weatherglass" of the status of America. The financial decline will be irreversible when America loses its USD hegemony. Though we cannot predict the future of the U. S., the American financial supremacy will not transfer to others unless the USD power is lost.

The "Idea of Decline" believes that the lowering status of the USD effects the position of America. As pointed out in the research study *Global Trends 2025: A Transformed World* by U. S. National Intelligence Council, despite the increasing capitals in dollar assets and the revaluation of the USD, the USD may still lose its absolutely unrivaled role as the reserve currency by 2025 and become the No. 1 among several currencies of equal status.[67] Michael Crawley, the professor of world peace and security study of Hampshire College, indicated that six factors, including the G-20 summit, USD weakness and emerging "BRIC" countries (Brazil, Russia, India, and China) demonstrated that the U. S. had become an "ordinary country."[68]

"Theorists of Thriving" consider the USD status will not decline, and the international currency system centering on the USD will continue to support the development of America. In their opinion, the view that the USD will lose its status as the base currency has appeared about four times but never realized.[69] According to French scholar Bruno Tertrais, the USD accounts for more than 2/3 of the global foreign exchange reserve and half of international commercial trade. In additon, half of international bonds are paid in USD,

---

65 Gideon Rachman, "Think Again: American Decline", Jan/Feb 2011, http://www.foreignpolicy.com/articles/2011/01/02/think_again_american_decline.

66 Nicholas Baverez, "Relative Decline of America," *French Le Monde*, September 21 2010, http://world.people.com.cn/GB/12804924.html.

67 U. S. National Intelligence Council, *Global Trends 2025: A Transformed World*, November, 2008, http://www.dni.gov/nic/PDF_2025/2025_Global_Trends_Final_Report.pdf.

68 Michael Crawley, "Six Signs for the Death of America Empire," Spain *Uprising*, November 5 2009, http://bt.xinhuanet.com/2009-11/19/content_18274546.htm.

69 Four shocks respectively appeared at late 1950s, when the Bretton woods system was weakened, 1970s, when the Bretton woods system was ended, late 1980s, when Japan grew up, USD became devaluated and stock market declined, and 2008, when the financial crisis broke out. Takenaka Masaharu (the professor of the Department of Economics of Japan Ryukoku University), "The USD-Based Currency Mechanism Will Maintain for More than 20 Years," Japan *Economists*. Quote from Li Changjiu, "How Long Can USD Keep Its Leading Role," *Economic Information Daily*, June 10 2010, http://finance.ifeng.com/opinion/hqgc/20100224/1849601.shtml.

demonstrating the comparative advantage of American financial system and enabling the country to issue low-price national debt and purchase high yield securities. One marked feature of American economy is the high proportion of high technology industry in the whole industrial production.[70] In a Chinese scholar, Song Guoyou's, opinion, the fall of USD exchange rate since 2003 is not terrible. Actually, the USD exchange rate had been falling for nearly 10 years, since late 1980s, dropping by over 40%, which was only reversed under the Clinton administration. The current USD devaluation is only a copy of the history. However, along with the devaluation of the USD, America ushered in the end of the Cold War and the establishment of the unipolar mechanism.[71] Takenaka Masaharu, a professor in the Department of Economics of Japan Ryukoku University, believes that the USD-based currency system will maintain for a long time unless America fails to manage the inflation risk, leading to serious inflation and significant devaluation of the USD, otherwise the "alternative currency" to replace the USD as the base currency will not turn up in short term.[72]

Innovation and competitiveness are also important factors contributing to the fall or rise of America. The "Theorists of Decline" see regression in innovation and enterprise competitiveness in America. As unveiled by French *Les Echos* on September 15, 2009, a technology innovation foundation made an assessment on the competitiveness based on 16 standards, with the U. S. ranking sixth, behind Sweden and Singapore. The American innovation crisis started in the late 1990's. "Brain drain" was serious in large public research labs and state-funded labs, with their best undergraduates feeling depressed due to the unattractive salary of researchers. In addition, non-applicable researches were going backwards since the U. S. lacked the political willingness to support the fundamental researches.[73] As indicated in the article *The Boring Age* in the weekly magazine *Time* in March 2010, the U. S., and even the whole world, is living in "an age of technological stagnation." The changes to life and industry brought by new inventions in the information age cannot be compared to the early and middle 20th century. Real revolutionary technological innovation can be rarely seen, especially in transport and energy area and the little output value

---

70 Bruno Tertrais (professor of French Foundation for Strategic Research), "Illusion of the Decline of America," French *Daily Echo*, December 18 2008, quote from Xinhua net, http://news.xinhuanet.com/world/2007-12/24/content_7302534.htm.

71 Song Guoyou, "Illusion of the Decline of America," *Orient Morning Post*, January 24 2008, from http://world.people.com.cn/GB/1030/6816575.html.

72 Takenaka Masaharu (the professor of the Department of Economics of Japan Ryukoku University), "The USD-Based Currency Mechanism Will Maintain for More than 20 Years," Japan Economists. Quote from Li Changjiu, "How Long Can USD Keep Its Leading Role," Economic Information Daily, June 10 2010, http://finance.ifeng.com/opinion/hqgc/20100224/1849601.shtml.

73 Quote from Ma Ye, *Several Literature on the Decline of America*, June 7 2010, http://www.xzass.org/html/news1237.html.

directly produced by high technology can only be utilized as a tool to create fictitious capital.[74]

Contrarily, the "Theorists of Thriving" think that the U. S. still possesses great vigor in technologies, talents, innovation and competitiveness. As reported by the *Wall Street Journal*, the plunging prices of materials and equipment stimulated talents to turn new ideas to inventions. More and more students from engineering departments of universities hope to join in the real research and development and share ideas and tools with other innovators, so a lot of innovation workshops spring up in America. In the next decade, individual inventions may play a more important role than research and development institutions. Internet brings more opportunities to capable, wise and resourceful Americans. American people have learned a lesson from their original value to seek ease and comfort. The general public becomes aware of deposit due to the loss of wealth and start to live within their means. Internet learners are increasing to improve their own skills.[75] As commented in the special column of the *New York Times*, you can always find the depression of the country in the American government and see the optimistic side of the country in Americans under 30, as the youth violence and crimes and teenage pregnancy has reduced in this generation.[76]

2. Soft Power and Smart Power

Americans, including Joseph Nye, in succession put forward both concepts of "soft power" and "smart power."[77] Though similar concepts, such as "American culture" and

---

74 Michael Lind, "The Boring Age", *Time*, Mar.11, 2010, http://www.time.com/time/specials/packages/printout/0,29239,1971133_1971110_1971120,00.html.

75 Quote from Canadian Chinese Online, *America Roars at the New Year, Who Said America Was Declining*, http://www.ccol.ca/news/View/5/3979.htm.

76 Ibid.

77 Joseph S. Nye proposed the concept of "smart power" in 2003. In 2004, Suzanne Nossel from U. S. Security and Peace Research Institute published an article *Smart Power* in the magazine *Foreign Affairs*, and further clarified the policy implication of "smart power," "this diplomatic strategy must be employed to effectively strike back against terrorists, go further by flexible application of various kinds of strengths and increase American interests in a stable alliance, institution and frame." (Suzanne Nossel, "Smart Power," *Foreign Affairs*, March/April,2004). In January 2006, Joseph S. Nye published an article entitled *Think Again: Soft Power* in *Foreign Policy* and indicated that it was wrong to only rely on hard or soft power, and the smart power, integrated with both, should be applied. (Joseph S. Nye, Jr., "Think Again: Soft Power", *Foreign Policy*, March 1, 2006). Later, CSIS established the Commission on Smart Power aiming to promote the influence and image of America. The "smart power" has been widely recognized by scholars and politicians including conservatives and has become the consensus in strategy, military and politics of America. He proposed in the Article *Get Smart: Combining Hard and Soft Power* in the July/August Issue of *Foreign Affairs* in 2009 that "the U. S. can become a smart power by reinvesting in global welfare (providing all people and their governments with anything they don't have). The leadership of America is necessary to develop economy, protect people's health, cope with the climate change and maintain an open and stable international economic order. Then America can rebuild necessary systems to deal with the severe challenges or the world through more investment on soft power to compensate the military and economic power." This is the real smart power." (Joseph S. Nye, Jr., "Get Smart: Combining Hard and Soft Power," *Foreign Affairs*, July/August 2009)

"ideology attraction" appeared in the debate on the rise and fall of America, the concept of "soft power" becomes popular and even an independent topic only in recent years.

According to the "Theorists of Decline," the decline of American soft power is revealed by the decline of the attraction of the American model, ideological attraction, ability for institutional innovation and international image. In Russian critic Sergei Kara Draganov's view, America and its ideological system and mechanism were hit hard by the financial crisis. Though the U. S. will get out of dilemma, it will lose more moral and political capitals.[78] Fred Hiatt from the *Washington Post* and Thomas Friedman from the *New York Times* questioned "whether American democratic system has been paralyzed" and pointed out that it was rare for Americans to doubt about model of their country like this. The French expert Corinna Carolina believed that the American political system "started to break down."[79] David Brooks, an American commentator declared that the prestige of American elite system had sharply fallen.[80] The "Smart Power Committee" of the U. S. Center for Strategic and International Studies considered that the image and influence of the U. S. was declining in recent years, while America had to inspire optimism and hopes instead of exporting fears. Some famous American scholars and critics even believed that the American age had ended before the new round of financial collapse and political mistakes.[81]

However, American "Theorists of Thriving" believe that the cultural soft power and diplomatic smart power can make up for economic and military hard power to maintain American leadership. As presented in an article in the magazine *Economist* in 2007, though the soft power of the U. S. was not so well respected as before, an investigation at the same time showed that people were still attracted by American value, freedom and openness in particular, which was demonstrated by immigrants and foreign commodities.[82] According to U. S. Secretary of State Hillary Clinton, the world without the U. S. cannot solve the most urgent problems. America shall employ all appropriate measures in global public welfare, public health and response to climate changes, provide people and governments of

---

78 Сергей Караганов, Мировой кризис: время созидать, 15.10.2008, http://www.rg.ru/2009/09/01/biznes-krizis.html. Quote from Sergei Kara Draganov, "Global Crisis: Chances for Creation," *Russia News*, October15 2008.

79 Corinna Carolina, "Americans Are Seeking Their Own Pattern," French *Le Monde*, December 31 2009. Quote from *China Education Newspaper*, March 21 2011, http://paper.jyb.cn/zgjyb/html/2011-03/21/content_43817.htm.

80 David Brooks, "The Power Elite", February 18, 2010, http://www.nytimes.com/2010/02/19/opinion/19brooks.html.

81 Peter Hartcher, "America's century: is the sun setting on an epoch", October 4, 2008, http://www.smh.com.au/news/world/americas-century-is-the-sun-setting-on-an-epoch/2008/10/03/1223013791575.html. 转引自 http://intl.ce.cn/zgysj/200810/08/t20081008_17000626.shtml.

82 "American power Still No.1", *Economist*, Jun 28th 2007, http://www.economist.com/node/9407806?story_id=9407806.

the world with anything that they cannot be obtained without the leadership of America and turn itself to a smart country to cope with global severe challenges.[83] Some scholars also pointed out talents flowing to America and immigrants would enhance American soft power and maintain its leadership. Ann Marie Slaughter, American liberal political scientist and the dean of Woodrow Wilson School at Princeton University, published an article in the first issue of *Diplomacy* in 2009, indicating that networking was the current standard to evaluate the strength. With the largest and most active networking, the U. S. will possess the global agenda, encourage innovation, promote sustainable development and continue to dominate the 21st century. Slaughter did not regard population as a criterion for the development potentials of countries, since more serious problems could result from more population. Despite being only 1/4 of the population of China and India, the U. S. can attract the best talents by its advanced education system and network system. The advantages of American society lie in its openness and population diversity, since innovation is derived from fierce competition. As predicted by Slaughter, 21st century would be another "Century of America."[84] According to estimations of demographers, the American population will be made up by a small number of non-Hispanics, 25% Hispanic Americans, 14% African Americans and 8% Asian Americans. The U. S. is the only developed country with increasing population and without population proportion decline, based on high-level immigrants. Immigrants can significantly promote the development of certain economic sectors. Each 1% increase of undergraduate immigrants will lead to a 6% rise of the number of patents per capita. Immigrants can also ameliorate the aging and old age problems, improve the soft power and promote the attraction of America.[85]

Available data indicates that Americans have received almost half of Nobel Prizes for Physics and Medicine and two-thirds for Economics. The U. S. Congress approved an act to set the visa indicators (H-1B) for experts applying to work in America to facilitate the entry of talents. The influx of foreign talents further strengthened American competitiveness in global economy. It is impossible for the country to constantly decline with the talent flow. In British politician Chris Patten's opinion, the U. S. is featured with

83 Philippe Naughton, "Hillary Clinton says 'smart power' will restore American leadership", January 13, 2009, http://www.timesonline.co.uk/tol/news/world/us_and_americas/article5510049.ece.

84 Anne-Marie Slaughter, "America's Edge-Power in the Networked Century", *Foreign Affairs*, January/February 2009. Soon after this article was published, Slaughter was appointed the head of Policy Planning Division of the Department of State and became a core member of diplomatic team of Obama. Now she has returned to Princeton University for teaching.

85 Joseph Nye, *Isolated America?*, Finance Net, August 11 2010, http://www.caijing.com.cn/2010-08-11/110495500.html.

strong soft power, especially in higher education and scientific research. Bright students came to study in America from every corner of the world. Among 50 top universities of the world, 42 are in America. Many foreign students choose to stay in the U. S. for scientific research after graduation, for example, working in National Aeronautics and Space Administration (NASA) or in Silicon Valley. The U. S. pays much attention to the investment in higher education, contributing to the thriving higher education industry. As shown by statistics, members of Organization for Economic Cooperation and Development (OECD) invest 1.3% of GDP in higher education, while the figure for America reaches up to 2.9%. Chris Patten said that, "All of these represent the soft power of America beyond comparison."[86]

3. Challenges from Emerging Powers with China as the Representative

In recent years, emerging developing countries represented by the BRIC countries attracted worldwide attention by their raising influence, especially China. As calculated by IMF, the contribution rate of developed countries to global economy dropped from 88.6% in 1990 to approximately 30% in 2010, while the contribution rate of BRIC (Brazil, Russia, India and China) grew from -0.6% in 1990 to over 60% in 2010. BRIC are leaders in stimulating economic growth, with China as the engine.[87] According to a survey made by Pew Research Center in 2009, most or relative majority people in 13 countries out of the 25 countries under investigation believed that China would replace the U. S. as the premiere superpower of the world. 87% Chinese, 50% of Brazilians and 45% Indians considered their countries were in the correct way of development, while only 31% British people, 30% Americans and 26% Frenchmen thought so.[88]

Relative decline of the international status of the U. S. is undoubtedly a result from the rising status of emerging developing countries. Gideon Rahman, the critic of *Financial Times*, pointed out the U. S. really began to decline this time due to the rise of other

---

86 Guo Lijuan, "Peng Dingkang: China and India Cannot Replace the Status of the U. S. in Recent Years,"*Lianhe Zaobao*, September 7 2010, http://www.zaobao.com/special/china/cnpol/pages3/cnpol100907a.shtml.

87 Emerging developing countries represented by BRIC have obtained more shares in IMF. The share of China in IMF has raised by 6.394%, ranking the 3rd of the world; the share of India has increased to 2.751%, ranking the 8th; the share of Russia has grown to 2.706%, ranking the 9th; the share of Brazil has developed to 2.316%, ranking the 10th. Edited by Lin Yaoqin et al., *Blue Book for Emerging Economies: Economic and Social Development Report for BRIC (2011)*, China Social Science Documentation Publishing House, 2011, P 1-20.

88 "New Pattern of World Powers Based on Globalization," *Economists*, December 16 2010, http://finance.ifeng.com/opinion/hwkzg/20101220/3082442.shtml.

countries.[89] In the view of Robin Niblett, the head of British Royal Institute of International Affairs, the proportion of America in "global strength" is declining in every aspect and it is difficult for the U. S. to play its influence, owing to the relative rise of the strengths of China, India, Russia and the EU.[90] The British critic Martin Jacques indicated in his book *When China Rules the World* that the rise of China and India would together end the world ruled by the West since 1800.[91] Fareed Zakaria wrote in *The Post-American World*, "Look around. The tallest building in the world is now in Taipei, and it will soon be overtaken by one being built in Dubai. The world's richest man is Mexican, and its largest publicly traded corporation is Chinese. Its number one caChina is not in Las Vegas but in Macao, which has also overtaken Vegas in annual gambling revenues. The biggest movie industry, in terms of both movies made and tickets sold, is Bollywood, not Hollywood. Even shopping, America's greatest sporting activity, has gone global. Of the top ten malls in the world, only one is in the United States; the world's biggest is in Beijing. But in every other dimension—industrial, financial, educational, social, cultural—the distribution of power is shifting, moving away from American dominance."[92] Neil Ferguson, a history professor at Harvard University, who was famous for proposing the concept of "Chimerica," pointed out that, the large number of American current account deficit was more and more relying on the funds of Asian central banks where China gradually became predominant.[93] According to the French critic Nicholas Baverez, competition of emerging countries has spread from industry to agriculture (Brazil) and service industry (India). The recession of the U. S. is inevitable, along with the rise of emerging powers. However, the end of American leadership may cause potential dangers to the world.[94]

There are many different opinions on when the Chinese economy will exceed America. The chief economist of Goldman, Jim O'Neil, predicted that Chinese economic aggregate would exceed America by 2027 and would be at least 10% stronger than the U. S. in 2050,

---

89 Gideon Rachman, "Think Again: American Decline", Jan/feb 2011, http://www.foreignpolicy.com/articles/2011/01/02/think_again_american_decline.

90 Robin Niblett, "Ready to Lead? Rethinking America's Role in a Changed World", February 2009, http://www.chathamhouse.org.uk/publications/papers/download/-/id/706/file/13443_r0209us_role.pdf.

91 Martin Jacques, *When China Rules the World*, China Citic Press, 2010.

92 Fareed Zakaria, *The Post American World*, New York: W. W. Norton & Company, 2008, p.3, http://www.cnl.com/documents/Post-American%20World.pdf.

93 Neil Ferguson, "Ten Years of Global Powers Moving to the East," UK *Financial Times*, December 31 2009, http://www.ftchinese.com/story/001030559/?print=y.

94 Nicholas Baverez, "Relative Decline of America," *French Le Monde*, September 21 2010, http://world.people.com.cn/GB/12804924.html.

when the total output value of BRIC and Japan would surpass the West.[95] As estimated by the American Economic Council, China was likely to become the largest economy of the world in 2012, according to the purchasing power parity index. The Standard Chartered Bank forecasted in November 2010 that Chinese economy would exceed the U. S. in 2020. According to *The Economist*, China would replace America as the largest economy by 2019 if the average annual economic growth of China and America respectively kept at 7.75% and 2.5%, the inflation was 4% and 1.5% and RMB saw a value rise of 3% each year in the next 10 years.[96] As predicted by IMF, the real-value-based economic scale of China would surpass America in 2016, since when the world would usher in the "Age of China."[97]

Most "Theorists of Decline" believe that the rise of emerging powers will facilitate the process of multi-polarization and prejudice the hegemony of America. The Japanese critic Yasushi Akashi pointed out that the world would come to an "age without polar" owing to the incapacity of the U. S. to maintain the unipolary system.[98] As emphasized by the Japanese scholar Sunohara Tsuyoshi, the current world system is an "age of collective polars" with the U. S. as the center. However, the U. S. has lost its strength, while emerging powers, including Russia, China and India and old powers of Europe and Japan have become potential "poles."[99] The expert on Belorussia, Yuri Baranschke, thought that we could clearly see the limit of America. As time goes by, Americans would gradually lose its ability to solve any crisis. The new situation of world politics and international economic relations adapts to the real political and economic pattern of major powers. China, Russia, EU, America and India constitute the multipolar world.[100]

However, the "Theorists of Thriving" remind people to not exaggerate the influence of the rise of emerging powers on the status of America. In Joseph Nye's opinion, though China is drawing close to America, it does not mean that China will necessarily become the

---

95 "Jim O'Neil, The Father of BRIC Countries: Chinese Economy Can Surpass America by 2027," *Southern Metropolitan Daily*, January 3 2011, http://finance.sina.com.cn/g/20110103/11359197142.shtml.

96 P. W. and D.H, "Save the Date," Dec 16th 2010, http://www.economist.com/blogs/dailychart/2010/12/save_date.

97 Brett Arends, "Cautionary Predictions of IMF: The Approach of the Age of China," *Wall Street Journal*, April 26 2011, http://cn.wsj.com/gb/20110426/roi072206.asp?source=whatnews2.

98 Yasushi Akashi, "Increasingly Complicated World Without Polars," *Current Affairs Comment*, January 18 2008. Quote from Xinhua net, http://news.xinhuanet.com/world/2008-01/25/content_7494610.htm.

99 Sunohara Tsuyoshi, "Age of Power Centralization: Trend of American Diplomacy and G8 Summit in 21st Century," Japan *Diplomatic Forum*, July 2008. Quote from China net, http://www.china.com.cn/international/txt/2008-06/23/content_15871258.htm.

100 Yuri Baranschke, "Inevitable Attack to Iran by America and Israel," website of Russian Strategic Culture Foundation, February 10 2009. Quote from http://xxbei.com/article/4603.htm.

strongest country. The U. S. economy ranked at the second place (second only to Switzerland) in the World Competitiveness Ranking of the World Economic Forum owing to its flexible labor market, high education level, political stability and stimulus to innovation, while China only ranked the 29th. The U. S. is still leading the biotechnology, nanotechnology and 2nd generation of Internet.[101] Some theorists also point out that the economic growth of China will slow down due to the decrease of the working-age population.[102] American scholar Robert Sartre indicated that the rise of China would not damage the interests of America, since it was not a zero-sum game.[103] In Ioannis Gatsiounis's opinion, China has become one of the world powers in terms of economy and other hidden influences, but its impact is a composite and is often checked by America. The U. S. will predominate over China in the trade with Africa and Latin America, etc. based on its diversified trade. Although China was the dominative trade partnership of other Asia-Pacific countries, it mainly relies on export of low-end products, while the U. S. controls the upper commodity supply chain. China is expanding its influence in many areas, but is outshone by the aid and direct foreign investment of America.[104]

"Theorists of Thriving" think that emerging countries will become another group of "meteors" following the Soviet Union, Germany and Japan that challenge the "star," America. Nina Hachigian and other American scholars pointed out that the rise of emerging powers was currently considered to be a threat to the leadership, overall prosperity and life style of America, and would destroy the leadership role of America. However, no power is the enemy of America now, which is rarely seen in history. None of "key powers," such as China, Europe, India, Japan and Russia, are directly challenging the military or ideology of America. Instead, their rise will facilitate the sustainable prosperity and development of the U. S. and even strengthen the American value. These countries share the same goal with the U. S., a stable world and better life of their people, providing America with abundant opportunities. The 21st century may become another American Century.[105] As indicated by

---

101 Joseph, S. Nye, The Future of American Power, *Foreign Affairs*, November and December 2010, http://www.foreignaffairs.com/articles/66796/joseph-s-nye-jr/the-future-of-american-power.

102 "Predictions by British *Economists*: China May Become the Economic Leader of the World by 2019," *Lianhe Zaobao*, December 20 2010, http://www.zaobao.com/special/china/cnpol/pages3/cnpol101220b.shtml.

103 Robert Sartre, "Rise of China: Impact on the Leadership of America in Asia," *India News*, June 11 2008. Quote from *Global Times*, P 06, June 13 2006, http://world.people.com.cn/GB/57506/4474685.html.

104 Ioannis Gatsiounis, "The China Dream: Why the Middle Kingdom Isn't Really Taking over the World", August 09, 2010, http://www.newsweek.com/2010/08/09/the-china-dream.html.

105 Nina Hachigian and Mona Sutphen, *The Next American Century: How The U. S. Can Thrive As Other Powers Rise*, Social Science Academic Press, January 2011, P 2-25.

Natalia Scherova from Russia, Russia has a weakness in the turbulent Central Asia, and China is worried about the triangle region between East India and the southern border of China.[106] Russia is beset by the "Dutch Disease"[107] and over-dependence on resources export.[108] Restrained by resources and environment, some emerging powers are faced with the problem of sustainable development of economy and society, in addition to the weak blow and risk resistance. The long-term accumulation of hidden troubles and conflicts may become the bottleneck for the development of emerging powers. Therefore, it is possible for the U. S. to display its superiority several years later.

III. Criteria to Measure the Rise and Fall of the U. S. and Major Variables for the Development Trend

Overall criteria and references shall be established to observe the change of the status of the U. S. in the world from an external academic perspective, including the verticle and horizontal scale and multiple angles of view. In order to predict the future of the American strength, we shall find out if any change occurs to the cause of the prosperity of the U. S. and whether its strategy conforms to the historical development.

The vertical scale for the measurement of the rise and fall of the current America refers to which development stage with which it is being compared. As indicated in *The Rise and Fall of the Great Powers* by Paul Kennedy, the proportion of the U. S. in the global wealth, production and trade has been declining since the 1960's.[109] Joseph Nye also admitted that the U. S., at the end of 20th century, possessed strength much weaker

---

106 Natalia Scherova, "Potential Overall Crisis of Asia," Russian *Morning News*, June 18 2010. Quote from http://www.globalview.cn/ReadNews.asp?NewsID=21759.

107 Dutch Disease, also known as resources curse, refers to the expansion of resource industry the the price of the development of other industries. In those years, Holland discovered petroleum and natural gas at the North Sea, leading to the value rise of Holland currencies and difficulties in export of other commodities, when Holland saw a slow economic growth and high unemployment rate.

108 For example, Andrei Illarionov, the economic adviser to Putin, emphasized that the resources such as petroleum would bring more harm than good to Russia and concerned the loss of competitiveness of Russian economy. As pointed out by Ryzhkov, the member of parliament, Russia was suffering "Petroleum Aids." According to the report of Economic Department of Russian Academy of Sciences, it at least will take 10 years to transform the economic structure of Russia. Only after 10 to 15 years can Russia became a real power instead of an resource-export-oriented country. Chang Zhe, "Amazing Value of Russian Resources," *Global Times*, June 15 2005, P19, http://world.people.com.cn/GB/14549/3477084.html.

109 Paul Kennedy, *The Rise and Fall of the Great Powers: Economic Change and Military Conflict from 1500 to 2000*, New York: Random House, 1987, p. 432.

than the mid 20th century.[110] Provided that the special period around 1945, when powers other than America were all severely damaged by WWII, is chosen as the reference, everyone will admit the relative strength decline of the U. S. and the impossibility to restore it to its original glory.

The American strength has developed in a curve of fluctuation in the history. The U. S. had replaced Britain to be the top economic power of the world in the late 1800's and early 1900's (U. S. GDP accounting for 23.6% of the world, while Britain accounting for 18.5% in 1900.)[111] After WWII, relative economic strength of the U. S. reached its peak in the 1950's, declined from 1960s to 1980s, revived in 1990s and declined relatively again since the beginning of this century. Its GDP accounted for 56% of the world in 1945, dropped to 34.4% in 1965 and fell to about 26% in 1970s. Under the Reagan administration (1981 - 1989), the proportion of U. S. GDP raised from 23.44% in 1981 to 32.32% in 1985, which later declined again along with the economic rise of Japan and West Germany. After Clinton took office (1993 - 2000), American economic strength saw a significant rise, with the GDP proportion of 24.2% in 1990 growing to 28.8% in 1999.[112] Under the Bush administration (2001 - 2009), the GDP proportion of the U. S. dropped from 28.36% in 2001 to 26.80% in 2008.[113] The trend has continued under the Obama administration. American GDP proportion in the world will fall to 19.88% in 2011 based on purchasing power parity.[114] However, different statistics can also be found. For instance, the entry of "American Economy" in Wikipedia displays that the American GDP amounted to 14.7 trillion USD in 2010, accounting for 25% of world economic output based on exchange rate calculation and accounting for 20% based on purchasing power parity.[115] Another statistic data displays shows that the proportion of American economy in the world has changed

---

110 Joseph S. Nye, Jr., *Bound to Lead: The Changing Nature of American Power*, New York: Basic Books, 1990, p. 5.

111 Gerald Segal, "The Myth of Chinese Power", *Newsweek*, September 20, 1999, http://www.southchinasea.org/docs/Newsweek-The-Myth-of-Chinese-Power.htm.

112 Zhen Bingxi, "Tendency of American Economic Strength at the Early 21st Century," *International Studies*, 1st issue 2001.

113 Mathew Shane, "Real Historical Gross Domestic Product (GDP) Shares and Growth Rates of GDP Shares for Baseline Countries/Regions (in percent) 1969-2010", December 22, 2010, http://www.ers.usda.gov/Data/Macroeconomics/Data/HistoricalGDPSharesValues.xls.

114 IMF, "GDP based on PPP share of world total", *World Economic Outlook (WEO) data*, Dec 04, 2010, http://www.econstats.com/weo/V012.htm.

115 "World Economic Outlook Database." International Monetary Fund. October 2009. http://www.imf.org/external/pubs/ft/weo/2009/02/weodata/weorept.aspx?sy=2006&ey=2009&scsm=1&ssd=1&sort=country&ds=.&br=1&c=111&s=NGDPD%2CNGDPDPC%2CPPPGDP%2CPPPPC%2CLP&grp=0&a=&pr.x=64&pr.y=8.

only a small amount in the previous four decades, which accounted for 26.7% of the world in 2009, slightly higher than 26.3% in 1975.[116]

The horizontal scale for the measurement of the rise and fall of the U. S. refers to which countries or regions will be compared. The American strength relatively declined in the 1960's compared to the Soviet Union in the 1960's. John F. Kennedy once complained in the Presidential election in 1960, "The American power has kept declining compared to the Soviet Union and the communism is steadily moving to every field of the world."[117] In the 1970's and 1980's, Japan and the "Four Asain Tigers" (Hong Kong, Singapore, South Korea and Taiwan) had made enormous progress in economy, while some European countries, including West Germany, exceeded the U. S. in the development speed. An American expert on Asia, Ezra Feivel Vogel, published the book *Japan as Number One* in 1979. In the preceeding 10 years, America had shown great concern to the challenge of Japanese manufacture technologies and trade policies. Since the 1990's, America saw better economic development than other major developed countries. The rise of emerging powers has constituted the major challenge to the strength and status of America, but America has continued to expand its economic and military advantages compared to Europe, Japan and most developing countries. Its status in the Western countries has risen, not fallen.

Multiple angles refer to criteria other than economy. The financial and economic index and economic development trend can only be regarded as one of the main bases. The ability of system and technology innovation, international competitiveness, domestic political cohesion, military ability, citizen quality, education level, talent flow, ideology and cultural soft power and influence on international organizations, etc. shall be taken into consideration to determine the development tendency of America. As analyzed by Chinese scholar Liu Weidong, "It is difficult to determine the overall decline of the status of America if only the financial strength or directly related factors are damaged while other elements did not suffer direct, substantial and negative influences."[118]

We must analyze whether any fundamental change has occurred in history to the main sources of American strong power, so as to determine whether America can maintain a long-term strength (not the international status as compared to other powers) in the future.

116 http://jccavalcanti.wordpress.com/2009/11/21/share-of-world-gdp-1969-2009.

117 Gideon Rachman, "Think Again: American Decline", Jan/Feb 2011, http://www.foreignpolicy.com/articles/2011/01/02/think_again_american_decline.

118 Liu Weidong, "Impact of the Financial Crisis to the International Status of America," *Ideological and Theoretical Education Guide*, 5th issue 2010, http://www.wyzxsx.com/Article/finance/201008/175841.html.

In one opinion, the following four internal causes can be summarized for the strong power of the U. S.:[119]

Firstly, its tradition and spirit of the rule of law maintain the long-term political stability of America. The rule of law in America, as represented by the sound constitutional government system and the deep-rooted tradition of law supreme, is the very foundation of the establishment of America, instead of the rule of man, as well as the fundamental institutional guarantee for a long and peaceful administration of the country, no matter small or large, weak or strong, separate or unified. The spirit of the rule of law also reflects in government officials and citizens' respect to the law.

Secondly, the uniform and continuous value of American society holds the internal cohesion of the country and strengthens patriotism. The value system centering on "freedom" is the foundation of the establishment of America. Freedom, democracy, civil rights, separation of the executive, legislative and judicial powers, separation of religion from politics, market economy based on inviolability of private property and the rule of law with constitution supreme is the core value system accepted by all American people that cross political, religious, class and ethnic boundaries. The complete set of the ideological system has maintained the social cohesion and national unity of America, despite several times of large-scale immigrant absorption.

Thirdly, the technological and institutional innovation plays as a strong driving force for social development. The innovative research and development and technological innovation have been the powerful driving forces for the social development of the country, and thus enable America to maintain its status as an economic power of the world in previous 100 years. The U. S. also attaches great importance to the reform and innovation of higher education and the introduction of foreign talents. It has established a complete national innovation system with the support of social forces represented by the government, enterprises and foundations. It also possesses a sound legislative system for technological innovation and emphasizes protection of intellectual property. Institutional innovation in education, science and technology, culture industry, social science and decision mechanism has increased the "soft power" of America.

Fourthly, the U. S. is featured with an advanced civil society and strong self-correction mechanism and ability, which can prevent development in a wrong direction and any serious strategic mistakes in foreign relations. The U. S. is the only country among modern

---

119 The statement refers to the study research *Reasons for the Great Power of America and Its Diplomatic Advantages and Characteristics* written by Wang Jisi, Zhao Mei, Zhu Wenli and Wang Dong in 2008.

powers where the government appeared after the society. Its motive power for self-adjustment comes from both the government and civil society. The prosperous civil society enables a gradual top-down improvement of the country, so as to ease social conflicts, solve the crisis and lead development in a direction that adapts to economic growth rules and social justice. The main engines to correct the institutional deficiencies and strategic mistakes lie in the extensive political participation by a large amount of non-governmental organizations, schools, churches, citizens and civic education.

On the other side, the capitalism corrosion, polarization of the rich and poor, partisan, corruption of politicians, ethnic conflicts, crisis of belief, various social handicaps, decline of government authority and savior mentality in foreign policies have existed in America for a long time. However, when no fundamental change is found in the four factors, the so-called decline of the U. S. is only a result upon the comparison with other countries.

Few people doubt the natural conditions and strength foundation of America when observing its rise and fall, so the long-term development of the country largely depends on its strategy. In other words, the major variable deciding the rise and fall of America is its strategic choice. The political and economic power of America are relatively more decentralized than other powers, such as China and Russia, while the social force has a greater impact on government decision. Therefore, we shall pay attention to both the social trend and government policies to find out the long-term strategy choice of America.

As pointed out by the Chinese scholar Song Wei, the reform of domestic and foreign strategies of America led by the financial crisis would ease its "over expansion" overseas, reduce international burdens, increase American benefits from the international order, improve the free market system and enhance the flexibility and vitality of American society.[120] Some American scholars indicated that the most urgent challenges to the U. S. mainly lay in the employment, medical care security, people's confidence in the government, innovation capacity of enterprises and the inadaptation of America to the new international pattern after the rise of emerging powers.[121]

Obama had basically taken the above-mentioned concerns into consideration and formulated strategies and policies to restore the strength and status of America. Obama's strategies on internal development mainly focus on construction of large-scale energy-conserving and environment-protective infrastructures, input increase on research

---

120 Song Wei, "The International Status of America Is Not Damaged by the Global Financial Crisis," 40th Issue of *International and StrategicStudies Report of Beijing University*, November 29 2009.

121 Nina Hachigian and Mona Sutphen's works, *The Next American Century: How the U. S. can Thrive as Other Powers Rise*, Social Science Academic Press, January 2011, P 3-15.

and development, development of clean energies, improvement of school hardware facilities, promotion of broadband network application, tax cut for 95% of families, extension of the coverage of medical care insurance, reduction of financial deficits and relaxation of the immigrant policies, showing his great determination to rally the power of America. Current governors have discovered that it is a new and highly potential economic growth point to increase the energy efficiency, develop technologies of clean energies and construct a low-carbon economy. Obama promised to lower the greenhouse gas emissions to the level of 1990 by 2020. It is a way to "facilitate the transformation of economic development pattern" of American characteristics.

However, the less effective plans on economic recovery and social reform by the Obama government, including economic stimulus, "quantitative relaxation," Plan for Doubling U. S. Exports in Five Years, financial regulation, medical care reform, education innovation and new immigration policies, have aroused constant dispute. The conservative "TEA (Tax Enough Already) Party," on behalf of grass-roots interests, came into the forefront, since strong reactions were triggered by the slow economic recovery, high unemployment rate and reform of all-people medical system. In the mid-term election of America in November 2010, Democrats lost their status as majority party in the House of Representatives, and scarcely maintained the majority seats in the Senate, symbolizing a right turn of American politics. However, the general direction of reform is not simply changed.

The foreign strategy adjustment of the U. S. basically accords to the domestic reform. The Obama administration transfers the main focuses in international affairs from the military security based on anti-terrorism and non-proliferation to the economic security aiming to maintain global financial stability and promote economic recovery. As the government places the economic recovery at the forefront, it means that Obama will put more investment in internal affairs and may reduce the budget on foreign aid and defense. More internal resistance and economic strength will further impede the external expansion of the U. S. Only through large investment on economic recovery, employment increase and energy reform can the U. S. maintain the superiority of the USD, restore the trade competitiveness of America, show the advantages of the American economic model and thus maintain the "leadership" and soft power of America.

Regarding international security, the current American government has no longer spoken of "Islamist militants" as the main opponent, or mentioned "war against terror" or "pre-emptive strategy." The focus of American security strategy has remained to be the Middle East, while it is an inexorable trend for the U. S. to "return to Asia." It still attached high importance to nuclear safety, proposed the "nuclear-weapon-free world" and advocated to hold the nuclear safety summit. It accepted the political multipolar pattern, but still dominated the military field. It attempted to develop the "smart power" in terms of politics and diplomacy to compensate insufficient hard power and keep the attraction of west value system. On one hand, since the western world has seen a more serious decline than the U. S., America needed to further strengthen its role as the leader of developed countries and promote the multilateral cooperation mechanisms, such as G-20, to maintain the dominance of the west in global order. On the other hand, the U. S. adopted cooperation, exploitation, disunion and diversion for emerging powers to prevent them from standing as an organization opposite against the West. This is the central task of the "new multi-partnership" diplomacy put forward by the Obama administration.

The diplomatic strategy of "smart power" is now regarded as the diplomatic guiding idea of Obama's government. The U. S. Secretary of State Hillary Clinton indicated that the leading role of America could be revived by strengthening diplomacy of smart power. She proposed that America would employ appropriate or comprehensive measures to enhance the smart power according to specific conditions, including diplomatic, economic, military, political, legal and cultural means.[122] The U. S. Secretary of Defense Robert Gates appealed to the government to increase the investment and efforts on soft power, including diplomacy, economic aid and communications, since American interests could not simply be protected with troops. He also asked the government to create a smart America by applying itself to global public undertakings and "provide people and governments of the world with anything that they cannot obtain without the leadership of America."[123]

The major adjustments on internal and external policies by Obama's government demonstrate that the U. S. has seen a relative decline of strength and status in the world, compared to the turn of the century, despite the denial from American leaders. Meanwhile,

---

122 Michelle Austein Brooks, "Hilary Clinton Attempts to Restore the Leadership of U. S. by Diplomatic Means," *American Reference* of IIP of State Department, January 13 2009, http://www.america.gov/st/usg-chinese/2009/January/20090114121325hmnietsua.1906702.html. On July 15 2009, U. S. Secretary of State Hilary made a speech in the Foreign Relations Committee. She systematically described the diplomatic strategyof "smart power" of Obama government and clarified the specific applications. She said frankly that the rigescent ideology and old operation model must be changed to realize the world peace and development under the leadership of America. America should avoid the balance of hegemony of the 20th century, mutual containment in the Cold War or unilateralism, but should advance with times and adapt to the reality. Hillary Rodham Clinton, "Foreign Policy Address at the Council on Foreign Relations", July 15, 2009, http://www.state.gov/secretary/rm/2009a/july/126071.htm.

123 Joseph S. Nye, Jr., "The War on Soft Power", April 12, 2011, http://www.foreignpolicy.com/articles/2011/04/12/the_war_on_soft_power.

some signs indicate the revival of American economic competitiveness, social vitality and technological innovation capacity, which proves the strong self-correction ability.

IV. Conclusion

The argument of the rise and fall of the U. S. has lasted for more than half a century and is likely to going on for another half a century. However, it is thought provoking that a country can play in the world stage as a leading role for a century or two.

The following assertion was made on a Chinese website: "It is a reality that the U. S. power is declining as free falling."[124] The American scholar Immanuel Wallerstein published an article *The Eagle Has Crash Landed* in 2002, while the bald eagle is regarded as the national bird of America and inlaid on the national emblem. It was strongly opposed by critics in the article *The Eagle Soars*.[125] Different people, with different emotions and policy orientations, insisting on different political stands, will necessarily reach different conclusions. They may even reach opposite conclusion based on unconventional academic analysis.

For a long time ago, Chinese academic circles, media and researchers have often made mistakes on the assessment of the strength and status of America, underestimating the strength and self-correction ability and overestimating the internal and external difficulties of the country, which was mainly resulted from the "political correctness." Of course, we have reasons to believe that the U. S. is experiencing an actual decline this time, due to the irresistible rise of emerging powers. However, the prediction on the rise of emerging powers is even more difficult than the prediction over America. Therefore, observers shall give a cautious answer to whether emerging powers can surpass America.

In consideration of historical, international and domestic factors, the following conclusions on the future of American strength can be reached:

Firstly, it is not the end for the development of American strength in terms of the natural conditions and development potentials of the country. It is featured with both "hard conditions," including the natural conditions and geographical position, and the "soft environment," including advantages of immigrant community and talents, rule of law, innovation mechanism, leberalistic value, authority decentralization and balancing system,

---

124 "What Is the Future of America," *Comments by Hugong*, December 2 2010, http://blog.chinaiiss.com/zzisl/blog/view/25165#.

125 James D. Hardy, Jr. and Leonard J. Hochberg, "The Eagle Soars: a comment on Wallenstein's 'The Eagle Has Crash Landed'", September 22, 2003, http://business.highbeam.com/438285/article-1G1-113757567/eagle-soars-comment-wallerstein-eagle-has-crash-landed.

large number of middle class, relatively open domestic market and powerful overseas expansion.[126] The country still possesses huge development potentials if no major change to the hard conditions (America attaches much attention to protection of environment and resources) and soft environment.

Secondly, in terms of vertical comparison (comparing to the past), the "unalterable quota," such as economic strength, military strength and technological strength, will continue to rise. The democratic and legal system and core values remain unchanged. The education level and social cohesion may lower slightly owing to large number of new immigrants entering the country. Civil society is still lively and the social ideological trend and politics are moving from right-wing conservatives to the middle.

Thirdly, in respect to horizontal comparison (comparing to other powers and strength center), the U. S. will maintain its role as the only superpower of the world in the next two or three decades. Its relative strength has reached the peak in the history despite many difficulties, while the situation of "one superpower and several major powers" will not appear. However, there is no basis to predict when the U. S. will start to decline. We shall not reach the conclusion that America will fall from the peak only based on the development in one or two years or because of one or two major incidents. The economic aggregate of China may catch up with the U. S. in about 10 years, but its comprehensive strength is far behind America, in addition to more uncertainties than America faces. As an emerging developing country, China still has no strength to contain America and the western world or rebuild the world order.

Fourthly, the domestic and international strategies of the U. S. are undergoing profound changes, which benefit the economic recovery, balance of social development, and the improvements of soft power and consolidation of international status. It will be America itself, the global economic and political development trend and other countries' attitudes towards America and policies that determine whether the U. S. can make forward-looking international strategy adjustments, cooperate with other powers and establish a more reasonable global governance mechanism.

---

126 Zi Zhongyun, *America in 20th Century*, first volume of *Coolly Observing the World: Revelations of A Hundred Years*, Sanlian Bookstore, 2007, P19.

Analysis of the Current Strength and Status of the United States: Comparison of Comprehensive Strength Among Major Powers

Huang Ping He Xingqiang Wang Wei Zhou Jing

Discussions of the decline of the status of the U. S., both inside and outside of the country, were increasingly aroused by major internal and external incidents of America in the 21st century.

This report aims to study the strength change of America based on published data in terms of "comprehensive strength,"[127] instead of directly discussing whether the U. S. has declined or studying on the topic subjectively.

To observe the "comprehensive strength" of a country, we need: (1) data even more comprehensive than this report, which later will be gradually improved in the tracking process; (2) a time span longer than this report, which will be gradually expanded in later observations;[128] (3) a field of vision broader than this report, instead of comparison among only a few countries or districts; (4) and introduction of important dimensions that cannot be incorperated in data, such as the system, culture and history, though the problem may become more complicated.

The report attempts to describe (**not analyze**) the variation of the comprehensive strength of the United States and provide a reference for further discussion.

I. Changes of the United States in Ten Years

Major changes occurred in the international pattern along with the disintegration of the

127 The concept of "comprehensive strength" was put forward by Deng Xiaoping. Different to the "smart power" (the smart combination of the hard and soft power) of American government, the comprehensive strength contains many meanings. It focuses to simply and clearly describe the "hardware" based on economy, society, population, politics, science and technology, education, military, energy and environment (some of them are not strengths but the foundations of strengths).

128 According to the traditions of the school of French yearbook, it shall start with the rise of America, which has been well explained in relative works (such as the *Long Twentith Century* by Giovanni Arrighi).

Soviet Union and Eastern Europe in the early 1990s, and the United States started to adjust its international strategy. Due to the terrorist attacks on September 11, 2001, America gave top priority to "anti-terrorism" to maintain the national security and successively launched the Afghan War and Iraq War. Afterwards, the country gradually realized internal stability and security. However, American economy saw a new round of crisis due to the global financial meltdown in 2008 developing from the subprime mortgage crisis of the U. S. in 2007. New changes in American economy and society under the effect of these incidents aroused discussions of more and more people on the status change of America.

1. Natural Resources and Infrastructure of the United States

The United States is rich in natural resources and is the third largest country (excluding the area of inland water, continental shelf and exclusive economic zones) with an area of 9.162 million square meters (16.378 million km^2 of Russia and 9.327 million km^2 of China). According to the Census, America has a population of 308.7 million, with an increase of 9.71% compared to the 281.4 million in 2000, ranking the third in the world. The area of woods in the U. S. amounts to 3.03 km^2, ranking fourth after Russia, which accounts for 33.1% of the American territory, being in the medium level of the current world. The arable area makes up 18.6% of the total area of the U. S., while the arable area per capita reaches 0.6 hectares, ranking the fifth of the world after Canada, Kazakhstan, Russia and Ukraine. In the front ranks of the world, its renewable fresh water resources of inland aggregate 28 trillion cubic meters, cimilar to China, Canada and Indonesia and only behind Brazil (No.1 of the world) and Russia (No.2). Its renewable fresh water resources of inland per capita is 9,199 m^3, higher than 6,511 m^3 of world average level, but far behind countries of rich tropical rainforests, such as Brazil and Ecuador.[129]

The United States is rich in energy resources. In 2009, American proven oil reserves amounted to 19.1 billion barrels by 2009, ranking the 12th in the world, while its output reached 9.14 million barrels a day, ranking the third in the world, only preceded by Russia and Saudi Arabia. The proven natural gas reserves was 245 trillion m^3, ranking the 5th of the world, while the output reached 21 trillion m^3, ranking 2nd worldwide. In 2008, the coal reserves amounted to 260.551 billion tons, which occupied 27.5% of the total reserves of the world, becoming the first worldwide, and the coal output was 1.01 billion tons in 2009, ranking the 2nd in the world. Regarding the electric power, it owned the world's No.1 net

---

129 The data of American population and natural resources is from the Census Bureau (www.census.gov) and indicators on the website of the World Bank (http://data.worldbank.org.cn/indicator).

generating capacity, total power consumption and total installed capacity in 2009, respectively amounting to 5.1 trillion kilowatt hours (kWh), 3.9 trillion kWh and 1.01 trillion (1010 GWe) watts. America also stands in the first place worldwide in energy production and consumption, respectively as 73.4 quadrillion BTU[130] and 99.5 quadrillion BTU in 2008. Its CO_2 emission generated from the use of fossil fuels was 5.4 billion metric tons in 2009, ranking the 2nd in the world. In 2007, the CO_2 emission per capita of the U. S. amounted to 19.3 metric tons, which was among the first ranks in the world, higher than developed economies, such as Japan, Germany, France and Italy, but lower than many rich oil-producing countries in the Middle East, such as Qatar and Bahrain.[131]

The United States is among the first ranked of the world in important indicators for infrastructure. By 2008, American Internet users amounted to 230 million, ranking 2nd in the world; 75.8 Americans out of 100 connected to the Internet, among the highest proportion in the world and same with most developed economies; and 24.02% Americans used fixed broadband Internet, similar to Germany and Japan and less than some small developed economies. In 2008, every one thousand Americans owned 820 vehicles, ranking No.1 among major economies, while the power consumption per capita was 13,638 kWh, only preceeded by Canada and some small developed economies such as Norway, Iceland and Sweden. By 2008, American railways stretched 227 thousand kilometers, far advanced compared to other countries (Russia, as the No. 2, only had a railway of 84 thousand kilometers). Its air traffic reached 9.05 million flights, much higher than the 1.85 million flights of China, who ranked 2nd worldwide. In 2008, the container throughput of the United States amounted to 40.34 million TEU (20 equivalent unit), the second highest in the world.[132]

2. Economic Aggregate of the United States

Economy is the most important latitude to observe the comprehensive strength of a country, while some of the variables of economy cannot be regarded as effective indicators of the "national power."

The overall economic strength of the United States has maintained as the No.1 of the world in the previous three decades. In absolute terms, the GDP of America amounted to

---

130 Quadrillion equals to the fifth power of thousand, i.e. 1000000000000000. BTU is a thermal unit of UK.

131 The data of American energy is from indicators on the website of the World Bank and the U. S. Energy Information Office (http://www.eia.gov/countries/country-data.cfm?fips=US). The unit for coals of America is short ton, which equals to 907.19 kg.

132 The data of American infrastructure is from indicators on the website of the World Bank and International Telecommunication Union (http://www.itu.int/zh/pages/default.aspx).

14.119 trillion US dollars (USD) in 2009, equal to the sum of the GDP of Japan, China and Germany, who were respectively No. 2, 3 and 4 in the world. According to the U. S. Bureau of Economic Analysis, the GDP of America saw a negative growth in 2009, but realized a positive growth in 2010. The GDP of America in 2010 was calculated to be 14.6604 trillion USD based on the current USD price. The American economy had significantly increased in the recent 10 years by 4.2 trillion USD, from 9.8988 trillion USD in 2000 to 14.119 trillion USD in 2009, including the 1 trillion USD growth only in 2007 and 2008. In the previous 30 years, the total GDP of America had grown by 11.5755 trillion, from 2.5435 trillion USD in 1979 to 14.119 trillion USD in 2009.[133]

The U. S. achieved GDP per capita of 45,918 USD in 2009, ranking the 9th in the world (only preceded by eight small economies including Luxembourg, Norway, Qatar, Switzerland, Denmark, Ireland, the Netherlands and the United Arab Emirates) and 1st among major developed countries, based on a population of 307 million, the highest among developed countries. The GDP per capita of America kept a steady growth from 2000 to 2008, but declined a little in 2009 (as shown in Figure 1). However, the GDP per capita in 2009 was still 10,000 USD higher than 2000.[134] In 2010, the GDP per capita of America hit a new ten year high based on the latest population data from the census and the return of the total GDP of America to the prior level before the financial crisis.

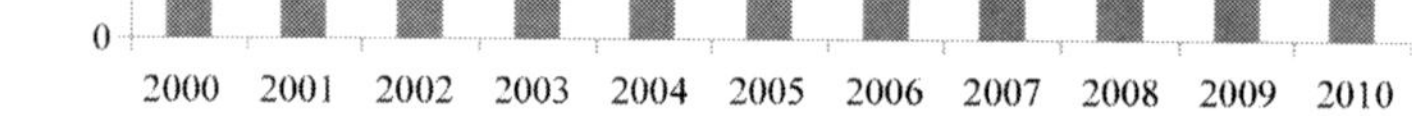

Figure 1 Variation of GDP per Capita of the U. S. from 2000 to 2010 (Unit: USD)
Data source: data of 2000 to 2009 comes from website of the World Bank (http://data.worldbank.org.cn/indicator); and the data of 2010 is calculated based on the total GDP of 2010 provided by the U. S. Bureau of Economic Analysis and the population data of 2010 provided by the U. S. Census Bureau.

133 The above data is from the website of the U. S. Bureau of Economic Analysis (http://www.bea.gov/national/index.htm#gdp) and indicators on the website of the World Bank (http://data.worldbank.org.cn/indicator).

134 In recent three decade, from 1980 to 2009, the GDP growth per capita of America based on PPP had always led the average growth rate of developed countries. The U. S. kept steady growth in this respect, having increased by 33.8 thousand USD in 30 years, from 12,180 USD in 1980 to 45,989 in 2009. See Klaus Schwab ed., *The Global Competitiveness Report 2010-2011*, World Economic Forum, Geneva, Switzerland2010, pp.360-361.

As shown in Figure 2, the proportion of American GDP in the global GDP decreased from 24% in 1980 to 20% in 2010 according to the data based on purchasing power parity (PPP) from the International Monetary Fund (IMF). The proportion will be a little higher as calculated upon the flexible price of GDP of the World Bank, but the variation tendency remains the same. According to the World Bank, the proportion of American GDP in the global GDP dropped from 27% in 1981 to 24% in 2009. It can be clearly seen in the data of the recent ten years that the overall economic strength of the U. S. has been decreasing, especially the last few years, as affected by the financial crisis. In terms of the data based on PPP from IMF, its GDP proportion in the world declined from 23.627% in 2000 to 20.218% in 2010. As estimated by IMF, the figure will further decline to 18.361% by 2015 and drop by more than 5% in 15 years. As calculated upon the flexible USD price of the World Bank, a more significant decline will be seen since the number dropped from 30.733% in 2000 to 24.284% in 2009.

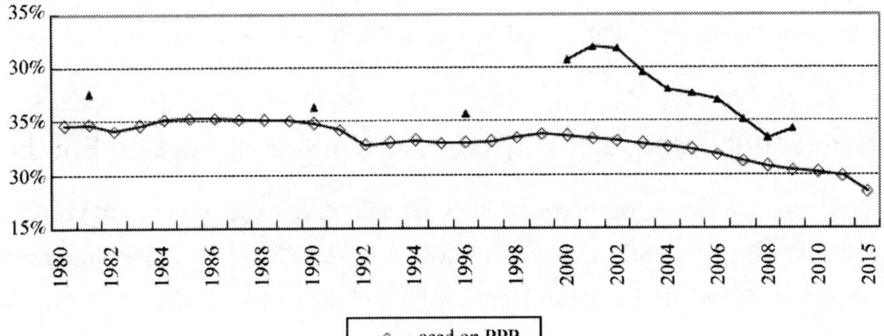

Figure 2 Variation of the Proportion of GDP of America in Global GDP (1980~2010)

Data source: PPP data comes from IMF World Economic Outlook in Maps-October 2010 Database. Data of 2011 and 2015 is estimated by IMF. The data based on current USD price is calculated upon the indicators on the website of the World Bank (http://data.worldbank.org.cn/indicator). Here, we only calculate the data of 1981, 1990, 1996 and 2000~2009.

The U. S. kept a basically steady growth in nominal and actual GDP in the recent ten years (as shown in Figure 3), which was interrupted by the financial crisis in 2008. As calculated based on the fixed USD price in 2000, the growth rate of GDP in America has reached 1.82% on average in the past ten years, but the actual GDP growth has achieved as high as 2.6% from 2000 to 2008 before the financial crisis. It is thus evident that the financial crisis had a significant impact on the economic growth of America. According to the U. S. Bureau of Economic Analysis, the actual GDP of America saw a growth of -2.6% in 2009, but turned to a positive growth of 2.9% in 2010.

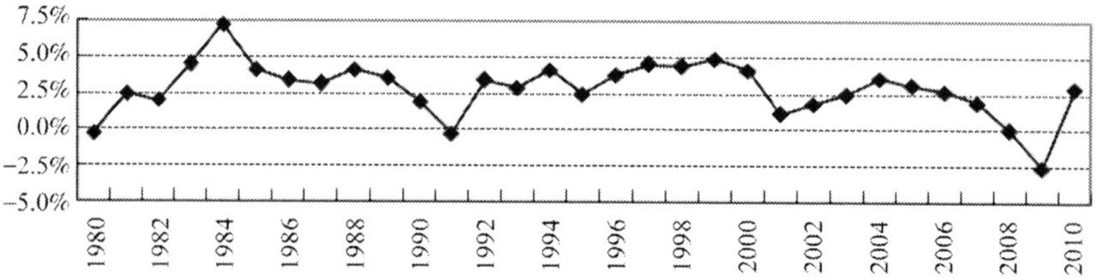

Figure 3 Growth Rate of Actual GDP of America from 1980 to 2010

Data source: the data from 1980 to 2009 comes from indicators on the website of the World Bank (http://data.worldbank.org.cn/indicator); and the data of 2010 is from the website of the U. S. Bureau of Economic Analysis (http://www.bea.gov/newsreleases/national/gdp/2011/txt/gdp4q10_3rd.txt)

The actual GDP of America has kept a steady growth in the previous three decades. Despite the negative growth in 1980, 1982 and 1991, the actual GDP of America maintained a growth rate around 3% most of the time. The average growth rate of actual GDP amounts to 2.54%. Therefore, comparatively, the GDP growth rate of America in recent ten years has obviously experienced a downward tendency. The average grow rate is 2.58% between 1980 and 1989, 3.21% between 1990 and 1999 and only 1.82% in the recent 10 years.

3. International Balance of Payments and Influx of Foreign Funds

The United States has led the world in goods and service export in recent years, which increased from 1 trillion USD in 2000 to 1.6 trillion USD in 2009. Its export volume equals to the export of the whole European Union (EU) and the export of China.[135] Affected by the Obama administration's strategy of doubling exports, the total volume of goods and service export of America has increased to 1.8 trillion USD. In terms of import, the large domestic market of America has attracted a large amount of imports worldwide, having increased from 1.5 trillion USD in 2000 to 2.6 trillion USD in 2008 and surpassing Japan, China and the overall import of the EU. Under the burden of the financial crisis, the import decreased to approximately 2 trillion USD in 2009 and developed slightly to 2.3 trillion USD in 2010. It is still the largest importer of the world.[136]

Despite the high export volume, the United States mainly relies on its large domestic market, instead of export, for economic development. The export dependence has kept about 10% in the recent decade, excluding 2008 and 2010 when the figure exceeded 12%

135 The data comes from indicators on the website of the World Bank (http://data.worldbank.org.cn/indicator).

136 The data comes from the website of the U. S. State Statistics Bureau: http://www.census.gov/foreign-trade/Press-Release/current_press_release/ft900.pdf

(as shown in Figure 4). America has maintained a minimum proportion of goods and service export in total GDP among major economies. The overall dependence on foreign trade (proportion of the total volume of import and export in GDP) of America has been maintained around 25% (excluding 2008, when the figure was higher than 30%), far lower than the world average level.[137]

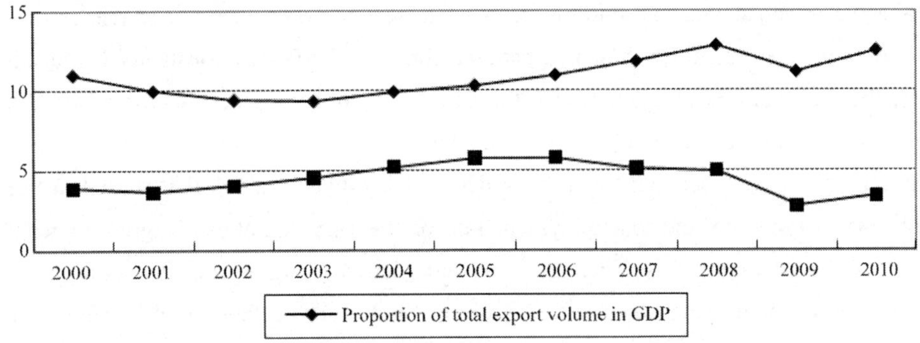

Figure 4 Proportions of the Total Export Volume and Adverse Trade Balance in GDP (%) from 2010 to 2010

Data source: the data from 2000 to 2008 comes from indicators on the website of the World Bank (http://data.worldbank.org.cn/indicator), and the data of 2009 and 2010 is calculated based on the statistics from the website of the U. S. Census Bureau (www.census.gov) and U. S. Bureau of Economic Analysis (www.bea.gov). Refer to http://www.census.gov/foreign-trade/Press-Release/current_press_release/ft900.pdf; and http://www.bea.gov/newsreleases/national/gdp/2011/txt/gdp4q10_3rd.txt.

The biggest problem of American international balance of payments lies in the high international trade deficit. The import of the U. S. is much higher than the export, leading to an increasing deficit in the international trade in the past decade, which grew from 382 billion USD in 2000 to 710.4 billion USD in 2008. As affected by the financial crisis in 2009, the deficit dropped to 386.4 billion USD, but later increased to 495.7 billion USD in 2010. Among the international trade, the goods trade generated an even higher deficit, while the service trade of the U. S. maintained a trade surplus in more than 10 years. The proportion of American trade deficit in GDP has also been increasing within the decade, from 3.84% in 2000 to 4.94% in 2008, with a peak of 5.74% in 2006. The proportion declined to 2.74% under the shock of the financial crisis in 2009,[138] but increased again to 3.38% in 2010.

137 The number is calculated based on the data from the website of the World Bank and the U. S. State Statistics Bureau.

138 The data is calculated based on the indicators on the website of the World Bank (http://data.worldbank.org.cn/indicator).

In some scholars' opinions, the huge trade deficit of the U. S. since the 1990s has reflected the economic vigor, flourishing demand of domestic market and upgrade of the industrial structure of America, instead of the economic crisis.[139] The trade deficit resulted from economic stability, strong social demand and low savings ratio. The financial hegemony of the USD and USD globalization make the huge deficit sustainable. In addition, USD acquired by surplus countries will be returned to America through their purchase of U. S. treasury securities, so the funds outflow led by the trade deficit do not become an issue.

However, the confidence of international funds on USD was constantly languishing since the financial crisis broke out in 2008. Due to the continuing devaluation of the USD, it was more and more difficult to make up the current account deficit with the surplus between American funds and financial projects, so the huge trade deficit started to bring problems. Meanwhile, the unemployment rate of the U. S. significantly grew under the attack of the financial crisis. Therefore, the trade deficit was then regarded as a political issue. Many congressmen and interest groups put trade deficit as the main factor contributing to the rise of the unemployment rate and threatening economic growth and even the economic security. Affected by the situation, the U. S. experienced a decline of import and a growth of protectionism in 2009.

In terms of foreign capital inducement, the net inflow volume of direct foreign investment in America (BoP) based on current USD price has basically stayed the first in the world for nearly 10 years, but the great impact on direct foreign investment was brought about by September 11th terrorist attacks. In 2000, the net inflow of direct foreign investment in America amounted to 321.3 billion USD, ranking the first worldwide. Only one year after the September 11th attacks, the direct foreign investment in America dropped to 84.3 billion USD in 2002, much lower than the 500 billion USD of Germany, since direct funds were transferred to safer European countries. In 2003, the figure further declined to a new low of 63.8 billion USD and the U. S. only got back to its first place world status with a net inflow of 146 billion until 2004. The net inflow volume of direct foreign investment in America respectively reached 243.2, 271.2 and 328.3 billion USD in 2006, 2007 and 2008, maintaining first place. The net inflow in 2009 dropped to 134.7 billion due to the financial crisis, only second to Luxembourg. (See Figure 5)

---

139 For example, Robert P. Murphy, "Perpetual Trade Deficits Can Be Good," Mises Daily, Tuesday, September 11, 2007; [US] Russ Roberts, *The Choice: A Fable of Free Trade and Protectionism*, translated by Liu Linna and Luan e, China Renmin University Press and Beijing University Press, 2001 edition; Yang Guangzhen, "Analysis of the International Competitiveness of the U. S. Based on Trade Deficit," *Economics News*, April 16 1999; Yu Yongding, "Analysis and Prediction of the World Economics," *World Economy*, 3rd Issue of 2002.

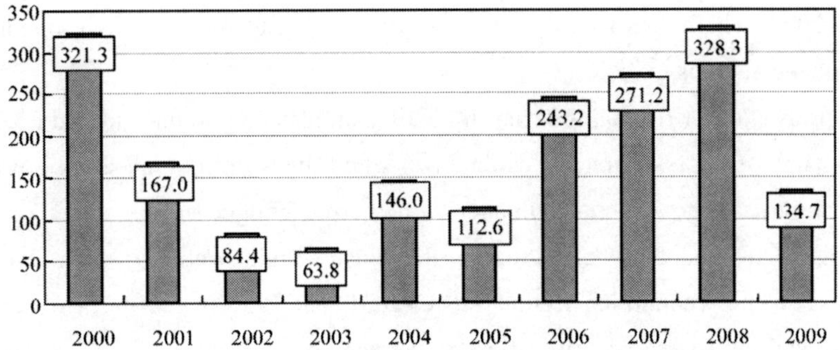

Figure 5 Total Foreign Investment in the U. S. from 2000 to 2009 (Unit: Billion USD)

Data source: indicators on the website of the World Bank (http://data.worldbank.org.cn/indicator)

In the recent decade, the U. S. has ranked the first in the absorption of direct foreign investment, except a few years when the foreign investment was lower than 100 billion USD as affected by "911" Incident. The investment environment of America, as it were, is still attracting most direct investment worldwide. Tracing back two decades, we can find that the net inflows of direct foreign trade in America had also maintained a premiere ranking in the 1990s, which was tens of billions USD between 1990 and 1996, exceeded 100 billion USD since 1997 and reached 289.4 billion in 1999.[140]

4. Government Debt and Financial Deficit

Government debt refers to total outstanding direct debt under fixed-term contracts on a certain date, including both internal and external debt. To be specific, it is the bonds issued by the government inside or outside the country or the loan borrowed from foreign governments and banks. As shown in Figure 6, the debt of the U. S. government has significantly increased from 3.395 trillion USD in 2000 to 7.561 trillion USD in 2009. The U. S. government has invested a large number of funds to cope with the financial crisis, so the government debt exceeded 13 trillion USD in June 2010. The proportion of government debt in GDP is regarded as an important indicator to evaluate the operation status of the state finance, and generally the proportion of 60% or 90% is set as the security line.[141] The proportion of American government debt in GDP had increased from 33% in 2001 to

140 The number and ranks related to FDI of America come from indicators on the website of the World Bank (http://data.worldbank.org.cn/indicator).

141 The government debt accounting for less than 60% or 90% of GDP will not damage the economy. The Maastricht Treaty signed at the foundation of EU expressly regulated that the government debt of EU members should not occupy more than 60% of GDP. According to the empirical research of American scholars Reinhart, Carman and Rogoff (2010), the government debt that exceeds 90% of GDP for a long time will cause adverse impact on macroeconomy.

54.6% in 2008, which was sharply raised to 90% owing to the great investment to cope with the financial crisis.

The proportion of **financial deficit** in GDP is another important standard to assess the financial status of the government, while 3% is often the warning line set by governments of most countries. The American finance turned from budget surplus under the Clinton administration to financial deficit under the Bush administration, which was mainly resulted from the economic decline since 2001 and the increasing expenditure on "anti-terrorism" and state security after the September 11th attacks, but was maintained around the warning line. However, in order to cope with the financial crisis, the U. S. government issued large-scale plans to rescue the market by stimulating the economy and adopting expansive financial policies after 2008, so the financial deficit sharply increased since then and exceeded 10% in 2009.

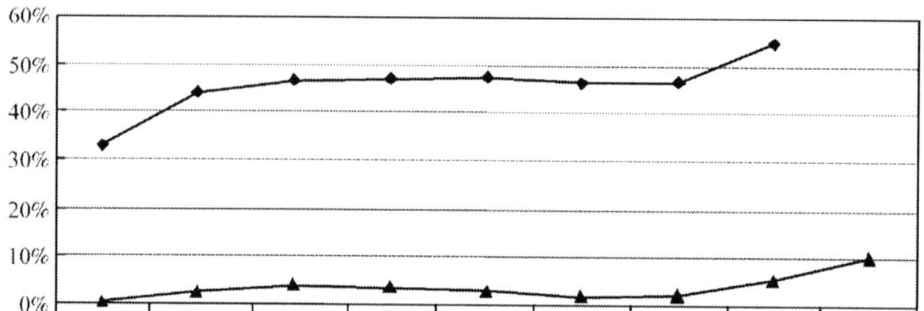

	2001	2002	2003	2004	2005	2006	2007	2008	2009
—◆— 债务率	33%	44.10%	46.80%	46.90%	47.20%	46.40%	46.60%	54.60%	
—▲— 赤字率	0.50%	2.60%	3.90%	3.60%	2.80%	1.80%	2.20%	5.40%	10.20%

Figure 6 Debt and Deficit Proportion of American Government (2001~2009)

In the picture, 债务率 refers to the debt proportion and 赤字率 means the deficit proportion. (Translator's note)

Data source: indicators on the website of the World Bank (http://data.worldbank.org.cn/indicator)

The proportion of government debt and the proportion of financial deficit in GDP are both important indicators to assess the credit rating of the government. The huge national debt and financial deficit have become one of the biggest economic problems of the American government since 2008. It had become the major goal of Republicans in U. S. Congress to reduce the financial deficit, and U. S. President Obama also incorporated the reduction of financial deficit in his State of the Union Address of 2011. Along with the increase of financial deficit of the American government, Democrats and Republicans developed fierce competition on the budget deficit and mutually accused the other side of the responsibility for the increasing financial crisis in recent two years. For the financial budget act of 2011 and 2012, Republicans criticized the Obama administration since their budget bill would increase the financial deficit, and were required to reduce the scale of budget. However, the government and Democrats considered their requirements on the reduction range to be unreasonable. Due to disputes by both parties, the U. S. federal government may collapse since Congress did not approve the financial budget bill. The total debt of America may exceed the upper limit set by Congress, 14.3 trillion USD, in 2011, which will definitely lead to more serious disputes on this issue.

5. Employment Status and Price Level

As shown in Figure 7, the unemployment rate of the U. S. had maintained between 4% and 6% from 2000 to 2008, which was within tolerance. Within the recent two decades, the unemployment rate reached as high as about 7% in the early 1990s, and dropped to a reasonable range along with the economic development. However, being affected by the financial crisis since 2009, the unemployment rate significantly rose to 9.3% in 2009 and 9.6% in 2010. Therefore, it became the most important problem of the Obama administration to create job opportunities and lower the unemployment rate, which took up the main effort and time of the government and affected the implementation of other domestic and foreign economic and trade policies.

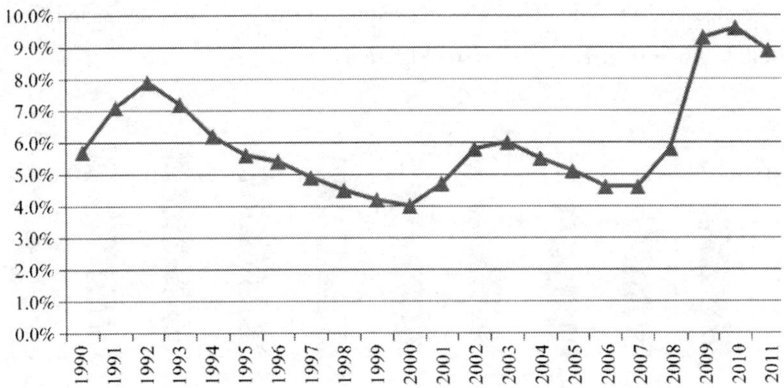

Figure 7 The Unemployment Rate of the U. S. (1990~2010)

Data source: data from 1990 to 2009 is from indicators on the website of the World Bank (http://data.worldbank.org.cn/indicator); and the data of 2010 and 2011 is from the website of the Bureau of Labor Statistics of the U. S. Department of Labor. Data of 2011 only includes the first quarter.

In recent ten years, the consumer price index (CPI) that reflects the price level has remained stable, with a growth rate below 4%, but it was influenced by the financial crisis in 2008. The CPI of America saw a growth of -0.36% in 2009, which meant that deflation occurred in America since Americans consumption expenditure significantly declined (see Figure 8).

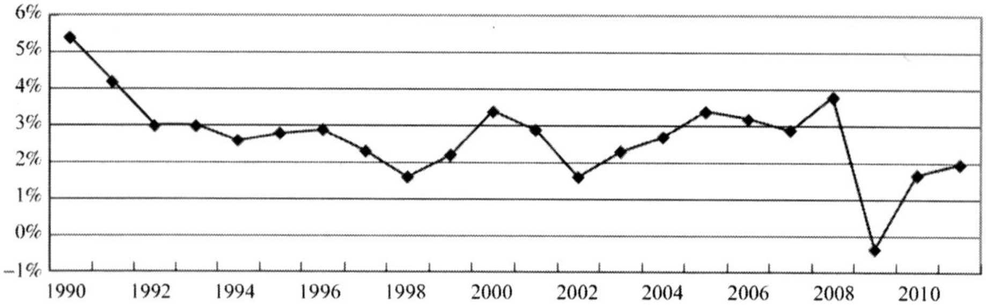

Figure 8 Growth Rate of CPI of the U. S. (1990~2011)

Data source: data from 1990 to 2009 is from indicators on the website of the World Bank (http://data.worldbank.org.cn/indicator); and the data of 2010 and 2011 is from the website of the Bureau of Labor Statistics of the U. S. Department of Labor. Data of 2011 only includes January and February.

6. National Income per Capita and Income Gap

Like GDP per capita, America has been in the front rank among advanced economies in the gross national income (GNI)[142] per capita for the past 10 years. Though it was lower than small economies such as Luxembourg, Norway, Switzerland, Denmark and Liechtenstein, it has ranked the first among major advanced economies, higher than Japan, Germany, France and the UK. The GNI per capita of the U. S. has increased from 34,890 USD in 2000 to 46,360 USD in 2009 (see Figure 9).

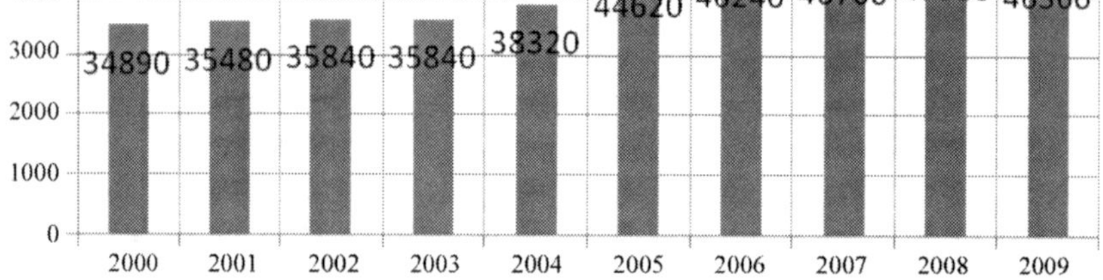

Figure 9 Variation of GNI per Capita in the United States from 2000 to 2009 (Unit: USD)

Data source: indicators on the website of the World Bank (http://data.worldbank.org.cn/indicator)

According to United Nations Development Programme (UNDP), American Gini coefficient between 2000 and 2010 was 0.408,[143] higher than most advanced economies

142 The gross national income (GNI) per capita (called GNP per capita before) was obtained by the GNI (converted to USD according to the World Bank Atlas) divided by the population of that year. This number is measured by the Atlas method of the World Bank.

143 http://hdr.undp.org/en/media/HDR_2010_EN_Table3_reprint.pdf

and some developing countries, which demonstrated that America was a country with a comparatively large gap between the rich and poor.

7. Dependence on Imported Energy

The United States is a big energy producer and consumer, as well as the biggest energy importer in the world. Despite great yield of domestic energy, it still relies increasingly on imported energy owing to its large economy. In the recent decade, the import volume of energy has remained to be 27% to 30% of the energy used (as shown in Figure 10). Since 1973, the international oil crisis has brought about the possibility of petroleum supply failure, so the U. S. government has been trying to adopt appropriate measures to reduce the dependence of America on overseas petroleum. However, the dependence has been increasing for several decades, which greatly constrained American economy and even diplomatic policies. Obama has vigorously promoted the development of clean energy since his inauguration, in order to improve the proportion of clean energy, also called alternative energy, and nuclear energy as a whole, which has been maintained between 10.6% and 10.9% in recent 10 years, lower than France, Japan, Canada, Germany and some other advanced economies.

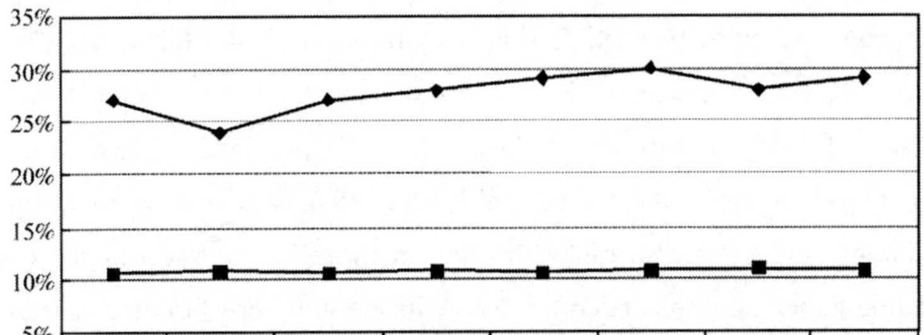

	2000	2001	2002	2003	2004	2005	2006	2007
◆ 进口能源	27.0%	24.0%	27.0%	28.0%	29.0%	30.0%	28.0%	29.0%
■ 可替代能源	10.6%	10.7%	10.6%	10.7%	10.6%	10.7%	10.9%	10.8%

Figure 10 Proportion of Imported Energy and Alternative Energy (Including Nuclear Energy) in Total Energy Consumption of the United States in Recent Ten Years

In the picture, 进口能源 refers to the imported energy and 可替代能源 means the alternative energy. (Translator's note)

Data source: indicators on the website of the World Bank (http://data.worldbank.org.cn/indicator)

8. Science & Technology Development and Education Level

As an important indicator of a country's comprehensive strength, the science and technology development level can guarantee the innovation ability and sustainable economic development of a country. The science and technology development level is revealed by the investment in research and development, technology possession, innovation ability, patent number, intellectual property protection, higher education and educational outlay, and the U. S. has led the world for long time in the above indicators.

The U. S. government has invested about 2.6% GDP in research and development in the recent ten years, and is high on the list of advanced countries. In terms of absolute quantity, the U. S. has ranked the first worldwide in investment in research and development for a long time, reaching 268 billion USD in 2000 and 340 billion USD in 2006.

America also led the world in income from copyright and license fees, having increased from 43.2 billion USD in 2000 to about 90 billion USD in 2009, much higher than Japan and Germany at the second position. The number of resident filings of patents in America has continued to rise, from 165 thousand in 2000 to 230 thousand in 2009 and the average number between 2005 and 2009 was 220 thousand, ranking the second for 10 years, only behind Japan.

The United States also had a long led on the number of published journals and articles on science and technology in the past ten years. According to the White Paper on Science and Technology 2010 published by the Department of Science and Technology of Japan, Americans had published 192,730 articles on science and technology in 1988, four times that of UK (in 2nd place) and 30 times of China (in 15th second). In 1998, Americans published 210,357 on this sector, three times of Japan (in 2nd place) and 10 times of China (in 9th place). In 2008, Americans published 275,625, two times of China (in 2nd place).[144] In addition, the U. S. also ranks the first in the relative "ratio of the cited" of American academic papers, and has been the No. 1 in the number of doctors in natural science for a long time.

The *Global Competitiveness Report 2010-2011* published by the World Economic Forum assessed and sorted the innovation of a country or economy from seven aspects. The U. S. ranked 6th in the "innovation ability" and "R&D expenses of enterprises" and in the top five in five other aspects, including "quality of scientific research institutions," "supply of scientists and engineers," "number of patents for each million people" and "cooperation between universities and industries on R&D," the last of which was led by America worldwide.

144 http://www.mext.go.jp/b_menu/hakusho/html/kagaku_e.htm

Table 1 Growth of Indicators of the Science and Technology Development Level in the U. S. (2000~2009):

	Investment on research and development (R&D) (100 million USD)	Proportion of R&D investment in GDP (%)	Income from copyright and license fees (100 million USD)	Number of resident filing of patents	Number of published articles on science and technology	Number of researchers out of each 1 million people
2000	2680	2.75	432	164795	192743	4481
2001	2780	2.76	407	177513	190593	4535
2002	2770	2.66	445	184245	190496	4566
2003	2890	2.66	467	188941	196432	4818
2004	3000	2.58	567	189536	202084	4648
2005	3230	2.61	644	207867	205516	4584
2006	3400	2.65	707	221784	209237	4663
2007	3755	2.67	856	241347	209695	
2008			898	231588		
2009			989			
World ranking	1		1	2	1	
Variation	Cumulative annual growth of 40% from 2000 to 2007	Average annual growth of 2.67% from 2000 to 2007	Cumulative annual growth of 129% from 2000 to 2009	Cumulative annual growth of 41% from 2000 to 2008	Cumulative annual growth of 8.8% from 2000 to 2007	Cumulative annual growth of 4.1% from 2000 to 2006

Data source: indicators on the website of the World Bank (http://data.worldbank.org.cn/indicator)

Regarding education, America has nearly doubled the educational outlays in the past ten years, increasing from 545.6 billion USD in 2000 to 972 billion USD in 2009. It ranks first in the world. However, its proportion of the educational outlays in the government expenditures and GDP is not outstanding, which respectively keeps at about 14% and 5.5%.[145] Over recent years, the education of middle and primary schools has been far behind major powers of the world. According to the *Global Competitiveness Report 2010-2011 of the World Economic Forum*, the enrollment rate of primary schools and middle schools only respectively ranked the 79th and 45th. Its quality of educational system and mathematics and science education only scored the 26th and 52nd. Both George W. Bush and Obama attempted to issue bills on education reform to increase the investment in primary and middle school education and rebuild the education evaluation system by various measures, in order to maintain the competitiveness of America in the future.

145 The data on American education comes from indicators on the website of the World Bank (http://data.worldbank.org.cn/indicator)

9. Military Expenditure and Military Development

The military expenditure of America amounted to 661 billion USD in 2009, accounting for 43% of the whole military expenditure of the world, equal to the sum of military expenditures of the 14 countries ranking from 2nd to 15th. The American military expenditure had increased by 75.8% from 2000 to 2009, reaching a military expenditure per capita of 2,100 USD, leading all other countries. The proportion of the military expenditure in GDP was also increasing, from 2.96% in 2000 to 4.68% in 2009.[146]

The U. S. now possesses a huge number of nuclear weapons. According to the Federation of American Scientists (FAS) and Natural Resources Defense Council (NRDC), America possessed 6,196 strategic nuclear warheads (including 1,700 intercontinental missiles, 3,120 submarine launched missiles and 1,376 warheads for strategic bombers) and 1,054 launching units (including 550 launchers for intercontinental missiles, 432 launchers for submarine launched missiles and 72 strategic bombers) in 2002. In the *Nuclear Posture Review* published by the George W. Bush administration in 2001, America aimed to reduce the number of strategic nuclear warheads to 3,820 and reduce the number of launching unit to 958 by 2007. As regulated in the Moscow Agreement signed by America and Russia in May 2002, America would reduce the number of strategic nuclear warheads to 3,556 and reduce launching unit to 958 by 2012.[147] After the Senate approved the New Strategic Arms Reduction Treaty (New START) between America and Russia at the end of 2010, scientists of FAS and NRDC published on the *Bulletin of the Atomic Scientists* that the actual strategic nuclear warheads and launching units were respectively estimated to be 1,968 and 798 in 2011, which would be 1,790 and 798 by 2018.[148]

The U. S. is far ahead of other countries in space exploration. According to the Union of Concerned Scientists, the number of satellites launched by America each year has been much higher than other countries in the recent decade, 258 times for the whole 10 years and 26 times per year. More than half satellites were for commercial use, 1/3 was for military use, while others were used for climate and maritime affairs as well as for civil use.[149] The total number of available satellites of the U. S. has exceeded the sum of other countries.

---

146 The data comes from the Stockholm International Peace Research Institute (SIPRI) Military Expenditure Database: http://www.sipri.org/research/armaments/milex/resultoutput/milex_15

147 http://www.nrdc.org/nuclear/nudb/datab1.asp

148 Kristensen, Hans M. and Norris, Robert S., "U. S. Nuclear Forces, 2011." *Bulletin of the Atomic Scientists* 2011 67: 66.Available at http://bos.sagepub.com/content/67/2/66.full.pdf+html

149 The data comes from the website of the Union of Concerned Scientists: http://www.ucsusa.org/

In terms of armed forces, the U. S. possesses a large army. As unveiled by the U. S. Department of Defense, America had armed forces of 1.611211 million people by June 30, 2010, including land forces, navy, Marine Corps and air forces, with 1.137235 million stationed within the country and 297.526 thousand people stationed overseas. 80,650 and 95,800 soldiers were respectively positioned in Iraq and Afghanistan (including reserve forces and the National Guard). Approximately 300 thousand soldiers were positioned in 150 countries worldwide. In 25 countries (in addition to Iraq and Afghanistan) were stationed more than 100 American soldiers. 77,882 soldiers were sent to NATO countries, while 50,087 were positioned in the Pacific area. 19,773 among the 300 thousand garrisons were positioned on naval vessels.[150]

As indicated in the *Base Structure Report* published by the Department of Defense, the U. S. had 4,999 military bases in total by 2010. It had 662 military bases overseas, including 20 large-scale, 12 medium-scale and 570 small-scale bases as well as 60 other various bases. 662 bases were located in 38 countries, mainly distributed in Germany (218 bases), Japan (115) and Korea (86), and could be divided into 276 land forces, 116 navies, 245 air forces and 25 Marine Corps.[151] The number of American military bases overseas has maintained between 600 and 800 in the adjustment within recent years, respectively as 737 overseas military bases in 2005 (16 large, 22 medium and 699 small bases), 823 in 2007 (14 large, 20 medium, 742 small and 47 other kinds of bases) and 716 in 2009 (13 large, 19 medium, 620 small and 64 other kinds of bases).[152]

Therefore, the U. S. has kept about 700 military bases overseas, approximately 300 thousand overseas garrisons (in addition to troops in Iraq and Afghanistan) and military presence all over the world. The military expenditure of America has increased along with the War Against Terrorism after the September 11th attacks. It stretched its military presence into the Middle East and Central Asia by Iraq War and Afghan War. America started to implement its *Global Posture Review* since 2004, which was regarded as the greatest military strategy adjustment since the Cold War. It aimed to improve the battle

---

150 Department of Defense, "Active Duty Military Personnel Strengths by Regional Area and by Country (309A),"June 30, 2010, available at :http://www.globalsecurity.org/military/library/report/2010/hst1006.pdf

151 Department of Defense, *Base Structure Report, Fiscal Year 2010 Baseline, pp.11, 28.* available at : http://www.acq.osd.mil/ie/download/bsr/BSR2010Baseline.pdf. large, medium and small bases are divided according to the plant replacement value of the base. A large-scale base has a plant replacement value above or equal to 1.715 billion USD, a medium-scale base values above or equal to 915 million USD, and a small-scale base has a value less than 915 million USD. Bases with a plant replacement value of 0 are classified as other bases.

152 Department of Defense, *Base Structure Report, Fiscal Year 2009 Baseline,p.23; Fiscal Year 2007 Baseline,p.23; Fiscal Year 2005 Baseline, p. 23.* Available at: https://kb.defense.gov/app/answers/detail/a_id/67/~/base-structure-reports.

effectiveness and flexibility of troops and alter the conventional pattern of overseas military deployment, i.e. establish more small-scale military bases worldwide for the convenience of maneuver deployment of American army, so as to ensure victory in the war against terrorism, cope with the global strength reorganization, maintain its relations with traditional allies and develop its relations with Eastern Europe, Africa and some Central Asian countries.

10. Population Variation Tendencies and Human Development Index

The concept of human development was generated in the 1980s, which defines development as the increase of incomes and also as to create an environment where people can develop their potentials according to their needs and interests and live an effective and innovative life. The United Nations Development Programme (UNDP) started to release the annual Human Development Report in 1990, based on seven indicators including social progress, economics, efficiency, equity, participation and freedom, sustainability and human security.[153]

Table 2 Population and Human Development Indicators of the U. S. (2000~2010)

Year	Rank in the UNDP human development index	Number of people obtaining the right of permanent residence in U. S.	Population growth rate (%)	Population (100 million people)*
2000	3	841002	1.12	2.81421906
2001	6	1058902	1.30	2.85081556
2002	6	1059356	0.95	2.87803914
2003	7	703542	0.88	2.90326418
2004	8	957883	0.94	2.93045739
2005	10	1122257	0.92	2.95753151
2006	8	1266129	0.96	2.98593212
2007	12	1052425	1.00	3.01579895
2008	12	1107126	0.93	3.04374846
2009	13	1130818	0.86	3.07006550
2010	4	1042625	0.57	3.08745538

Data source: rank in the UNDP human development index: http://hdr.undp.org/en/reports/global/hdr2010/

Number of people obtaining the right of permanent residence in U. S.: http://www.dhs.gov/files/statistics/publications/yearbook.shtm

Population and growth rate of America: http://www.census.gov/popest/states/tables/NST-EST2009-01.xls

*: Data of 2000 and 2010 was provided by the census of that year, while the other data was estimated by the U. S. Census Bureau.

153 See the concept and indicators of human development in the introduction of human development by UNDP: http://hdr.undp.org/en/humandev/. More details on the assessment system will also be discovered.

The U. S. has always ranked first among developed economies for many years. It has maintained a growth rate of about 1% in previous decades, but slowed down in recent years. America was still the country that attracted most foreign immigrants among developed countries. About 1 million people had obtained the right of permanent residence in the U. S. each year in the recent decade, excluding 2003 and 2004 when the figure dropped to 700 to 900 thousand after the September 11th attacks, but later it returned to the previous level. In 2006, 1.26 million people obtained the right of permanent residence in the U. S. and 1.04 million in 2010.

II. Comparison and Analysis

The economic and social status and the national strength variation are described above. We will compare the economic and social status of the U. S. to the EU, Russia, China, Japan and India as below, to provide reference for the discussion on the relative strength variation of America. As the only superpower of the world, the United States is undoubtedly the strongest country. However, the EU, Russia, China, Japan and India have their own comparative advantages in different areas of the economic and social development.

1. Biocapacity and Energy Dependence

Resources are essential to social production, so the resource self-sufficiency constitutes an important indicator for the independent economic and social development of a country. Natural resources include both non-renewable resources, such as petroleum, minerals and coals, and renewable resources, such as forests, lakes and arable lands. The current resource issues lie in reducing non-renewable resources and the use of renewable resources in a speed faster than reproduction speed of resources. Currently, the economic policies prefer a green growth pattern, while the ecological environment has become the important factor deciding the competitive edge in the 21st century. In view of this, biocapacity is regarded as an indicator to evaluate the comprehensive strength, which measures the natural resources or the total area of the land and water that can absorb waste discharge in man's activities under general engineering conditions.[154]

154 The actual value of lands of different production efficiency and utilization can be measured based on the standard unit, global hectare (gha). In countries of high production efficiency, a hectare of land can be converted into several global hectares; while in countries of low production efficiency, a hectare of land only equals to a fraction of global hectare. The lands in different applications, such as the arable land, forest, sea and swamp, become comparable owing to the standard measurement.

According to the annual report of the Global Footprint Network in 2010, the countries of top ten biocapacity (in descending order) include Brazil, China, America, Russia, India, Canada, Australia, Indonesia, Argentina and France.[155] In terms of the total biocapacity, America is only second to China and far surpasses France, Germany, UK, Japan and Italy (even exceeding the sum of total biocapacity of those countries) (as shown in Figure 11). On the other hand, the ecological requirements of the U. S. are also only preceded by China and surpass the sum of France, Germany, UK, Japan and Italy.

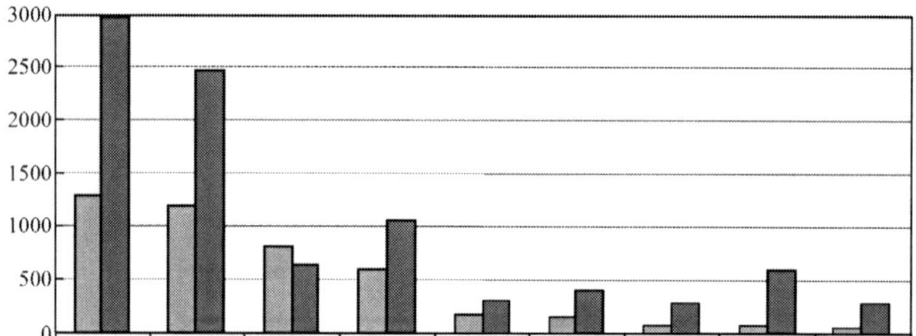

	中国	美国	俄罗斯	印度	法国	德国	英国	日本	意大利
生态承载	1307.2	1193.9	815.83	594.33	185.34	158.48	81.90	76.32	67.85
生态需求	2959.2	2468.0	625.75	1063.4	309.42	418.46	299.05	602.45	296.00

Figure 11 Comparison of Biocapacity (Unit: million global hectares)

In the picture, 中国 refers to China, 美国 for the U. S., 俄罗斯 for Russia, 印度 for India, 法国 for France, 德国 for Germany, 英国 for UK, 日本 for Japan, 意大利 for Italy, 生态承载 for biocapacity and 生态需求 for ecological demands. (Translator's note)

Data source: *The Ecological Footprint Atlas 2010*.

The population must be taken into consideration when biocapacity is assessed. Russia leads the world in biocapacity per person. America and France rank higher than the average level of Europe (2.89) but lower than average level of North America (4.93); the biocapacity per person of Germany is higher than the world average level (1.78) but lower than the average level of Europe; the UK, Italy and China's biocapacity per person is higher than the average level of Asia (0.82) but lower than the world average level; and the biocapacity per person of Japan and India is lower than the average level of Asia. It should be noted that the demands on resources of a country could be satisfied by domestic production and international import. With import volume per capita as the standard, the U. S. (0.01) and China (0.03) are substantially at the same level, solely relying on imported resources; Germany (0.36) and France (0.74) more rely on imported resources; and Japan

155 Ewing B., D. Moore, S. Goldfinger, A. Oursler, A. Reed, and M. Wackernagel, *The Ecological Footprint Atlas 2010*, Oakland: Global Footprint Network, 2010, p.18.

(1.18), the UK (1.51) and Italy (1.91) are highly relying on imported resources (as shown in Table 3).

Table 3 Comparison of Resources–Capacity per Capita (Unit: global hectare)

Country	*Population (million)*	*Resources output*	*Resources import*	*Resources export*	*Resources consumption*	*Capacity*	*Net export*
Russia	141.94	5.15	0.69	1.43	4.41	5.75	0.74
America	308.67	7.99	1.62	1.61	8	3.87	−0.01
France	61.71	4.27	3.23	2.49	5.01	3	−0.74
Germany	82.34	4.72	3.97	3.6	5.08	1.92	−0.36
UK	61.13	3.38	2.84	1.33	4.89	1.34	−1.51
Italy	59.31	3.08	3.5	1.59	4.99	1.14	−1.91
China	1336.55	2.19	0.4	0.37	2.21	0.98	−0.03
Japan	127.4	3.55	2.05	0.87	4.73	0.6	−1.18
India	1164.67	0.91	0.06	0.06	0.91	0.51	0
World Average	6670.80	2.70			2.70	1.78	

Data source: *The Ecological Footprint Atlas 2010.*

Energy is an essential strategic resource for economic and social development. This report also incorporates the dependence of all countries on imported energy. The higher the dependence of a country on imported energy may lead to greater constraints on the stability and security of energy supply. On the whole, developed countries such as America, Japan and Europe are not as good as emerging economies such as Russia, China and India in this aspect, while the U. S. is better than the EU and Japan (as shown in Figure 12). However,

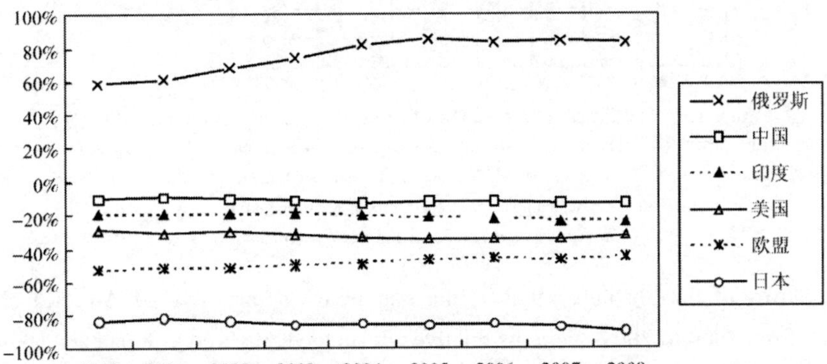

Figure 12 Proportion of the Energy Export in the Total Energy Consumption

In the picture, 俄罗斯 refers to Russia, 中国 for China, 印度 for India, 美国 for the U. S., 欧盟 for EU, and 日本 for Japan. (Translator's note)

Data source: http://www.census.gov; http://epp.eurostat.ec.europa.eu; http://www.stat.go.jp; http://data.worldbank.org.cn; and *China Statistical Yearbook*.

Russia does not only satisfy its own domestic demands but also exports enormous energy, with an export volume equal to 60% to 80% of domestic use. The dependence of Japan on imported energy has slowly increased from 2000 to 2009, while the EU saw a reduction of dependence on imported energy from 53.2% in 2000 to 45.2% in 2009. The dependence of America, China and India on imported energy has increased by a small margin in 10 years, but China's dependence on imported energy is significantly lower than India and America.

2. Gross Domestic Product (GDP) and per Capita GDP

GDP of the U. S. topped the world in 2000, higher than the EU, Japan and China. By 2003, GDP of the EU had surpassed the U. S. for the first time and occupied the first place since then, followed by the U. S., Japan and China. A significant variation can be discovered in the proportions of America, EU, Japan and China in the global GDP from 2000 to 2009, as well as the variation of their economic status (as shown in Figure 13). In terms of the absolute number, the U. S. and EU constitute the first echelon of the world economy, and the economic scale of each exceeds the sum of Japan and China. Japan and China are placed as the second echelon, each of which surpasses the sum of Russia and India.

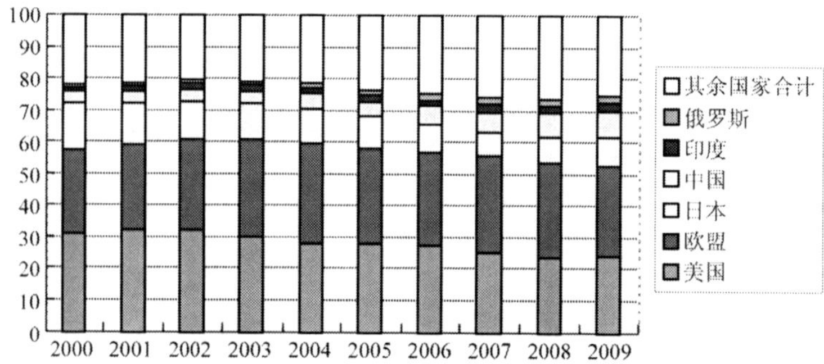

Figure 13 The Proportion of GDP of Major Economies in Global GDP (%)

In the picture, 其余国家合计 means the sum of other countries, 俄罗斯 means Russia, 印度 means India, 中国 means China, 日本 means Japan, 欧盟 means EU, and 美国 means America. (Translator's note)

Data source: http://www.bea.gov; http://epp.eurostat.ec.europa.eu; http://www.stat.go.jp; *China Statistical Yearbook*; and http://worldbank.org/.

In terms of the absolute number, the gap between the GDP of America and EU widened from 2000 to 2009, while its relative advantage compared to Japan and China also increased (as shown in Figure 14). China was 8753.024 billion USD smaller than the GDP of America in 2000 and was 10.780239 trillion USD smaller in 2007. As affected by the global economic crisis, the gap was narrowed to 9134.27 billion USD. Based on the estimation of IMF, the gap between total GDP of China and America will be 8879 billion USD in 2000 and 8735 billion USD in 2011.

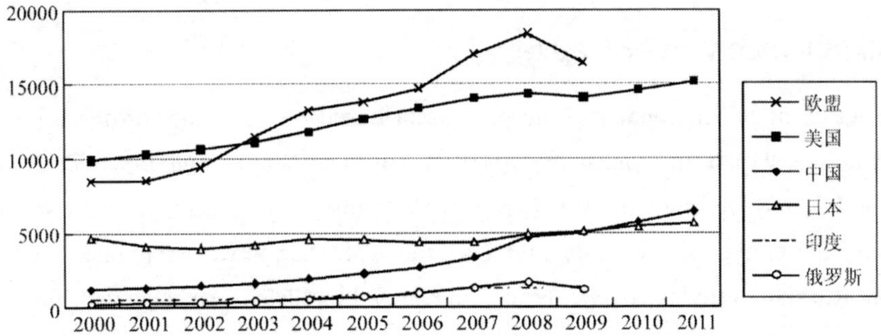

Figure 14 Comparison Between the Economic Scale of America and Major Economies (Unit: billion USD)
In the picture, 欧盟 means EU, 美国 means America, 中国 means China, 日本 means Japan, 印度 means India and 俄罗斯 means Russia (Translator's note)
The data of 2000~2009 comes from http://www.bea.gov; http://epp.eurostat.ec.europa.eu; http://www.stat.go.jp; http://data.worldbank.org.cn; and *China Statistical Yearbook*. The data of 2010 and 2011 comes from IMF: Economic Outlook Database.

Regarding the GDP per capita, the U. S. leads over Japan, China and even the EU, which has a larger economic aggregate. Here lists the multiple ratios between the GDP per capita of America and of Japan, China, Russia and India.[156] In 2000, Japan led the U. S. slightly in the GDP per capita but has fallen behind America later.[157] Regarding emerging economies, China's GDP per capita was 37 times smaller than America ten years ago, but now was only 10 times smaller. Russia narrowed its gap with America, developing its GDP per capita, which was 20 to 5 times smaller than America. India has developed from 80 times smaller to 40 times smaller than America (as shown in Figure 15).

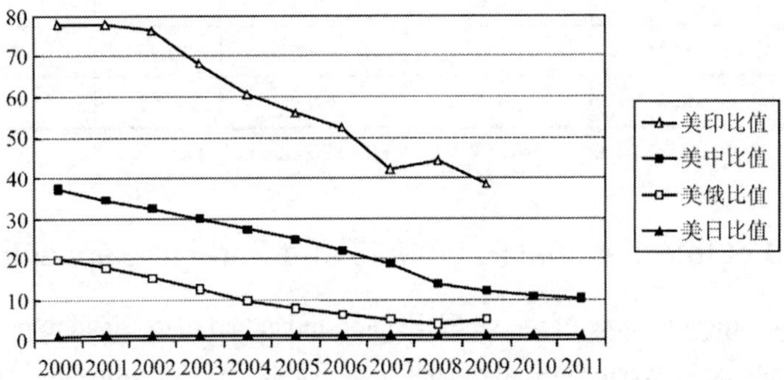

Figure 15 Ratio of GDP per Capita of the U. S., Japan, China, Russia and India
In the picture, 美印比值 means ratio of America to India, 美中比值 means ratio of America to China, 美俄比值 means ratio of America to Russia and 美日比值 means ratio of America to Japan
The data of 2000~2009 comes from http://www.bea.gov; http://www.stat.go.jp; http://data.worldbank.org.cn; and *China Statistical Yearbook*. The data of 2010 and 2011 comes from IMF: Economic Outlook Database.

156 The ratio is calculated based on the data of the World Bank (http://data.worldbank.org.cn/indicator).

157 EU is similar to this situation. It is not drawn in the figure since it is almost the same with the "ratio of America to Japan."

3. National Income per Capita

In terms of the national income per capita based on PPP, the top three countries were America, Japan and Germany in 1990, America, France and Japan in 2000 and America, UK and Germany in 2008 (as shown in Table 4). In contrast to the rise and fall of Japan, Germany, France, Italy and UK, the U. S. has always remained in the top position. Russian national income per capita equaled to 40% of America in 1990, 21% in 2000 and 33% in 2008. Generally speaking, the United States and UK had doubled the income per capita from 1990 to 2008, with a higher speed than Japan, Germany, France, Italy and Russia. Comparatively, China and India, especially China has developed faster than others.

Table 4 National Income per Capita Based on PPP (Unit: USD)

Country	*1990①*	*2000②*	*2008③*	③/①	②/①	③/②
U. S.	22940	35190	46970	2.05	1.53	1.33
Japan	18870	25910	35220	1.87	1.37	1.36
Germany	18630	25670	35940	1.93	1.38	1.40
France	17860	26380	34400	1.93	1.48	1.30
Italy	17360	25370	30250	1.74	1.46	1.19
UK	15860	25590	36130	2.28	1.61	1.41
Russia	9100	7430	15630	1.72	0.82	2.10
India	860	1500	2960	3.44	1.74	1.97
China	800	2330	6020	7.53	2.91	2.58

Data source: *World Health Statistics 2010* of World Health Organization (WHO)

4. Balance of International Payments and Foreign Capital Inflow

The total export volume of the U. S., EU and Japan had maintained to be 10% of GDP of these countries between 2000 and 2009 (see Table 5). Regarding the surplus of the international payments, the proportion of the trade deficit in the GDP of the U. S. dropped from 3.84% to 2.74%. Between 2000 and 2009, the dependence of America, EU and Japan on foreign trade between 2000 and 2009 was lower than China, Russia and India. The latter three countries, with an "export oriented economy," had contributed a great deal to economic growth by international trade, revealing better performance than America, EU and India.

Table 5　Comparison of Dependence on Foreign Trade and International Payments

Year	*Proportion of export in GDP*						*Proportion of trade surplus in GDP*					
	U. S.	EU	Jap-an	Chi-na	Ind-ia	Ru-ssia	U. S.	EU	Jap-an	Chi-na	Ind-ia	Ru-ssia
2000	11.0	—	9.8	20.8	13.2	44.1	−3.8	—	2.5	2.0	−0.9	20.0
2001	10.0	10.3	9.4	20.1	12.8	36.9	−3.6	−0.4	1.7	1.7	−0.9	12.7
2002	9.4	10.0	10.1	22.4	14.5	35.2	−4.0	0.1	2.4	2.1	−1.0	10.8
2003	9.3	9.7	10.6	26.7	14.8	35.2	−4.5	−0.1	2.4	1.6	−1.3	11.4
2004	9.9	9.1	11.7	30.7	17.6	34.4	−5.2	−0.6	2.8	1.7	−1.8	12.3
2005	10.3	9.7	12.5	34.1	19.3	35.2	−5.7	−1.0	2.1	4.6	−2.7	13.7
2006	11.0	9.2	14.1	36.5	21.3	33.7	−5.7	−2.4	1.9	6.7	−3.0	12.7
2007	11.8	10.0	15.5	37.1	20.4	30.2	−5.1	−1.6	2.4	8.0	−4.0	8.6
2008	12.8	10.5	15.3	30.5	23.5	31.2	−4.9	−2.0	0.8	6.4	−5.4	9.2
2009	11.2	9.3	10.7	24.1	19.6	27.7	−2.7	−0.9	0.9	3.9	−4.4	7.4
2010	—	—	—	—	—	—	−3.3	−0.3	2.8	6.2	−2.2	5.1
2011	—	—	—	—	—	—	−3.4	−0.2	2.4	6.5	−2.0	4.6

The data of 2000-2009 comes from http://www.bea.gov; http://epp.eurostat.ec.europa.eu; http://www.stat.go.jp; and *China Statistical Yearbook*. The data of 2010 and 2011 comes from IMF: Economic Outlook Database.

The U. S. has remained to be the first choice of foreign investment in view of the total foreign direct investment (FDI). Its annual FDI had been always higher than Japan, China, Russia and India (See Figure 16). America also led the utilization of foreign investment. On the other hand, the foreign scale does not only reflect the investment environment of a country, but also its domestic investment level. The private savings have been smaller than private investment in America since the 1980s, so not enough funds could be provided to satisfy the overall investment demands. Therefore, America needed to attract more international investments to maintain the economic growth.

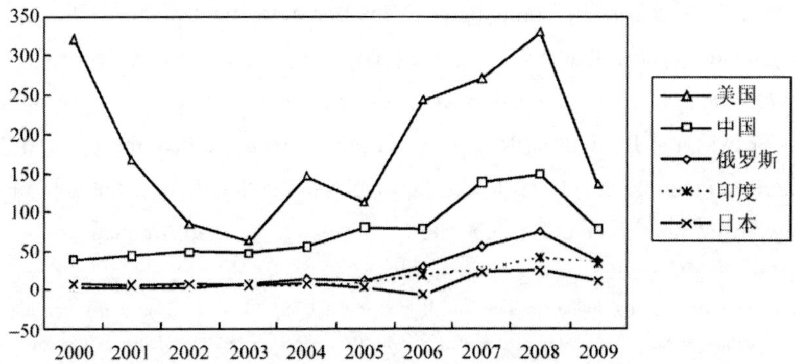

Figure 16　Total Amount of FDI of Various Countries (Unit: billion USD)

In the picture, 美国 means the U. S., 中国 means China, 俄罗斯 means Russia, 印度 means India and 日本 means Japan.

Data source: http://data.worldbank.org.cn

5. Price Level and Employment Status

The U. S. and EU share similar price levels according to their consumer price index, both of which have controlled the index within the acceptable range of 4% and basically maintained the stability of price level (as shown in Figure 17). In short, America and EU kept a stable price level and avoided the inflation, like Russia and India, and deflation like Japan.

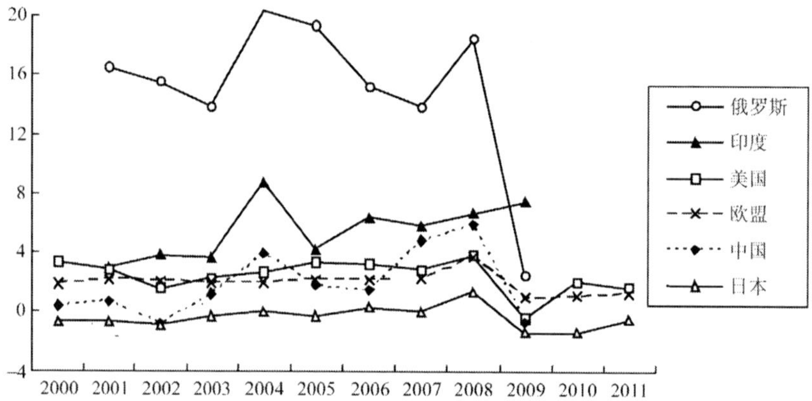

Figure 17 Comparison of Consumer Price Index (%)

In the picture, 俄罗斯 means Russia, 印度 means India, 美国 means America, 欧盟 means EU, 中国 means China and 日本 means Japan

The data of 2000~2009 comes from http://www.bls.gov; http://epp.eurostat.ec.europa.eu; http://www.stat.go.jp; and *China Statistical Yearbook*. The data of 2010 and 2011 comes from IMF: Economic Outlook Database.

In terms of employment status, the unemployment rate in America stayed under 6% from 2000 to 2008, but it had come close to or even surpassed 9% for the successive three years since 2009. The unemployment problem has become one of America's most urgent social problems. Based on the comparison of the unemployment of the U. S., EU, Russia, Japan and China, it is clear that American unemployment had been lower than EU and Russia between 2000 and 2008, but exceeded them in 2009 (as shown in Figure 18). According to the estimation of IMF, the EU will suffer higher unemployment rate than the U. S. in 2010 and 2011. American unemployment was lower than Japan in 2000 and 2011, but kept higher than Japan afterwards. China's unemployment rate was always lower than America.[158]

158 Besides, the reason for the higher unemployment rate of the U. S., EU and Japan than China may lie in the industrial structure. The added value of the tertiary industry in the U. S., EU and Japan may account for 70% or even 80% of GDP, while the added value of both secondary and tertiary industry of China respectively account for 40% of GDP. The employment opportunities in labor intensive industries have significantly exceed America, EU and Japan and thus decrease the unemployment rate of China. It is a "suprise" brought about by the industrial structure that China has a lower unemployment rate than America, EU and Japan.

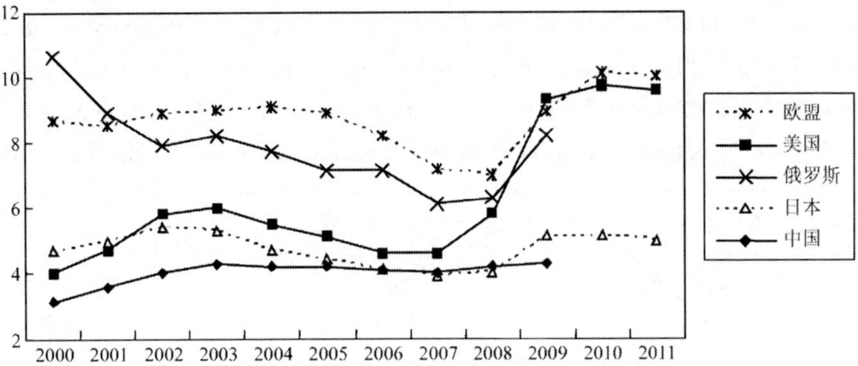

Figure 18 Unemployment Rate of Countries (%)

In the picture, 欧盟 means EU, 美国 means America, 俄罗斯 means Russia, 日本 means Japan and 中国 means China.
The data of 2000~2009 comes from http://www.bea.gov; http://epp.eurostat.ec.europa.eu; http://www.stat.go.jp; http://data.worldbank.org.cn/; and *China Statistical Yearbook*. The data of 2010 and 2011 comes from IMF: Economic Outlook Database.

6. Government Debt and Financial Deficit

Government debt refers to the bonds issued by the government inside or outside the country or loans borrowed from foreign governments and banks. The proportion of government debt in GDP is an important indicator to evaluate the financial status of a country. The U. S. had maintained a proportion of around 35% between 2000 and 2007, which exceeded 40% in 2008, 50% in 2009 and even 90% in 2010 (as shown in Figure 19).

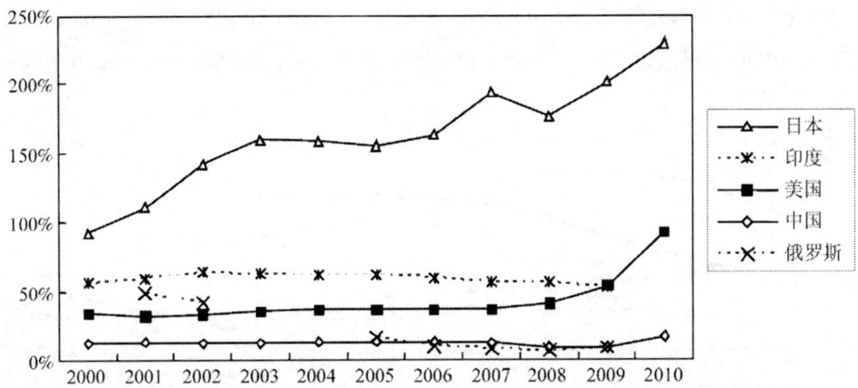

Figure 19 Proportion of Government Debt in GDP

In the picture, 日本 refers to Japan, 印度 means India, 美国 means the U. S., 中国 means China and 俄罗斯 means Russia.
Data source: http://stats.oecd.org; http://data.worldbank.org.cn/; and *China Statistical Yearbook*.
The data of 2010 is an estimated value.

The proportion of financial deficit in GDP had exceeded the warning line (3%) in America in 2008 and even got close to 10% in 2009. As predicted by IMF, the deficit proportion would fall in 2010, but get close to 7%, and would remain above 5% in 2011 (as shown in Figure 20). Comparatively, though the deficit proportion of the EU had exceeded 4% in 2009 and 2010, it will fall back to a little higher than 3%. Japan maintained a ratio of 4%. China had controlled the proportion of financial deficit in GDP under the warning line.

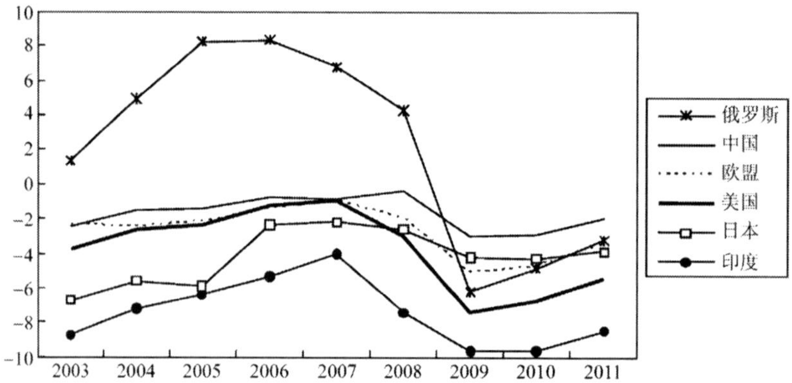

Figure 20 Proportion of Financial Surplus in GDP of Countries (%)

In the picture, 俄罗斯 means Russia, 中国 means China, 欧盟 means EU, 美国 means America, 日本 means Japan and 印度 means India.

Data source: IMF: Economic Outlook Database.

7. Military Forces

The U. S. had exceeded the sum of Germany, UK, France, China and Japan in the absolute number of military expenditure between 2000 and 2009 and constantly rose its proportion of military expenditure in GDP from less than 3% in 2000 to approximately 5% in 2009 (as shown in Figure 21). Comparatively, only Russia, among major economies, had

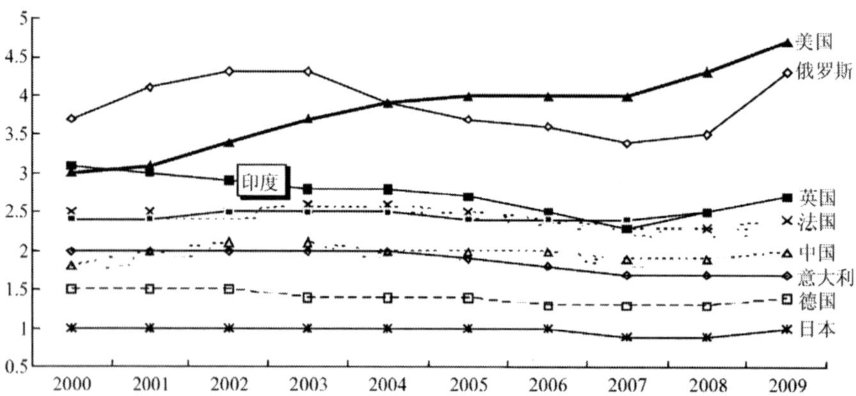

Figure 21 The Proportion of Military Expenditure in GDP of Countries (%)

In the picture, 美国 refers to the U. S., 俄罗斯 for Russia, 英国 for UK, 法国 for France, 中国 for China, 意大利 for Italy, 德国 for Germany and 日本 for Japan. (Translator's note)

Data source: http://data.worldbank.org.cn

reached or even surpassed American proportion of military expenditure. India maintained a proportion of about 3%, which was higher than UK and France, the two permanent members of the UN Security Council, in most years. China has the lowest military expenditure proportion in the five permanent members of the UN Security Council all the time, nearly the same as Italy. As constrained by the Peace Constitution, Japan and Germany had a lower proportion of military expenditure.

The ability of space exploration comprehensively reflects the technological level and carrying and projection ability of a country. According to the Union of Concerned Scientists, a total of 651 satellites had been launched between 2000 and 2010 worldwide. In the report respectively lists the number of times for launching satellites by nine countries including the U. S. and Russia (as shown in Table 6).[159] In this period, the number of satellites launched by America at any year surpassed Russia, China, France, Japan, India, Italy, UK and Germany. Between 2000 and 2007, the U. S. had occupied about 1/2 of the total number of satellites independently launched by the nine countries, which was decreased to about 1/3 between 2008 and 2010. The satellites launched by the U. S. roughly equaled to the sum of other eight countries from 2000 to 2010.[160]

Table 6 Statistics of the Satellites "Independently" Launched by Various Countries Each Year Between 2000 and 2010

Year	*00*	*01*	*02*	*03*	*04*	*05*	*06*	*07*	*08*	*09*	*10*	*Total**
U. S.	31	20	28	24	17	16	28	24	16	32	22	258
Russia	2	7	4	7	4	5	4	9	11	15	13	81
China	1	0	2	3	6	1	4	5	12	6	19	59
France	5	3	5	1	2	2	5	1	5	7	3	39
Japan	0	0	1	3	0	3	4	1	4	4	2	22
India	1	1	2	4	1	3	0	3	2	2	2	21
Italy	0	2	1	0	0	0	0	2	2	2	7	16
UK	0	0	0	2	0	2	0	1	0	6	2	13
Germany	0	1	0	0	0	0	1	3	3	1	0	9
Total	40	34	43	44	30	32	46	49	55	75	70	518

* Including the satellites launched for other countries and excluding the satellites co-launched with other countries.
Data source: http://www.ucsusa.org

159 The database has provided other indicators on the space exploration capacity of all countries, such as the launching weight, satellite weight, trajectory information, running period, perigee and apogee, which play an essential role in the measurement of the space exploration capacity of all countries.

160 The European Space Agency (ESA) is not taken into consideration here, nor the launching success ratio and accident rate of all countries. Therefore, the discussion here is not comprehensive enough. Further data and in-depth analysis are needed to compare the space exploration capacity of all countries.

In terms of the applications of new satellites in America, 1/3 were for military use, 1/5 for government services such as weather and maritime affairs, over 1/2 for commercial use and the rest for civil use (as shown in Table 7). Among the new satellites launched between 2000 and 2010, the new satellites for military use launched by America were five times that of China, while Russia's were four times that of China. In addition, China had only one satellite that assumed two different kinds of tasks, but Russia had 29 and the U. S. had more than 40. Regarding the public service provided by satellites, America and China had better performance than Russia. The U. S. remained ahead of Russia in the combination of commercial and civil use, both of which were followed by China. In fact, the new satellites of the U. S. had surpassed the sum of "BRIC" (Brazil, Russia, India and China) countries. In particular, the new satellites for commercial and civil use launched by the U. S. were one time more than the sum of the four countries.

Table 7 Applications of New Satellites Launched Between 2000 and 2010

Applicatio-n	*Military*	*Governme-nt*	*Commerce*	*Civil*	*Total**
U. S.	75	48	125	21	226
Brazil	0	0	5	0	5
Russia	62	7	44	4	90
India	3	19	0	3	22
China	16	40	6	4	65

* Including the satellites launched by others for the purpose of American use and the foreign satellites that independently launched, co-launched and jointly used by America.

Data source: http://www.ucsusa.org

8. Science, Technology and Education Level

The U. S. and Japan maintained advantages in science and technology compared to China.[161] According to the *Global Competitiveness Report 2010-2011*, the U. S. ranked the 9th, 17th and 1st respectively in the higher education, technical possessions and innovation ability, while Japan ranked 20th, 28th and 4th, and China ranked 60th, 78th and 26th on the three indicators.[162] Despite the long time it took for China to achieve a qualitative leap, the gap with America and Japan on quantity is shrinking.

161 A substantial gap exists in the science and technology development level of EU members, so it is difficult to measure it with a uniform scale. We emphasize on the comparison of the development of America, Japan and China.

162 Klaus Schwab ed., The Global Competitiveness Report2010–2011 *World Economic Forum*, Geneva, Switzerland 2010, respectively in p.340, p.196, p.128.

The ratio of expenditure on science, technology and education to the military expenditure of China and America is compared here.[163] For America, the ratio dropped from 1.92 in 2000 to 1.51 in 2009 (as shown in Figure 22). For China, the ratio was around four between 2000 and 2005 but was maintained around 2.5 since 2006, which mainly resulted from the 40.7% reduction of educational expenditure in 2006. China saw a growth of educational expenditure of 44.6% in 2007 and 38.4% in 2008, and exceeded the level of 2006 by 18.7%. Without other considerations, China emphasized more on the development of science, technology and education than the U. S. in the choice between science, technology and education and military ability.

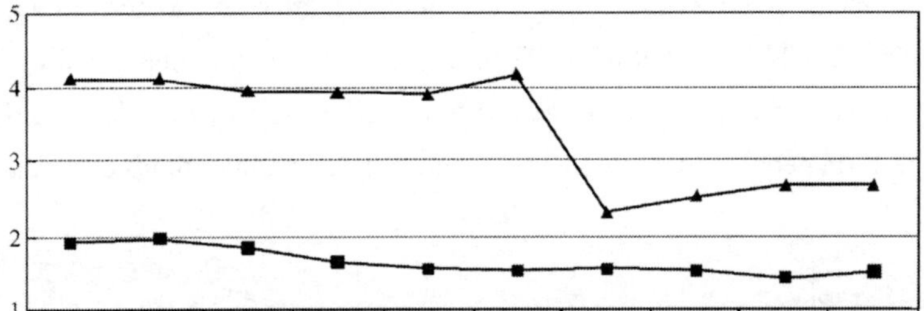

	2000	2001	2002	2003	2004	2005	2006	2007	2008	2009
中国	4.12	4.10	3.94	3.90	3.90	4.16	2.30	2.51	2.67	2.66
美国	1.92	1.96	1.85	1.65	1.55	1.53	1.56	1.52	1.44	1.51

Figure 22 Ratio of the Expenditure on Science, Technology and Education to the Military Expenditure

In the Picture, 中国 means China and 美国 means America.

The U. S. has exceededChina in the number of patents applied by American residents from 2000 to 2007, but was surpassed by China in 2008 (as shown in Figure 23). It only

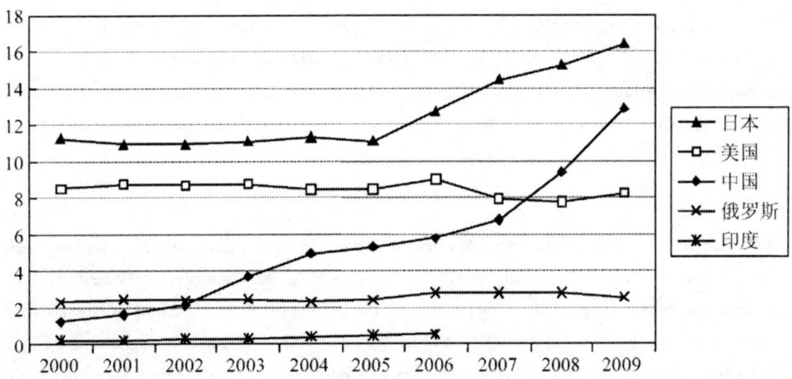

Figure 23 Number of Patents Applied by Residents (unit: 10 thousand)

In this picture, 日本 means Japan, 美国 for the U. S., 中国 for China, 俄罗斯 for Russia and 印度 for India.

Data source: http://www.uspto.gov; http://www.jpo.go.jp; http://data.worldbank.org.cn; and *China Statistical Yearbook*.

163 "Ratio" is calculated based on the data of the World Bank (http://data.worldbank.org.cn/indicator)

took eight years for China to exceed the U. S., who was originally several times stronger than China in this respect. Japan has been ahead of America in the number of patents applied by residents and further increased a lead from 2000 to 2009. The number of patents applied by Japanese residents was nine times that of China in 2000, but only surpassed China in 30% in 2009. America was behind Japan and surpassed by China, but it was 3-4 times of Russia in this respect and had a long lead on India.[164]

In terms of the number of new doctors each year, the U. S. maintained its advantage against Japan in the absolute quantity, but gradually caught up with by China (as shown in Figure 24).[165] India had less new doctors each year than Japan before 2002, but has exceeded Japan since 2003.[166] The ratio of new American doctors to Japanese doctors dropped from 3.342 in 2000 to 2.995 in 2009. With a population equal to 1/4 of China's population and 2.5 times of Japanese population, it is clear that the "number of new doctors among million people" of America is 1.2 times of Japan and 4 times of China.

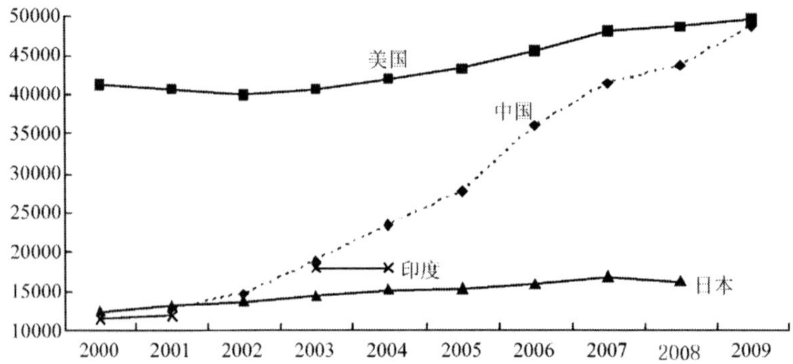

Figure 24 Number of New Doctors Each Year (unit: one person)

In the picture, 美国 means the U. S., 中国 for China, 印度 for India and 日本 for Japan.

Data source; http://www.nsf.gov; http://www.mext.go.jp; and http://www.ugc.ac.in. Data of China from 2001 to 2004 comes from *Statistical Communique of the National Educational Development*, and the data from 2005 to 2008 from *China Statistical Yearbook*.

164 China is far behind U. S. based on the "number of patents owned by each million people," let alone Japan.

165 Russia is not incorporated in the comparison owing to its special academic degree system. Two things about Russian scientific research team shall be clarified here. Firstly, the number of students in Russian higher schools significantly decreased owing to the decline of the birth rate. Secondly, the research team suffers the aging problem and serious brain drain. According to the age structure of schools under Russian Ministry of Education and senior researchers of research institutions, 20.5% of doctors are younger than 50, and 79.5% of doctors are more than 50 years old; and 50.1% of associate doctors are younger than 50 and 49.9% associate doctors are older than 50. See details in Russian National Conditions Net: http://euroasia.cass.cn/ cate/1001.htm.

166 The University Grant Commission of India has submitted annual report but did not publish the complete report, so the data of years after 2005 is not collected here.

9. Population Variation Tendencies and Human Development Index

The demographic factor, as an important indicator in evaluatinh the comprehensive strength of a country, plays different roles in various links of socialized production. On the one hand, it determines the labor sufficiency and overall scale of the consumer market; and on the other hand, it affects the social resources per capita and efficiency of social distribution. In 2000, the population of China surpassed the sum of EU, America and Japan. India, with a population above 1 billion, was only second to China, which was 200 million more than America, three times of Russia and four times of Japan. By 2009, Chinese population had increased by 70 million in 10 years, India increased by 130 million, EU grew by more than 10 million, America grew by more than 20 million, Japan increased by less than 1 million and Russia decreased by approximately 4.5 million.

India and America continued a population growth rate over 10%, higher than China and EU (as shown in Figure 25). On the whole, the population growth rate of the EU was increasing, while India, America and China saw a slower growth rate.[167] The zero or even negative population growth rate had become a serious social issue for Japan and Russia. China and India, in addition to the large population base, shared a higher population growth rate than the EU and Japan. Comparatively, Japan and Russia are faced with the pressure of a shrinking population.

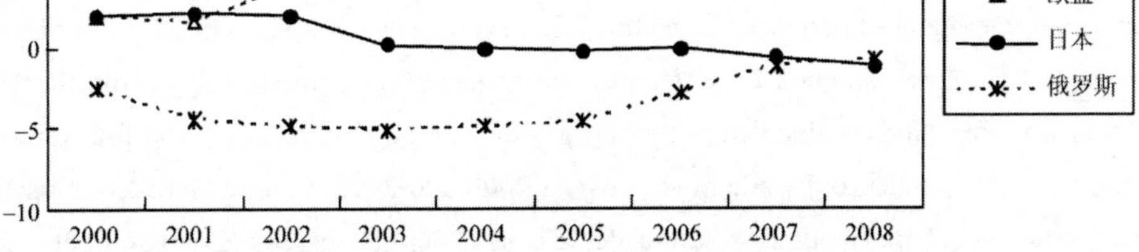

Figure 25 Population Growth Rate of Various Countries (‰)
In the picture, 印度 means India, 美国 for America, 中国 for China, 欧盟 for EU, 日本 for Japan and 俄罗斯 for Russia.
Data source: http://data.worldbank.org.cn.

167 The increase of the growth rate of EU largely depends on the constant European Union enlargement.

In terms of the proportion of people over 65 years old in total population, Japan and EU are faced with the great pressure of aging, with Russia and America ranking the second and third place, and then followed by China and India (as shown in Figure 26). This proportion also reflects the medical care level of a country. Between 2000 and 2009, Japan had ranked the first in the medical care development level, closely followed by EU and America, while China had a comparatively low medical care level.

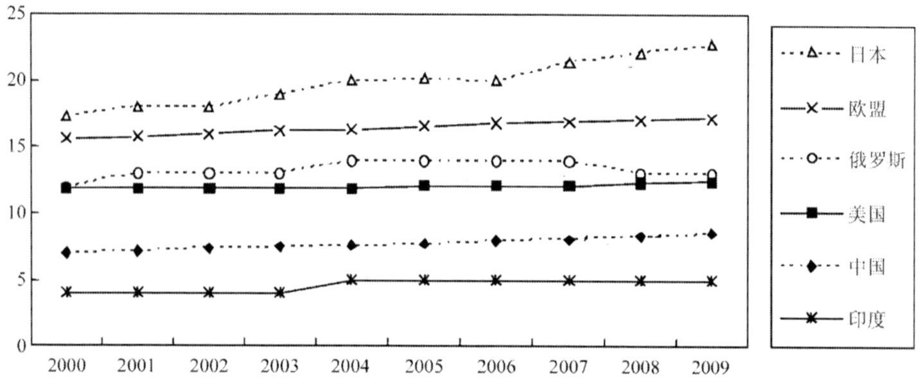

Figure 26 Proportion of People Above 65 Years old in the Total Population (%)
In the picture, 日本 means Japan, 欧盟 for EU, 俄罗斯 for Russia, 美国 for America, 中国 for China and 印度 for India.
Data source: http://www.census.gov; http://www.stat.go.jp; http://epp.eurostat.ec.europa.eu; http://data.worldbank.org.cn; and *China Statistical Yearbook*.

UNDP assesses the achievements of various countries on health and longevity, education universalization and decent life based on HDI. According to the annual *Human Development Report* of UNDP, developed countries had experienced a rise and fall between 2000 and 2010. Italy went up between 2000 and 2005, while America, Japan, UK, France and Germany experienced a decline. However, between 2005 and 2010, the U. S., France and Germany stopped their decline and began to pick up steadily, while the UK continued to drop and declined from the top position to the bottom of the top four powers of the EU. To summarize the situation between 2000 and 2010, despite Germany's rise in ranks, other developed countries saw a decline in different degrees. Comparatively, the U. S. still led over others though it faced a decline.[168]

168 http://hdr.undp.org

Table 9 HDI of Various Countries

Year	1980	1990	2000	2005	2010
U. S.	0.810	0.857	0.893	0.895	0.902
Germany		0.782		0.878	0.885
Japan	0.768	0.814	0.855	0.873	0.884
France	0.711	0.766	0.834	0.856	0.872
Italy	0.703	0.764	0.825	0.838	0.854
UK	0.737	0.770	0.823	0.845	0.849
Russia		0.692	0.662	0.693	0.719
China	0.368	0.460	0.567	0.616	0.663
India	0.320	0.389	0.440	0.482	0.519
World average	0.455	0.526	0.570	0.598	0.624

Data source: http://hdr.undp.org

10. Public Satisfaction Towards the National Development Direction

The national cohesion is an important factor of the comprehensive strength. The public satisfaction towards the national development direction can reflect the national cohesion to a certain degree. According to the survey of Pew Research Center, 72% of Chinese interviewees answered "satisfied" to the current status of the country. More than half of British, Americans and Indians felt "unsatisfied" to the current status of their countries. 70% of interviewees in France, Germany and Russia felt "unsatisfied" about the current status of their countries (as shown in Figure 27).

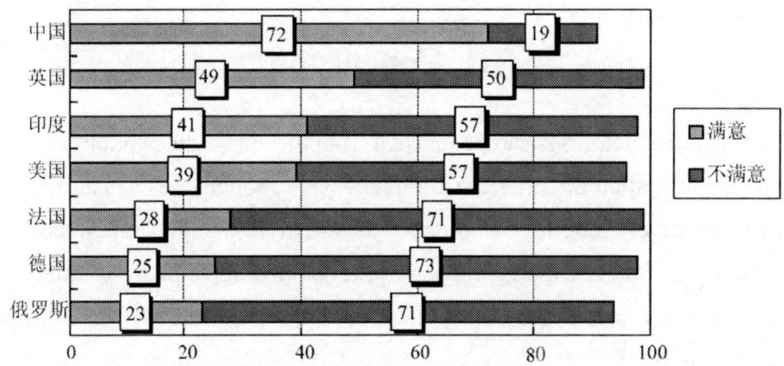

Figure 27 Public Satisfaction About the "Current Status" of Their Countries in 2005

In the picture, 中国 means China, 英国 for UK, 印度 for India, 美国 for the U. S., 法国 for France, 德国 for Germany, 俄罗斯 for Russia, 满意 for satisfied and 不满意 for unsatisfied.

Data source: http://pewglobal.org/

According to the survey on the public satisfaction to the national development direction, American people had shown a declining satisfaction towards the national development direction between 2002 and 2008, which improved in 2009, but dropped again in 2010. The satisfaction of French people reached a peak in 2003, dropped in 2006 and increased afterwards, but below 30%. Comparatively, Chinese and Indian people became increasingly satisfied about the national development direction from 2002 to 2010. Russia saw constant rise in 2008, but a decline after 2009 in this respect. Based on the comparison between the survey in 2002 and 2010, the public satisfaction of China and India had improved significantly; Japan, Germany and Russia experienced a small increase; and the U. S., UK and France lost their people's satisfaction to different degrees (as shown in Table 10).

Table 10 Public Satisfaction Towards the National Development Direction (%)

Year	China	India	Germ-any	Russi-a	UK	U. S.	Fran-ce	Japan	Italy
2002	48	7	31	20	32	41	32	12	24
2003			25	27	46		44		29
2004			20	26	38	39	32		
2005	72	41	25	23	44	39	28		
2006	81	31	29	32	35	29	20	27	
2007	83	42	33	36	30	25	22	22	16
2008	86	41	34	54	30	23	29	23	
2009	87	53	43	27	21	36	27	25	
2010	87	45	39	34	31	30	26	20	

Data source: http://pewglobal.org

III. Conclusion

The following conclusions can be reached from the above descriptions:

Firstly, the formation of American comprehensive strength was a historical process, so it takes a comparatively long time to observe its variation, though some incidents (such as the disintegration of Soviet Union and Eastern Europe, the September 11th attacks, financial storm and economic crisis) may also play an important role in the variation of its comprehensive strength.

Secondly, the variation of American comprehensive strength can be discussed from the perspective of both absolute value and relative value. In terms of the absolute value, the U. S. maintained a sound development in many areas (such as the economic aggregate);

and regarding the relative value (speed and ratio), it has experienced improvements in some areas and declines in other areas. Its decline in the proportion in the world economy attracts most attention.

Thirdly, the comprehensive strength of the U. S. shall be compared to other countries and districts for analysis on its variation. Based on the comparison with EU, Japan, China, Russia and India, it has relatively declined in some areas, though signs were still not obvious in many aspects. In particular, the public satisfaction towards the national development direction of the U. S. continued declining and was positioned at the low level among developed countries, according to the survey of Pew Research Center. However, after the disintegration of the Soviet Union and Eastern Europe, the U. S. has led in the science, technology and military on the whole, without any challengers.

Fourthly, regarding the variation of comprehensive strength of various countries (or districts), the tendency of multipolarity can be seen, but the multi-polar world has not been established yet. Though the EU and Asia are comprehensively the strongest only after the U. S., EU is still undergoing integration, but has not formed a national strength, and no member of the EU can be the equal of America. It is an even longer way for Asian countries (such as China, Japan and India mentioned in this report) to form a united regional force.

Finally, this report only lists the actual variation occurred in some resects (some are still in the process, such as the financial crisis and its consequences). No causality is pointed out here since this report does not conduct an in-depth analysis.

The United States After the Financial Crisis

Chen Baosen

The subprime mortgage crisis broke out in the United States at the beginning of 2007 and developed into a serious financial crisis second only to the Great Depression (1929~1933). The large-scale financial derivatives trading among giant financial institutions for profits and negligent supervision of the government, which ultimately led to the recession of the U. S. itself and many countries worldwide were the main causes for the financial crisis. For the U. S., the recession lasted 18 months, from December 2007 to July 2009, and was distinguished as the "Great Recession" because of its longevity and the seriousness of the damages it caused. However, the economic recovery of the U. S. experienced difficulties after the end of the recession. It was only until the fourth quarter of 2010, when the GDP on an annual basis exceeded the peak value before recession,[169] but employment still saw a bleak future. People held different views on the future of the U. S. after the financial crisis, that the U. S. would either revive or decline. For example, David Walker, the Comptroller General of the General Accounting Office, compared the U. S. to the Eastern Roman Empire that was going to collapse. According to his article published in the United Kingdom's Financial Times, "Americans lack the real spiritual power and political attachment, while the U. S. government is on a 'burning platform' of unsustainable policies and practices on education, environmental protection and energy sources, leading to the failure of economic recovery. It is similar to the Eastern Roman Empire facing the stagnant economy and terrible plague." Russian President Medvedev thought, "The financial crisis in 2008 symbolized that the global leadership of the U. S. was coming to an end." Michael Ignatieff, the Chief of the Liberal Party of Canada, once said, "The peak period of the U. S. strength has passed." On the contrary, Time magazine believed that 21st century was still going to be the century of the U. S. "Though the U. S. has made some severe errors worldwide, it was still the super power of extreme inclusiveness. Other

169 As published by the Bureau of Economic Research of the Department of Commerce in January 2011, the GDP on an annual basis of the fourth quarter of 2010 amounted to 13382.5 billion US dollars, which was 13312.2 billion US dollars in 2008

countries maintain prosperous based on the world peace under the power of US; while the rising of second-class powers influences surrounding areas to greet the constant power projection from US with more joy. This is the best method to ensure that this century will be another U. S. century."

Multi-party collaboration is necessary to comprehensively analyze the future development of America. Here we will only discuss the rise and fall of the U. S. from economic points of view.

View of the Rise and Fall of the U. S. from the Perspective of Periodic Crises

The decline of a great power means that a top power of the world experiences a constant decline of dominance in global politics, economics and military, etc. and completely loses its superiority in the end. The assessment on the severity of the recent financial crisis shall be regarded as the starting point to analyze whether the U. S. is undergoing a decline or starting a decline. In other words, it must be clarified that whether the financial crisis is a slight, serious, or mortal blow to the country as opposed to previous periodic economic recessions.

Most authorities of American economic circles considered this financial crisis to be a terrible blow to American economics. For example, the former president of the Federal Reserve (Fed) Alan Greenspan said on many occasions that this financial crisis happened once every hundred years. Henry Paulson, the U. S. Secretary of Treasure during the George W. Bush administration, felt "no longer fresh" about the financial crisis and bankruptcy of financial institutions, but he believed that "the financial crisis since 2007 was far more serious, bringing greater risks to economics and American people," and would "cause tremendous harm to the world."[170] In fact, Americans suffered the most in the crisis in addition to the financial sector. American household wealth had reached a peak of approximately 66 trillion U. S. dollars (USD) in 2007, which had declined by 17.5 trillion USD by 2009, a greater figure than the annual GDP of America. Millions of families could not afford their monthly mortgage due to financial troubles, therefore lost their ownership of houses and became homeless. In addition, the unemployment rate reached as high as around 10%, representing an unemployed population of 15 million. All these led to American civilians' hatred towards Wall Street.

---

170 [US] Henry M.Paulson, *On the Brink* (translated by Qiao Jiangtao et al.), China Citic Press, April 2010, P 373-374.

It also deserves our attention that the periodic economic crisis cannot be avoided in the American market. There is no essential distinction between the current financial crisis and previous financial crises. The current financial crisis is now revealed in the overproduction of the real estate sector instead of previous manufacturing sector and shows a great shock to American economics owing to the financial collapse led by financial scandals, but it was not necessarily more serious than previous periodic economic crises. In the 20th century, the U. S. had experienced two greater reverses, the Great Depression, which lasted from 1929 to 1933, and the "stagflation" of America and rise of Japan and Germany in the 1970s and 1980s. Many people, including Americans, predicted that the U. S. would decline, but the country had made it through these difficulties. Compared to the Great Depression of a GDP decline of 44% and an unemployment rate of 25%, the current financial crisis only lasted for six quarters, with a GDP decline by 2.6%, i.e. a reduction of 257 billion USD. The "stagflation" in America in the 1980s also significantly shocked the American economics and provided grounds for Paul Kennedy, a British historian at Yale University and specialist in international relations and economics, to predict the decline of America. At that time, the automobile, steel and semi-conductor sector of the U. S. were all defeated by Japan in terms of quality and cost, having aroused the awareness of suffering American businesses. America did its best to catch up with Japan and finally brought about a decisive turn in the information technology (IT) revolution. During the current financial crisis, the U. S. maintained unbeaten real economy. Despite no significant technical breakthrough, the U. S. kept continued developing in ICT (Information, communications and technology) and other fields and maintained a strong technical power. Favorable factors contributing to American superior status and competitiveness in the world lay in its technical innovation, which can improve the labor productivity and help the authority release social contradictions, and the space for the adjustment of policies owing to two parties ruling in turn.

In general, this financial crisis hit the virtual economy harder than the real economy, Wall Street harder than Main Street, and the soft power harder than the hard power. The collapse of the "fairy tale" of Wall Street deflated the pride of Americans. It was only a serious setback compared to previous economic crises, so it is possible for American economy to get back on track based on adjustments since the country had gone through even more serious crises.

View of the Rise and Fall of the U. S. from the Perspective of Economic Strength and Status

The economic strength and status of the U. S. is an important reference with which to observe the rise and fall of American economy, including the following ten factors: the gross domestic product (GDP) and GDP per capita, labor productivity, science and technology, educational level, fiscal solvency, financial strength, sovereign currency, multinational operation, human resources and natural resources.

1. GDP and GDP per Capita Reveal a Country's Ability to Accumulate Wealth and its Level of Prosperity

According to the world development indicator of the World Bank, the U. S. took up 23.4% of global GDP in 2008, while Japan occupied 8.1%, Germany 6%, France 4.7%, United Kingdom 4.4%, Italy 3.9% and Canada 2.3%. In terms of the growth rate of GDP, the U. S. enjoyed a slightly faster growth speed than other developed countries in the 28 years from 1980 to 2008. Regarding the gross national income (GNI) per capita[171] that reflects the level of prosperity, the U. S. reached 46,360 USD, while Japan equaled to 83% of America, Germany and France 92%, UK 89%, Canada 91% and Italy 76%. The above statistics indicate that the advantages of the U. S. to other major developed countries lie in the higher proportion of global GDP, faster GDP growth rate and higher level of prosperity. However, the GDP of the European Union (EU) (including 27 countries) had surpassed America in gross amount.[172] Nevertheless, the U. S. could play to its advantage in economic scale as a sovereign state of centralized power and unified policies. The EU still needs to make long-term effort to improve its political and economic system to catch up with America.

Compared to emerging powers, the disadvantage of the U. S. lies in the slow growth rate of GDP, but a vast economic chasm still exists in the economic scale and level of prosperity between emerging powers and America. It calls for the continuous efforts of several generations of emerging powers to catch up to America in economic scale and even more efforts to surpass America in the level of prosperity.

2. Labor Productivity

Labor productivity refers to production per man-hour, which depends the competitiveness of an enterprise and a country. The improvement of labor productivity means to produce the same or more physical and intellectual products in fewer man-hours.

---

171 GNI includes the GDP of a country and the incomes from other countries (such as interests and dividends) deducting the incomes of other countries obtained from the country.

172 See the Nation's Comparison in CIA website. The GDP of EU (27 countries) in 2009 amounted to 15.9 trillion USD, while America was 14.6 trillion.

The U. S. leads major developed countries in this respect. Given the labor productivity of the American manufacturing sector in 1973 as 100, Japan equaled to 55%, Germany 73%, France 66%, UK 52%, Holland 77% and Sweden 66%. In 1996, Japan equaled to 74%, Germany 82%, France 84%, UK 67%, Holland 97% and Sweden 90%. It demonstrated that the U. S. still led over major competitors despite the narrowing gap. According to the statistics of America in 2010, the average annual growth rate of non-agricultural labor productivity was 2.1% from 1995 to 2000 and maintained 2.1% between 2000 and 2008, while EU reached 2.1% and 1.5% in these two periods. America saw a significant edge in this aspect.

According to the research report of New York Federal Reserve (Fed) in 2007,[173] Japan and Europe had experienced a leap of labor productivity in the 1960s, when the annual growth rate of the labor productivity in Japan reached as high as 8%, and EU of 15 countries achieved 5%. However, their growth rate slowed since then for two reasons. Firstly, their marginal utility of capital input reduced after they had narrowed their gap with America. Secondly, they needed innovation, instead of imitation as before, to improve technologies, and they could not keep up with the U. S. in innovation.

The report also attached importance to the growth rate of labor productivity in emerging economies and revealed the results as 6.4% in China and 4.4% in India. It also indicated that the U. S. did not need to worry about the emerging economies, since China's labor productivity only accounted for 15% of the U. S. and it took a long time for China to catch up with America.

3. Science and Technology

The Defense Research Institute of the Research and Development (RAND) Corporation in the U. S. published the report on the U. S. Competitiveness in Science and Technology in 2008, where it compared America to other countries in terms of several important indicators that reveal the science and technology development level. Based on the comparison, they came to the conclusion that the U. S. was still leading the world in science and technology. (1) The expenditure on research and development of other countries did not significantly exceed America, who took up 40% of the total expense. China, India and Korea increased their input in science and technology and achieved considerable results, but they only occupied small proportions in the times of quotation of

---

173 *Current Issues in Economics and Finance* of the Federal Reserve Bank of New York, Volume 13, Number 8, September 2007.

patents, scientific publications and research results. (2) The science and technology teams of other countries still fell behind America. EU of 15 countries saw a growth of talented personnel similar to America, while Japan maintained a slower growth rate. In fact, 70% of Noble Prize winners were working in America. (3) EU of 15 countries and Japan were slower in the growth of innovation patents. The U. S. accounted for 38% of the patents of technical invention in the Organization for Economic Cooperation and Development (OECD) industrial countries, 49% of the quoted publications and 63% of the frequent cited publications. The U. S. has a strong awareness of unexpected development, keeps alert about the development of other countries and attempts to adopt appropriate measures to maintain its superiority, though it is leading the world in science and technology development.

4. Educational Level

Education is the foundation to improve moral qualities, intellectual ability and physical fitness of human resources. The U. S. was the first country in the world that implemented compulsory education, having created the most important base for an innovative country. American universities are very competitive, especially research institutes and laboratories of universities, where a wealth of excellent talents in science and technology are born, because they are heavily subsidized by the government and enterprises. American universities have taken up 2/3 of expenditure on fundamental research. In terms of the number of Nobel Prize winners, American Noble Prize winners have accounted for 39% of the world and 47% in science, medical science and economics, with a total of 315 prizewinners winning 317 prizes. According to statistics, the expenditure on universities has taken up 2.4% of total GDP of America, while the average figure of other OECD countries has been around 1.5%. The federal government has assumed 32% of expenses on universities but only 7% of middle and primary schools, which can explain why American universities gain higher reputation than its middle and primary schools.

5. Fiscal Solvency

The fiscal solvency of a country, which originates from economy, decides its ability to maintain state apparatus, provide public service, adjust income distribution and cope with sudden emergencies. Despite the low proportion of financial income in GDP of the U. S., it still leads the world in the fiscal solvency owing to the premiere gross product created annually by the country. The primary task of U. S. President Barack Obama after his inauguration was to overcome the financial crisis. Therefore, he adopted financial incentives and gave first rank to solving the financial crisis, which led to a historic high of financial deficit. The accumulated deficit was estimated to about 1.96 billion USD by 2015, accounting for 102% of GDP. The net debt would reach 14 trillion USD after the deduction of government bonds of various government departments, making up 73% of GDP and exceeding the internationally recognized warning line of deficit. In some people's opinions, runaway inflation would occur when the national debt of the U. S. rose to 150% of GDP. However, it seems unlikely for the EU-style sovereign debt crisis to happen in America based on the current situation. There are two reasons for this conclusion. Firstly, the large amount of deficit aims to stimulate the economy. Obama will reduce the deficit as he promised when the economy has recovered. Secondly, the status of the USD as the currency for international reserves enables America to support the national debt with sovereign currency, which is called the policy of "quantitative easing" of Fed. Thirdly, America is featured with special international credit owing to its economic scale and prosperity, and three rating organizations to define the rating of American national debt are headquartered in America.

6. Financial Strength

The financial strength of a country depends the expanding ability of the economy. The large-scale financial strength of the U. S. is revealed by its abundant funds, strong and diversified financial intermediaries and the active financial market. The funds for the financial market originate from national savings, while national savings have formed and been managed by various funding pools, such as bank savings, pension funds, insurance funds and mutual currency market funds, etc.

American pension funds and mutual funds have made up approximately 46% of the world. The U. S. is the country with the largest number of annual insurance income, followed by Japan, and the two countries have taken up 40% of global insurance funds, though their population only accounts for 7% of the world. America also possesses the largest and most active stock market, with a total stock value in 2008 of 3.7 times more than Japan and a trading volume of 6.2 times more than Japan, the second largest stock market. American bond market is extremely flourishing, which accounts for 39% of the world. Mortgage-backed debt securities, making up one fourth of the American bond market, amount to a total of 9.2 trillion USD. The subprime mortgage securities are estimated to be between 500 billion and 1.4 trillion USD. The country also possesses several world-famous banks.

A variety of financial companies are classified as financial intermediaries, including hedge funds, private equity funds, venture capital funds and mutual currency market funds. Strong financial intermediaries facilitate the introduction of financial resources to the real economy. However, the unrestrained expansion of financial activities in aim to gain profits may spell disaster to the real economy, which is exactly the root for the financial crisis this time. The financial crisis has greatly damaged American finance, but it may provide opportunities for the sound development of American finance industry if the finance industry can serve the real economy based on the *Financial Reform Act*. The financial crisis has prejudiced the strength and status of the American finance industry, but has not fundamentally changed the superiority of American finance in the world.

7. Sovereign Currency

As the major reserve currency of the world, the means of exchange and pricing tools of the USD have great influence over the global financial activities. According to IMF and the European Central Bank, the USD took up 65% of international reserves by December 2006 before the financial crisis, while the euro accounted for 25%, Japanese yen for 6%, British pound for 3% and other currencies for 1%. After the crisis, the USD made up 61.6% of international reserves by September 2009, while the euro accounted for 27.7%, Japanese yen for 3.2%, British pound for 4.3% and other currencies for around 3%. The change of the proportion mainly resulted from the change of exchange rate. The USD plays an important role in international settlement and accounts for 62% of the total amount. The USD settlement is the most common method in both Asia and Europe and is even adopted by euro area in the trade with economies outside the area.

As unveiled by a report by the U. S. Council on Foreign Relations in 2010, the status of the USD as the world reserve currency will not change in a short amount of time. According to the article "Two Fairy Tales on USD" published in the third issue of the *Quarterly Capital Flow Report* of 2010 by the Council, assets will remain to be priced by USD. The inflow national debt of America reached a record high in 12 months by July 2010. According to the report, the foreign investment on inflow securities market remain stable despite the significant decline of foreign official capital invested on American national debt in 2010 based on the official data.

8. Transnational Operation

Transnational operation is an integral part of the globalization strategy of American enterprises and has significantly improved the competitiveness of America. American transnational companies have led in the foreign direct investment (FDI). In 1990, American

FDI accounted for 35% of total global FDI, ranking first among developed countries and three times that of the UK, the No. 2 of FDI. The U. S. maintained an FDI proportion of 33.8% in 2009, which declined to 22.7% in 2009 due to the financial crisis but still maintained two times more than the second place France. FDI of the U. S. had reduced year by year in the three years of financial crisis, with a decline of 16% in 2008 and 25% in 2009, but it was still lower than 43%, the average decline rate of the world. Therefore, the proportion of American FDI had increased from 17% in 2007 to 22% in 2009.

In addition to the first place of FDI in the world, American transnational companies possess strong competitiveness worldwide. 139 out of the Top 500 transnational companies chosen by Fortune 500 magazine in 2010, i.e. more than 1/4, came from America, followed by 71 Japanese companies, 46 Chinese companies, 39 French companies, 37 German companies, 20 British companies, 11 Italian companies and 8 Canadian companies. The annual income of the 139 American transnational companies amounted to 6.9772 trillion USD, accounting for 30.8% of the total income of Top 500 companies.

9. Human Resources

Currently, some countries saw an increasing population while others experienced declining fertility rate. The U. S. is the former, contributing to the better economy of America. By 2010, the American population rose to 307 million, 2.1 times of Russia, 2.4 times of Japan and 3.7 times of Germany. America has kept a growth rate above 8% each ten years for a consecutive 50 years. The population increase of the U. S. mainly resulted from an influx of immigrants and a high birth rate. The influx of immigrants to America had amounted to 11 million from 1990 to 2000, accounting for 1/3 of the population growth in America. The increase rate of population who was born in foreign countries had amounted to 16% from 2000 to 2005. Diverse population facilitates the development of America. Meanwhile, the age structure of the U. S. lays the foundation for the constant development and prosperity of the country. The aging population exerts great pressure on many countries, but America does not greatly suffer in this issue, since its population aged over 65 only accounts for 12% and the average age of Americans is 36, which is rarely seen in developed countries. However, the U. S. is faced with challenges to improve the quality of minorities and enhance the national reunification.

10. Natural Resources

The U. S. is richly endowed with superior climate, water, land, mineral resources, etc. Mostly located in temperate and subtropical zone, the country is featured with agreeable climate and abundant precipitation. Water resources of the U. S., with overall abundance and high quantity per capita, are richer in the north than the south, ranking fourth only after Brazil, Russia and Canada. America possesses adequate land resources and its area of arable land accounts for 19% of its territory, leading the world. Its area of arable land per capita amounts to 0.6 hectare, 2 times of the global average level, with 40% located in the main land. It owns rich mineral resources and is the country with the most verified reserves of the world. The characteristics of American mineral resources lie in its abundant supply and abundance of different resources, being richest in non-metal mineral resources with widest distribution, followed by metal resources and energies with wide but unbalanced distribution. Rich natural resources lay a solid foundation for economic development. However, people may acquire the "Dutch Disease"[174] based on too great natural resources, which has not happened in America yet. The country has given full play to its rich natural resources.

The above ten factors reflect the current economic strength and status of America. It takes long-term efforts for other major developed countries or emerging powers to catch up with or even surpass America. It is still too early to discuss the decline of America.

Militarism and the Decline of Powers

The U. S. was shocked by the book, *The Rise and Fall of the Great Powers*, written by Paul Kennedy, the famous American historian, in the 1980s. It predicted that the U. S. and Soviet Union would decline, because it was demonstrated by the 500-year-experiences that the rise of economy of great powers would necessarily lead to military expansion and conflicts among powers and would finally result in the decline of great powers. It is worth researching whether or not the U. S. will decline due to militarism.

In addition to economy, the U. S. is even stronger in military. The country accounts for 5% of world population, 25% of world economy and as high as 46.5% of world expenditure on military. According to the article "America, World's Top Military Forever?" by Bernd Debusmann published by Reuters on October 1 2010, American presidents "all believe that the U. S. shall garrison all around the world and shall have the right to intervene in global affairs," and "the Obama administration is no exception, while

174 Dutch Disease, also known as resources curse, refers to the expansion of resource industry the the price of the development of other industries. In those years, Holland discovered petroleum and natural gas at the North Sea, leading to the value rise of Holland currencies and difficulties in export of other commodities, when Holland saw a slow economic growth and high unemployment rate. (Translator's note)

no sign indicates his difference with other presidents after the World War II." It is believed that the globalization strategy of big funds and large enterprises is the root of the militarism of America. It also resulted from the close relation between the development of military and national defense and the development of high technology, so the authority attaches great importance to the investment on military. Based on the history, the science and technology development of America was derived from both business and military demand. The research and development demand and profits brought about by the war are reflected in several respects.

Firstly, the war brought together many top-class scientists to conduct research and development for the war, which facilitated daily scientific research and development. In 1916, it was voted by the National Academy of Sciences (NAS) that all scientific elite nationwide were to be brought under the unified allocation of the state. Later, George E. Hale, the famous astrophysicist and founder of the Carl Tyke Lab, and scientist Noyce Milliken jointly established the National Research Council (NRC) under the control of scientists. They demonstrated by their research achievements that scientists were more useful than the military department on solutions to chemical warfare or detection of submarines.

Another important achievement brought by World War I was the popularity of the achievements made by pioneers in research and development and important labs as well as their organization methods and management experiences. The scientific and technical achievements made in World War I also bridged the "pure" science and "applied" science. For example, the AT&T Company gathered their best researchers to utilize the facilities provided by the government to research the detection of submarines and had succeeded.

World War II even played a more important role in the promotion of science and technology. Therefore, WWII was regarded as the "Great Age of Science," when atom bombs, radars, proximity fuze, antibiotics, digital electronic computers and many new materials, theories and analysis technologies were jointly developed by scientists in universities and labs. They made significant contributions to solve war demands. Nuclear power plants, satellite communications and civilian industry products such as personal computers were developed based on these inventions. During the war, on one hand, the government allocated large amounts of funds to ensure large-scale scientific researches; and on the other hand, the intellectual resources could be well mobilized to realize some important goals.

The end of WWII did not inhibit American efforts on military technologies, owing to the start of the Cold War between the U. S. and the Soviet Union. In a quarter of a century after 1945, its expenses on national defense researches had been increasing in a geometric ratio. During the 1950s, the only important capital source for the physical research of the U. S. was the U. S. Department of Defense and the Atomic Energy Commission (AEC). 80% of the research projects of the federal budget were related to national defense in 1960. The development of quantum electronics was wholly funded by the expense on military researches after the war.

After the disintegration of the Soviet Union, America did not remove its focus from military but continued to research, develop and produce modernized weapons in order to maintain its status as the premiere military presence. Therefore, the war, in addition to the business demand, is necessary to promote the technological innovation of America.

The war can facilitate the science and technology development, which does not necessarily mean that all wars waged by the U. S. are favorable for the country to maintain its dominance. Wars can be divided into just wars and unjust wars. In terms of World War II, it stimulated Americans' patriotic enthusiasm as a just war, which meanwhile facilitated the domestic political unity, technological progress and social harmony. In contrast, the Vietnam War caused political break-up and economic stagflation. The Iraq War launched by George W. Bush also brought about adverse effects. The desire of the U. S. to dominate the world is reflected by the monopolistic companies seeking profits worldwide, which aroused the risk of militarism. However, Americans' love for peace and opposition against the war may restrain warmongers. The historical lessons indicated in *The Rise and Fall of the Great Powers*, written by Paul Kennedy, are also applicable for America. It depends on the result of the struggle between strengths that whether America will decline due to militarism.

View of the Rise and Fall of the U. S. Based on History

Two points are emphasized by the historical materialism to view the rise and fall of a country. The first is the social system reform. The rise and fall of a country is led by the new production relations that can further improve social productivity, such as the evolution from the feudal society to the capitalist society. In this course, the old feudal countries were destined to decline while the new emerging capitalist countries were destined to rise, such as the rise of the UK in the 18th century. The second point is that the countries following the beaten path will decline while innovative countries will rise, typically represented by the rise of the U. S. and decline of the UK in the 19th century.

Historians regard the period of 1815 – 1914 as the "Century of Britain." However, the

UK lost the game among great powers after two world wars and was defeated by America. Four lessons could be learned by the UK, which also warned Americans.

Firstly, the UK lost its leading position in the technological revolution. Though the victory in the Napoleonic Wars was the symbol for the rise of Britain, it was exactly the First Industrial Revolution started by Britain that laid a solid foundation for the Century of Britain, i.e. the invention of steamers and the rise of big factories. Besides, the Industrial Revolution further promoted the capitalist mode of production. Britain lost its leadership in the Second Industrial Revolution, i.e. the Electric Revolution at the end of 19th century. A passage written by a British factory inspector in 1901 was cited in *An Industrial History of Modern Britain* by J. H. Clapham "The country had led in the steam age all the way, but it seemed we had fallen behind America and other countries in the electric era." Electric companies were rarely seen in the UK between 1886 and 1888, while "central electrical stations can be found nearly in every city or town with a population above 20 thousand." In other words, the U. S. was the standard-bearer in the Second Industrial Revolution based on electricity, like Britain did in the First Industrial Revolution. It was because the British Empire was high on colonialist wars to make super profits from colonies by imperial preference, leading to the reduction of British capitalists' pioneering spirit. In addition, British bureaucracy and old-fashioned regulations inhibited its economic development either. Americans had drawn a lesson from the experiences of Britain. All American presidents had given priority to the leadership of technological innovation. Obama aimed to grab the commanding elevation of the technological innovation in the new century by focusing on new energies and a green economy.

The second lesson drawn from the decline of Britain lay in the lagging of the enterprise system. Thomas K. McGraw indicated in his book *Creating Modern Capitalism* that "nearly no large enterprise existed in steel, chemical industry or other sectors that needed large-scale production in 1919, which was regarded as the symbol of the failure of Britain by many critics. In American capitalist world, unions of companies replaced enterprises controlled by families, with managers who drew their salaries from the union as leaders. The famous historian Thomas K. McGraw gave a cutting comment that Britain was featured with "individual capitalism." He also mentioned that "only a few large-scale companies were founded in UK in the Second Industrial Revolution, compared to America, Germany and Japan. Therefore, Britain would fall behind these countries since large-scale companies were easier to implement innovation and carry out a new form of scale economy."[175] Instead of the old family

175 [US] Thomas K. McGraw, *Creating Modern Capitalism*, translated by Zhao Wenshu and Xiao Suozhang et al., Jiangsu People's Press, 2000, P82–83.

enterprises, the U. S. gave birth to innovative enterprises and continued system innovation after the transformation to rule by the manager level. The country also attached importance to the study on successful experiences of other countries on enterprise management and draw lessons therefrom, in order to maintain the enterprise vitality.

The third cause for the decline of Britain was the breakdown of the colonial system. The British Empire was born with a weakness because it was a country established on the basis of colonies. At its golden age in 1914, its colonies had an area 111 times larger than its main land, which provided the country with a monopolistic market and extensive investment choices. Britain closely tied colonies to the metropolitan country with export and investment. By the end of 1913, the British investment on the Britain Empire occupied nearly half of foreign investment, 1.7 billion pounds out of 3.763 billion pounds. The plunder in colonies led to the parasitic and corruptive British economy. The British colonial system was knocked down by the national liberation movement starting from the Russian October Revolution and World War II. According to the comparison, the U. S. is naturally endowed with more favorable conditions. The United States of America, with the continent of North America as the main body, formed an integrated large market based on the 50 states, including 48 interlocking states. Though most Americans were immigrates, they had combined as one, except the barrier between the white and minorities. They identified a strong sense of nationhood and would not disintegrate as the British Empire did.

Fourthly, Britain lost the leadership of English pound. Since the British economy was brought to the brink of bankruptcy and the financial and fiscal strength was greatly damaged by the two world wars, English pounds lost its leadership in the international currency system. It failed to remain its dominance in currency system at the establishment of the Bretton Woods system in 1944 and completely abandoned its central position in international finance in 1947. Americans also drew a lesson from this experience and is now exerting great efforts to maintain the superiority of the USD. It can keep its position in a long term owing to its adequate economic strength.

In conclusion, the U. S. takes the rise and fall of the British Empire as a mirror and draws lessons to maintain its edge.

View of the Rise and Fall of the U. S. Based on the Law of Social Development

Whether the U. S. is going to decline is a different issue against whether the American capitalism can prevent decline. If we say no to the former question, the answer to the latter one will be yes. The historical materialism unveils the law of social development from the low level to high level and impermanence of any social form. The incompatibility between productivity and production relations drives the reform of economic forms and social progress, which is also applicable for the capitalism. Americans find this opinion hard to accept, because they consider their current social form to be the highest, representing freedom, equality, fairness and justice. America is featured with innovative spirit in economic system but with self-complacency in terms of politics. However, the current serious financial crisis and economic regression enable Americans to realize the following.

Firstly, this social form of the U. S. is good at creating wealth but hard to share the wealth among participants, which will necessarily lead to the unconquerable polarization both in domestic and international circumstances. Despite the prosperity brought by the society, it exerts most attack to grassroots people and disadvantaged groups in regression, and adversely influences other weak countries. Freedom, equality, fairness and justice can never be realized for mass victims after the periodic crises.

Secondly, it has taken and will still take a long time for socialism to develop from fantasy to science, which generated based on the resentment against capitalism. It is an innovation that must experience failures or setbacks. Socialism generated in the poorest rank of the old system, so it is encountered with huge pressure exerted by the old order and may easily be extinguished. However, the new social system will enable a stronger and more prosperous economy after having gone through these pressures and will realize common prosperity and social harmony. It needs a model to make socialism attractive to all people. It is a long way but also an inexorable trend.

Thirdly, the two-party system of the U. S., bringing both positive and negative influence on the development of America, aimed to essentially safeguard the old system, so it will not promote the country to transform to a more advanced social system. Republicans expressly speak for the monopolistic capital in Wall Street, while Democrats are restrained by the narrow mind of interest groups, though it claims to protect interests of disadvantaged groups and sometimes improves the system. The greed of Wall Street and the American government's desire to dominate the world are the roots for the contradictions between American governing class and masses and between the U. S. and other countries, which also brew various crises.

Fourthly, emerging market economy countries, with large area and great population, had become free and independent sovereign states after having thrown off the colonial or semi-colonial yoke. They are now emerging powers for the new century and taking the road to shake off poverty and make the country strong and the people rich. They had found the way that was suitable for them after having drawn necessary lessons to succeed, so they are undergoing a quicker development. The economic globalization, reform of the market economy system and the freedom from dogmatism jointly contribute to its development. A significant change is occurring in the contest of strength of emerging economies and developed countries. The contest among powers is a course turning quantitative change into qualitative change, while the rise and fall of a country is a tortuous way from leadership, stalemate to decline. Ignorance or overestimation of this change shall be avoided.

Fifthly, all countries compete with each other to establish a powerful country with rich people in the diversified world. Competition is favorable to countries under peaceful circumstances. The final winner will go to any country that can effectively create wealth and find a way to share achievements, realize common prosperity and overcome the crises and troubles generated in the current world economic order. Instead of politics of interest groups, it needs a party that thinks in people's position, learns well, understands the law of social development, is broad-minded and is able to learn from other countries, to lead masses to realize our ideals. Fortunately, we are going the right way.

The Current China-U. S. Relations

Yuan Peng Wang Honggang

2010 marked a new historic beginning for the China-U. S. relations after a tumultuous 30 years relationship. The repositioning of the China-U. S. relations was realized under the background of rapid reform of international order, constant adjustment of regional order and profound economic and social transformation of both countries in 2010, a year that inherited both the past and ushered in the future. This year was destined to be significant moment in history. All-around conflicts and competitions never before seen broke out in 2010, and the bilateral relations saw a great uncertainty. Both countries attempted to reach a new balance and stability under the new circumstances by more frequent and profound interaction, struggle and competition and mutual adjustments.

I.

The following important features can be concluded from the China-U. S. relations in 2010:

Firstly, the relations were volatile in 2010, in contrast with the basically positive and steady China-U. S. relations in 2009. The most significant feature of the China-U. S. relations in 2009 was the stability after a positive start. U. S. President Obama broke away from the "historical law" that the change of government would definitely lead to volatile China-U. S. relations. On the contrary, both countries rapidly established the "positive, cooperative and comprehensive" keynote for the bilateral relations and upgraded the "strategic economy dialogue" to the "strategic and economic dialogue." Ministerial exchange visits were conducted soon after the inauguration of Obama, including Obama's visit to China during his first year of term and exchange visits of leaders of legislative bodies of both countries, such as Pelosi and Wu Bangguo. The two countries announced the second China-U. S. Joint Statement after 1997, for the first time established the common task to improve the "strategic trust" and pushed the positive China-U. S. relations to a new high. However, the China-U. S. relations took a sudden turn for the worse soon after. The opposition emerged after Obama's visit to China, since they considered the President to have returned empty-handed, thus exerting domestic pressure on Obama; both countries ended the Copenhagen Climate Conference in anger due to significant differentiating opinions on the climate change; and the China-U. S. relations further cooled down owing to "Google issue," sales of weapons to Taiwan, America's meeting with Dalai, and conflicts of the exchange rate. In particular, the "core benefits" crisis, led by the Yellow Sea and South China Sea issue, greatly worsened the bilateral relations and damaged the sound atmosphere previously created by both countries. Despite both parties' efforts to intercede, the China-U. S. relation development remained significantly volatile.

Secondly, conflicts and competition, having become more comprehensive and profound than before, were more prominent and given with different strategic and historical connotation. The previous conflicts between China and the U. S. were concentrated in fewer fields, while current conflicts now concern every aspect of China-U. S. relations. These conflicts are occirng with increasing frequency, respectively related to Chinese core interests (sales of weapons to Taiwan and meeting with Dalai) in Taiwan and Tibet, sensitive network security issue (Google issue), long-term development of China (exchange rate of RMB and climate change), crisis of military confrontation (Yellow Sea and South China Sea) and the special meaning of "the rise and fall of great powers," "power transfer" and "world No.1 vs No. 2," having aroused widespread concern from the world. The optimistic view once held by scholars started to become pessimistic. American scholars, including David Lampton, Shen Dawei and Li Kanru, etc., wrote articles to express their concern on the China-U. S. relations. The scholars who were previously pessimistic expressed their deepening concerns. For example, James Mann, an American scholar, considered it to be impossible to transform China by getting touch with the country and was necessary to adopt other policies to respond to the stronger China.[176] Chinese scholars regarded the U. S. as "competitor rather than a partner."[177] Some Chinese scholars even considered the "mighty combat between China and the U. S. to be inevitable." Some radical scholars and media started to promote topics such as "strategic containment of China by the U. S.," "C-shaped ring of encirclement" and "new Cold War between China and America."

Thirdly, the China-U. S. relations became more sensitive, fragile and more subject to accidents and "third party factors." In 2010, the strategic mindset of both states varied due to a number of factors, so both attached more importance to any behavior of the counterpart, making bilateral relations more sensitive and fragile. In the case of the "Cheonan Incident,"

176 Mann, James. "Behold China". *The New Republic.* April 8, 2010.

177 Refer to the interview with Professor Yan Xuetong in the *International Herald Leader* of March 22 2010.

which was not directly related to China or the U. S., the two countries began to struggle over the sea due to the development of the Incident and misinformed reports by media. For another example, the "core interests" became the hot issue between strategic circles of the two countries soon after speculation by the American media, exercising great influence over the decision-making of both countries. Again, the conflicts between the two countries on the South China Sea and Diaoyu Island issues partly resulted from the instigation of Japan and ASEAN. The reasons why these issues became so important in the relationship between China and the U. S. lies in America's overall plan, based on its Asia-Pacific strategy, and the declining tolerance of China-U. S. relations to accidents and "third party factors."

Fourthly, the high-level interaction went against public opinion. In the previous year, the two countries kept close interaction on an official level, with a basic mutual understanding of one other, despite various differences in China-U. S. relations. However, public opinion was quite the opposite. High officials of both countries met at a small meeting. James Steinberg, Jeffrey Bader, Tom Donilon and Lawrence Summers had successively visited China as special envoys of Obama; and Dai Binguo and Hillary Clinton and Wang Qishan and Timothy Geithner respectively met in Hainan and Qingdao. In the National Security Strategy Report, the U. S. kept a positive policy on China, looked forward to China playing a responsible leading role and further upgraded the status of China from the original "party interested." The Report on Military Power of the People's Republic of China adjusted the attitude towards China and reduced the stimulation against China. Meanwhile, the two countries continued their cooperation on several major international issues in multi-lateral occasions, such as the Global Summit on Nuclear Safety and the G-20 Summit. This cooperation revealed that both governments maintained a positive attitude to bilateral relations, took general interests into account and had effectively maintained fundamentally steady relations. However, violent quarrels occurred between the media and public opinions of both countries. American public opinions increasingly criticized China for its arrogant and tough diplomacy and Chinese domestic policies such as independent innovation. Chinese public opinions strengthened the criticism and counterattack against America, while some media and scholars discussed on whether major plots were included in American policies on China.

II.

The dramatic change in the 2010 China-U. S. relations mainly resulted from the major changes in the background of the China-U. S. relations in the "post-crisis era," leading to further adjustments on Obama's policies on China, creating a new environment for bilateral relations and leading to new issues. The above-mentioned features, as the direct results of the adjustments on Obama's policies on China, revealed the necessity and urgency to alter the framework of the China-U. S. relations.

In the post-crisis era, historic changes occurred in the large, medium and small environment for the China-U. S. relations, which appeared in 2009 and were strengthened in 2010, contributing to the tendency of China-U. S. relation development. In terms of the large environment, the global financial crisis in 2008 had increased its impact and incurred great loss in America, the EU and Japan. Emerging powers rose as a group, so the power rapidly transferred from the Western to non-Western world and the relative comprehensive strength and development momentum underwent tremendous changes (especially the relative strength between China and America);[178] and the international system that had regulated China-U. S. relations for a long time changed due to the transition of strategies of various countries, frequent realignment and regrouping and succession of the old global system by the new system. The tendency was reflected from the beginning of the crisis and strengthened in 2010. Regarding the medium environment, the peace between China and America in the Asia-Pacific area since the September 11th terrorist attacks came to an end. Along with the transfer of American strategic focus to the Asia-Pacific region, this area has meanwhile become the core area for America to maintain its leading role in the world in the "post-anti-terrorism age" and the important strategic base for China to rise and explore the development space. The role of global anti-terrorism cooperation in strengthening bilateral relations was weakened, while the geopolitics competition between two states became increasingly fierce, which was demonstrated by the brutal geopolitics conflicts between the two countries in the Asia-Pacific area in 2010. In terms of the small environment, the public opinions that supported the stable bilateral relations reduced. Americans generated unhealthy crisis awareness based on their discontent of the economic depression, helplessness to the subject of political polarization and anxiety about the fate of the country, and thus became more sensitive and restless against the external world, especially towards the behaviors of China. And in China, strong nationalism was generated owing to its increasing economic strength and people's historical memory of China, so public opinions became more sensitive to and less tolerant of American policies.

The changes of the environment magnified the problems in Obama's policies on China

---

178 Freeman, Chas W. "The United States, China and the New Global Geometry." Remarks at the Hopkins-Nanjing Center, Nov. 10, 2010. http://www.mepc.org/articles-commentary/speeches/united-states-china-and-new-global-geometry.

to some degree and forced the government to adjust its policies on China again, which led to significant changes in the China-U. S. relations. At the beginning of this term, Obama inherited and developed the strategy on China formed in the second term of the Bush administration with the "party interested" as the symbol. It was seen in the following: 1) In terms of the importance of China-U. S. relations, President Obama and the Secretary of State Hillary Clinton emphasized that China-U. S. relations were the "most important bilateral relations" in the 21st century; 2) The U. S. turned its expectation on China to be the "responsible party interested" to the "responsible leading role";[179] 3) Regarding the position of the China-U. S. relations, the "constructive cooperation" was upgraded to the "full range of positive cooperation" and "partnership to cope with common challenges";[180] 4) The new ideas of "pulling together in times of troubles" and "arriving at the same end by different means" were put forward in terms of the role of China and the opinion on the development of China; 5) The two governments proposed the new concept of "strategic guarantee" to stabilize the China-U. S. relations. [181]

However, these new strategies on China were not demonstrated well. The significant changes in the China-U. S. relations in 2010 were largely resulted from the adjustments and corrections of Obama administration on policies on China. To be specific, firstly, the Obama administration turned the idea of "expressing friendship," which obtained no achievement, to "expressing strength," due to domestic political pressures. Obama did not obtain common support for his initial policies on China, making it difficult to implement these policies. Along with the accelerating rise of China in the post-crisis era, the American strategic circle saw a significant change on the understanding of China. They became pessimistic and passive in the development direction and strategic purpose of China, considered that it was more possible for China to become the major competitor of the U. S., doubted the future of China and increasingly believed that "China of peaceful rise was also a challenge." Therefore, Obama's visit to China in November 2009 invited widespread criticism inside America, his performance in the Copenhagen Conference on Climate Change in December was satirized by Americans, and the new idea of "strategic guarantee" put forward by James Steinberg was disparagingly referred to as "only another better wording" of "appeasement."[182] Obama had to adopt tougher polices on China to promote

179 "National Security Strategy," May 2010, http://www.whitehouse.gov/sites/default/files/rss_viewer/national_security_strategy.pdf.

180 *Sino-U. S. Joint Statement*, November 17 2009, http://world.people.com.cn/GB/10394969.html.

181 Steinberg, James. "Administration's Vision of the U. S.-China Relationship," Keynote Address at Center for New American Security. September 24, 2009. http://www.state.gov/s/d/2009/129686.htm

182 Currie, Kelley. "The Doctrine of 'Strategic Reassurance.'" *Wall Street Journal*. October 22, 2009.

its domestic support. Secondly, Obama's frustrations brought by his over expectations on China led to more troubles in the China-U. S. relations in 2010. The Obama administration hoped to obtain China's support on various practical issues, such as anti-terrorism in Afghanistan and Pakistan, financial recovery and cooperation on climate changes by expressing his positive support to China. The enthusiasm for quick success and instant benefits unveiled the Obama administration's anxiety to regain leadership, which did not comply with the development of China-U. S. relations. In addition, the two countries did not share the same benefits on these issues, so China did not act as the U. S. predicted. The U. S. rapidly adjusted the strategy again. For example, U. S. Secretary of Defense Robert M. Gates and U. S. Secretary of State Hillary Clinton frequently expressed American's attitude on the South China Sea issue in high profile situations to warn China. Thirdly, the Obama administration could not prevent the profound conflicts in the bilateral relations and thus could not realize its policies on China as he said, which made attacks to China-U. S. relations. For example, Obama administration stuck to selling weapons to Taiwan and meeting with Dalai, which disappointed China and damaged the fragile strategic trust between the two countries.

More importantly, the changes in the environment highlighted, or even aggravated, deep-seated issues in the bilateral relations, such as the "ambiguous positioning" and "loose support," leading to volatile China-U. S. relations in 2010. The strategic framework, which has supported the steady development of both countries in the previous 30 years, was loosened by the changes in domestic and international conditions. Firstly, the economic situation has changed. Both countries have increasing conflicts on independent innovation, investment access and exchange rate of RMB on higher level and in larger scale. Economic relations between the two states turned from the complementation between the "largest developed country" and the "largest developing country" to the competition between "largest economic power" and "second largest economic power," since the international rules of "disorderly competition" has gradually replaced the "orderly competition." Secondly, the room for political cooperation is reducing. Geopolitical competition becomes fierce on regional issues such as the Korean peninsula issue, Iran's nuclear issue and Burma issue, which reduced enthusiastic cooperation and raised the difficulties for cooperation, since any conflict between the two countries are regarded as bad relations between a "rising country" and a "hegemonist power." Thirdly, based on decreasing strategic trust, both parties tend to formulate policies from a pessimistic perspective, mutually condemn the other party, forming a vicious circle. America's preventive measures against China are increasingly considered to be "containment," while the rational behaviors of China to safeguard national interests are regarded as "arrogance."[183] Increasing and more serious troubles have occurred in China-U. S. relations due to changes in the strategic support of both countries and the traditional strategic frame. We shall see the inevitability rather than contingency in the constant conflicts between both countries in 2010. The frequent and more serious conflicts did not result from accidents or the policy choice of a country, but were generated because the original framework that had supported the China-U. S. relations could no longer adapt to the new conditions under the dramatic change of relative strengths, adjustments of the international system and the political transformation of both countries.

The ambiguous positioning of China-U. S. relations has increasingly become an outstanding issue, along with the loosened relation framework. The positioning of China-U. S. relations has remained ambiguous for the 20 years since the end of the Cold War. People can clearly understand what the China-U. S. relations are neither "enemy" nor "ally", but have no clear and uniform idea on what the China-U. S. relations are. The ambiguous positioning did not fundamentally affect the bilateral relations because, on one hand, the long-term mutual cooperation and significant gap of strength between the two countries have diluted the structural conflicts in the bilateral relations, and, on the other hand, both parties were trying to find out the correct way without long-term positive expectations. However, the positive factors that have supported the stable bilateral relations for 30 years are currently fading away, the negative factors have gradually became the focus, and the strategic circles and people of the two countries turned to a negative prediction for the future of China-U. S. relations, so the ambiguous positioning of China-U. S. relations exerts more effect on bilateral relations. Two states have to find out the clear answer to the following questions: "What is the nature of China-U. S. relations?" and "What is the future of China-U. S. relations?"

III.

As the most important and complicated bilateral relations, the ambiguous positioning and uncertain development direction under the dramatic changes of environment are great threats to the world. On one hand, both countries are experiencing difficulties understanding the other side and may possibly make wrong strategic decisions because of this. The narrowing gap between Chinese and American strength, the opposite development momentum and the worsening public opinion environment may aggravate the negative side

---

183 Lieberthal, Kenneth. "The U. S. and China: Mending Fences." *Los Angeles Times*. 2011. Jan. 17. P. A11.

of China-U. S. relations, i.e. both parties may examine the other's behaviors and guess its intent upon supposing itself to be the "victim" and regarding the defensive behaviors of the counterparty as aggressive behavior, prepare itself based on the worst possibilities and get caught up in a vicious circle.[184] For example, the recent defensive position of China to defend its territory and sovereignty over territorial waters was interpreted to be a signal that China would abandon the policy of "hiding one's capacities and biding one's time" and the commitment of "peace and development" by American strategic circle and public opinions, who guessed that China would employ "Chinese-style Monroe Doctrine" and kick the U. S. out from the Asia-Pacific area.[185] Meanwhile, America's frequent joint military exercises with Japan and South Korea directed at the Korea issue and behaviors in the security deployment in Asia-Pacific area, which, in China's opinions, was attempting to further contain China. The mutual strategic trust has been greatly damaged by this kind of suspicion. The negative trend may lead to major strategic mistakes without any timely prevention. On the other hand, based on the strategic mistakes, the China-U. S. relations may become the competition between great powers and lead to another "Cold War." The competition between China and the U. S. in 2010 revealed the structural conflicts between the "No.1 of the world" America and "No. 2 economy of the world" China,[186] which were especially reflected in the competition in Asia-Pacific area by the two countries. According to Henry Kissinger, the powers of the 21st century had little experience in participation in the joint actions of powers, and both China and the U. S. had not prepared themselves for the equal relations at the cost of restrained self-freedom. Challenges aroused by China to America were somewhat similar to the threats of Germany to the UK one hundred years ago. If decision makers of both countries do not adopt firm measures to stop the negative trend, the structural conflicts will strengthen the hostile relations, just as the Germany-UK relations that finally turned from friendship to confrontation.[187]

---

184 Shambaugh, David. "A New China Requires a New Strategy." *Current History*. Sep. 2010. p. 225; Garrett, Banning. "U. S.-China Relations: Gone Fishing," *The Globalist*. Nov. 24, 2010. http://www.theglobalist.com/storyid.aspx?StoryId=8820.

185 You can refer to: Bosco, Joseph. China's growing threat, *The Washington Times*. November 29, 2010, http://www.washingtontimes.com/news/2010/nov/29/chinas-growing-threat/; and Wang, Vincent."China-ASEAN Free Trade Area: A Chinese 'Monroe Doctrine' or 'Peaceful Rise'?" *China Brief* of the Jamestown Foundation. 2009.Vol. 9 http://www.jamestown.org/programs/chinabrief/single/?tx_ttnews[tt_news]=35434&tx_ttnews[backPid]=25&cHash=8650 60aaab; and Ames Holmes and Toshi Yoshihara, "A Chinese Monroe Doctrine?", Defense News, Sep. 20, 2010, http://www.defensenews.com/story.php?i=4784169

186 Yuan Peng, "What's the Future of Sino-U. S. Relations," *Diplomatic Commentaries*, 2nd issue 2010, P6.

187 Refer to Kissinger, Henry A. "Reining in Pyongyang." *The Washington Post*. June 8, 2009. http://www.washingtonpost.com/wp-dyn/content/article/2009/06/07/AR2009060702097.html; Kissinger, Henry A.

China-U. S. relations in the post-crisis era have come to a point of strategic decision and a critical moment to redefine the relations.[188] A wrong decision may lead to confrontation between powers and a "lose-lose" situation, while a correct decision may promote the China-U. S. relations and set up a good model for the friendly relations between the two powers in different systems, cultures and historical development stages. Therefore, decision makers and strategic circles of the two countries sought for appropriate methods, adjusting itself to compromise to the other party and attempting to promote the balance and stability of China-U. S. relations.

Regarding the U. S., despite some changes in the policies on China, the Obama administration has not fundamentally changed the keynote policies on China and still held a high expectation. Though the Obama administration felt frustrated on the relations with China for a time and found it difficult to establish friendly relations with China, the U. S. government was in a complicated mental status, with dissatisfaction and emphasis and disappointment and expectations. The American domestic conditions, with high unemployment rate, high deficit and high debt, created a heavy burden on American economic recovery and largely contributed to the continuance of Obama's time in office. Therefore, Obama paid greatest attention to the economy, the basis to rebuild the global leadership of America. In terms of foreign affairs, the U. S. has been challenged by their withdrawal from Afghanistan and Pakistan, the Korea and Iran issues, the reform of international system and the rise of non-Western countries in groups. Obama knew that it was impossible to solve any of these difficulties without the cooperation of China. Through the competition and cooperation in 2010, the Obama administration gradually realized that it did not necessarily mean that China would confront the U. S., though it would not accept all of America's requirements. America had no ability to stop the rise of China and could not afford the price of hostile relations between the two countries, and it's the choice of America to decide whether the rise of China would damage the fundamental benefits of America. The U. S. had to seek cooperation with China to cope with domestic and international difficulties. Therefore, the fierce conflicts between China and America in

---

"Rebalancing Relations With China." *The Washington Post*. August 19, 2009. http://www.washingtonpost.com/wp-dyn/content/article/2009/08/18/AR2009081802850.html and Bennhold, Katrin. "Mutual Trust Called Crucial to U. S.-China Relations," *The New York Times*. September 12, 2010. http://www.nytimes.com/2010/09/13/world/europe/13geneva.html

188 Clinton, Hillary R. "A Broad Vision of U. S.-China Relations in the 21st Century," Jan. 14, 2011. http://www.state.gov/secretary/rm/2011/01/154653.htm; and Gewirtz, Paul. "What America and China Must not Forget," *The International Herald Tribune*. Jan. 19, 2011. P. 6.

2010 helped the Obama administration in more rational and practical expectations and positioning of China-U. S. relations.[189]

China also wished for steady and healthy relations with the U. S. to maintain comparatively favorable strategic opportunities and stable domestic and foreign environment. China's relations with the outside world are seeing the key historical point after the 30-year reform and opening-up. Economically, China now has a deeper mutual dependence with other countries, shares the common benefits and damages with the world economy and needs external support to the current economic transformation and economic development in the future. In terms of politics and security, China has initially established its status as a world power, but its role in and impact on the world is still to be confirmed. Both expectations and suspicions exist in China's future. Under these circumstances, Chinese diplomacy shall avoid violent ups and downs or criticisms from other countries. Chinese diplomacy will be greatly attached by any problem in China-U. S. relations. It will help overcome any distrust between China and the U. S. and reduce the interference caused by "third party factors" on China-U. S. relations by maintaining the stable and favorable China-U. S. relations and respecting American contributions to global order and its leadership without damages to the own interests of China. The fierce competition between China and the U. S. in 2010 and the change of surroundings incurred therefrom, will further enable Chinese decision makers and strategic circles to realize the deep interactive relationship between the "primary" surrounding environment and "key" countries (especially the U. S.), the necessity to continue to conceal capacities and bide the time and insist on peaceful development, and the significance to seek for a favorable interaction with the U. S., which meets the fundamental interests of China and shall be regarded as the periodic focus to develop the China-U. S. relations.

In addition, both countries share the same strategic idea that it is not only necessary, but also possible, to prevent strategic confrontation and deepen strategic cooperation. Decision makers of the two countries know that it will be favorable for both if cooperating, and unfavorable for both if struggling, and will deem it as the guidance for the development of China-U. S. relations. Numerous channels for dialogues and cooperation also lay a solid foundation for stable relations. Both countries share compatible interests in maintaining global maintenance and seeking common prosperity. As powers that are capable and responsible to change the world, both countries are featured with strong strategic initiatives

---

189 Kerry, John. "U. S.-China Relations: A View from the U. S. Senate." Speech at the Center for American Progress. Dec. 7, 2010. http://www.americanprogress.org/events/2010/12/inf/kerrytranscript.pdf/.

in recreating the world order and great flexibility in the future development. China-U. S. relations may step into a new relations model of "being harmonious based on differences," "pulling together in times of trouble" and "common progress" based on their positive wills.

In the latter half of 2010, especially toward the end of the year, the two countries begant frequent interaction to prepare for President Hu Jintao's visit to America, which aimed to show their attention on this visit, leading public opinions and creating a favorable environment. Bill Gate's visit to China symbolized that the military interaction between the two countries had restarted. The U. S. Secretary of State Hillary Clinton, former senior official Henry Kissinger and Brzeginsky, and Dai Bingguo and Cui Tiankai from China made frequent speeches on China-U. S. relations, with the purpose to promote China-U. S. relations. Chinese President Hu Jintao paid a state visit to the U. S. from January 18 to January 21, 2011 and was regarded as the most important meeting between Chinese and American leaders since Deng Xiaoping's visit to America in 1979.[190] During this period, leaders of the two countries exchanged opinions on major issues, having significantly improved mutual consensus and trust. The new positioning of "cooperation partnership," confirmed in the Joint Declaration, has laid a solid foundation for the long-term strategic stability of China-U. S. relations. The new positioning has summarized and recognized the achievements in the 30-year development of China-U. S. relations, responded to the constant ups and downs of bilateral relations and clearly answered the question "What would be the future of China-U. S. relations?" in the second decade of 21st century. The positioning facilitated solutions to long-term problems, turned the critical development direction of China-U. S. relations, clarified the essential attribute of the bilateral relations, prevented the upgrading of potential structural conflicts, promoted the mutual dependence based on differences, explored the cooperation space, helped the unified planning to maintain an appropriate strategic distance between China and the U. S., provided space for both countries to administrate foreign relations, dispelled international society's doubts on damages to their security owing to China-U. S. confrontation or sacrifice of their interests due to shared governance of the U. S. and China, prevented a small number of countries from obtaining easy gains from the tight China-U. S. relations, and most importantly, attempted to establish a new model for powers in the 21st century where powers compete, cooperate and ensure common prosperity instead of damages under the conditions of globalization and multipolar world and become the "cooperation relations model for countries of different political systems, historical and cultural backgrounds and economic

190 Brzezinski, Zbigniew. "How to Stay Friends with China." *The New York Times*. Jan. 2, 2011. P. A21.

development level."[191]

IV.

The China-U. S. relations of 2010 started with the "Meeting of Hu Jintao and Obama." The bilateral relations have seemed calm since then. However, the stability may be affected by the conventional conflicts, new difficulties and accidents.

Firstly, both countries maintain stable bilateral relations without the solution to any one long-term structural conflict, so their relations are very fragile. The relations may be adversely influenced by the impact of the United States' strategic movement eastward on the security environment of China and the challenges on the core benefits of China by inherent dual characters in American policies on China. When the Obama administration would provoke China on issues related to Taiwan, Xinjiang, Tibet and human rights, Obama would necessarily pay more attention to make up the bilateral relations. In particular, the frequent turbulence and government transfer in the Middle East and North Africa cause China-U. S. relations to become more sensitive and uncertain. Therefore, decision makers of both countries are attaching a great deal of importance on how to maintain their own geographical, political and economic benefits in the Middle East and North Africa without conflicts, how to cope with the derivative effect of the "Jasmine Revolution"[192] and human rights issue. The competition will be intensified upon the mismanagement of these issues, even fiercer than the situation in 2010 and harder to handle, which may easily cause the disorder of the bilateral relations.

Secondly, in terms of the domestic political conditions of America, the stability of China-U. S. relations was realized by the promotion of U. S. administration, but the opposition will be the negative factor that always exists in the China-U. S. relations. Owing to the political characteristics of America, the promotion of the bilateral relations by the chief executives of both countries may be inhibited by the U. S. Congress, the military and a small amount of anti-China forces, while the relations may move "two steps forward and then a step back." Soon after Clinton's visit to China in 1998, the Cox Report was issued[193]

191 Sino-U. S. Joint Statement, *People's Daily*, P2, Jan. 20, 2011.

192 A peddler in Tunis set himself on fire in protest against the maltreatment of law enforcers, which finally led to the end of the term of Tunisian President bin Ali. (Translator's note)

193 The Report of the Select Committee on U. S. National Security and Military/Commercial Concerns with the People's Republic of China, commonly known as the Cox Report after Representative Christopher Cox, is a

and Wen Ho Lee case[194] occurred. We shall clearly see the current U. S. policies on China and China-U. S. relations are realized by various forces and wills, especially the administrations of both states, so we are not clear about whether the relations now meet the expectations of domestic forces of America. The activities of the domestic opposition in the U. S. may attack the bilateral relations that get back on the track not long ago.

Thirdly, the decisions of the two governments are increasingly restrained by public opinions and diversified strategic estimates. Decision-makers of both countries have to conduct "grand strategic thinking" in an era of "crushing ideas," make decisions meeting the grand strategy and ensure the execution. As discovered from the history of China-U. S. relations, the breakthroughs in the bilateral relations in the beginning and end of 1970s were made based on comparatively concentrated rights of foreign decisions. After the Cold War, diversified ideas on security interests and security threats arose in America. More and more government departments have joined in foreign policy-making along with the globalization, so it is difficult to recreate the foreign decision-making process like before, which was originally led by a diplomatic strongman.[195] Meanwhile, the environment for decision making of China-U. S. relations has greatly changed. The rights of decision making in policies related to China became decentralized even inside the administration department. At the "strategic and economic dialogue" between China and U. S. held each year, nearly all ministers of American government attended. Despite different national conditions and decision-making process in China, the rights are increasingly decentralized, and more diversified perspectives are employed in decision making to some degree.[196] This means that the two countries shall not only pay attention to strategies, but also need to consider the preference of various departments and diversified values of nongovernmental bodies in order to maintain correct, appropriate and controllable relations.

---

classified U. S. government document reporting on the People's Republic of China's covert operations within the United States. (Translator's note)

194 Dr. Wen Ho Lee (Chinese: 李文和) is a Taiwan-born Taiwanese American scientist who worked for the University of California at the Los Alamos National Laboratory. He created simulations of nuclear explosions for the purposes of scientific inquiry, as well as for improving the safety and reliability of the US nuclear arsenal. A federal grand jury indicted him of stealing secrets about U. S. nuclear arsenal for the People's Republic of China (PRC) in December 1999.

195 Ignatius, David. "Obama Needs a Machiavelli." *The Washington Post*. July 8, 2010. P. A15.

196 Related researches can be referred to Jakobson, Linda and Knox, Dean. "New Foreign Policy Actors in China." *SIPRI Policy Paper*. No.26, Sep. 2010; Shambaugh, David. "Coping with a Conflicted China." *The Washington Quarterly*. Winter 2011. p. 7-27. And Higgins, Andrew. "Hu's Visit Spotlights China's Two Faces." *The Washington Post*. Jan. 16, 2011. P. A01 etc.

In terms of China, the foreign relations with the U. S. in the new age are in demand of more complicated, balanced and careful planning along with the increasingly diversified national attribute, varied national interests and complicated international conditions. Decision makers and strategic circles have to clearly think about how to correctly assess the strength and status of the U. S. and its relative strength to China, how to deal with conventional difficulties, including American sales of weapons to Taiwan and meeting with Dalai, how to improve relations with the U. S. in sea, air, space and network, how to cope with the new challenges brought by the changes of domestic political conditions of the U. S. and how to appropriately respond to other issues in China-U. S. relations.

Current China-U. S. Trade Relations

Wang Rongjun

I. Features of China-U. S. Trade and Investment Relations after the "Great Recession"

1. China-U. S. Trade Relations Suffer Slightly from the Financial Crisis and Recovers Rapidly

The "Great Recession," lasting from December 2007 to June 2009, was the longest and most serious economic crisis since the Great Depression in 1929. The "Great Recession" severely damaged the foreign trade of America, including China-U. S. trade relations. The trade between China and the U. S. had experienced a rapid growth before 2008. As shown in Table 1, America's import from China had maintained a constant growth from the 1980s to 2008, with an annual growth rate of more than 21%, according to statistics from America. However, the growth rate of China's export to America dropped under 10% in 2008, while all the export, import and total volume of China-U. S. trade significantly declined in 2009.[197]

Table 1. Balance of China-U. S. Trade of Goods: 1980~2010
Unit: billion U. S. dollars (USD)

Year	Import from America		Export to America		Balance of Trade		Proportion in the Total Goods Trade Volume of America (%)	Proportion in the Total Goods Import Volume of America (%)	Proportion in the Total Goods Export Volume of America (%)
	Stat. from China	Stat. from U. S.	Stat. from China	Stat. from U. S.	Stat. from China	Stat. from U. S.	Statistics from U. S.	Statistics from U. S.	Statistics from U. S.
1980	3.82	3.8	0.98	1.1	−2.84	2.7	1.0	0.45	1.7
1990	6.58	4.8	5.19	15.2	−1.39	−10.4	2.2	3.1	1.2
2000	22.4	16.3	52.1	100.1	29.7	−83.8	5.8	8.2	2.1
2005	48.7	41.8	162.9	243.5	114.2	−201.6	11.1	14.6	4.6
2006	59.2	55.2	203.5	287.8	144.3	−232.5	11.9	15.5	5.3
2007	69.4	65.2	232.7	321.5	163.3	−256.3	12.4	16.5	5.6
2008	81.4	71.5	252.3	337.8	170.9	−266.3	12.0	16.1	5.5
2009	77.4	69.6	220.8	296.4	143.4	−226.8	14.0	19.0	6.6
2010	102.0	91.9	283.3	364.9	181.3	−273.1	14.3	19.1	7.2

197 Data from Chinese statistics also shows a constant growth in overall trend, with an annual growth rate of 18.3%, but a small decline in the export to America between 1985 and 1986.

Data source: USITC DataWeb, U. S. Census Bureau and the Chinese General Administration of Customs. Proportions before 2005 are estimated by the author based on the census-based statistics of goods trade from America.

The status of both countries in the other country's foreign trade was not influenced by the decline. Since 2007, China has replaced Canada as the largest exporter to America, while America has become the largest importing country of China. China is the second largest trade partner (only second to Canada) of America and has become the third largest importer from America after having surpassed Japan in 2007 (after Canada and Mexico, as shown in Table 2). Along with America's economic recovery in 2010, the China-U. S. trade relations have also been restored. Export from China to America has grown rapidly and its proportion in America's import developed from approximately 16% in 2009 to 19% in 2010. The China-U. S. goods trade is accounting for 14.3% of total goods trade volume of America. In recent years, America has seen the quickest growth rate in the export to China, which had increased by 263% from 2001 to 2009, much more rapidly than export to any other major trade partners. Under the economic recession of global economy, the decline of America's export to China in 2009 was much slighter than other major trade partners and the overall decline by 18.7% of the trade of America. The proportion of goods exported to China in the total goods export volume of America has grown from 5.5% in 2008 to 7.2% in 2010.

Table 2 Top 5 Goods Trade Partners of America in 2010
Unit: one billion USD

Rank	Country	America's Export	America's Import	Total Trade Volume	Proportion in the Total Trade Volume
—	Total amount of all countries	1,278.1	1,912.1	3,190.2	100.0%
1	Canada	248.8	276.5	525.3	16.5%
2	China	91.9	364.9	456.8	14.3%
3	Mexico	163.3	229.7	393.0	12.3%
4	Japan	60.5	120.3	180.9	5.7%
5	Germany	48.2	82.7	130.9	4.1%

Data source: U. S. Census and Foreign Trade Division

2. America's Trade Deficit with China Hit a New Record

According to China's statistics, the export of China to America has increased from 5.19 billion USD in 1990 to 383.3 billion USD in 2010, with an average annual growth rate of 22.1%. According to America's statistics, the figure increased from 15.2 billion USD in 1990 to 364.9 billion USD, with an average annual growth rate of 17.2%. For the same period, America's trade deficit with China grew from -1.39 billion USD to 181.3 billion USD, according to statistics of China, and from 10.4 billion USD to 273.1 billion USD according to America's statistics. Since China experienced a greater decline in the export to America than in the import from America in 2009, America's trade deficit with China improved from 2008, with a reduction of 39.5 billion USD. However, this has not improved the unbalanced China-U. S. trade, because the decline of the overall foreign trade of America was greater than its trade deficit with China. By 2009, America's trade deficit with China accounted for as high as 2/3 of the total trade deficit of America, compared to 1/3 in 2008. The export of China to America returned to growth along with the economic recovery of America. America's trade deficit with China has occupied approximately 55% of the total trade deficit of America, much larger than any other major trade partner, having exceeded the sum of goods trade deficit with the European Union of 27 countries, Mexico, Japan and Canada (see Table 3).[198]

Table 3 Goods Trade Balance of the U. S. and Its Major Trade Partners From 2008 to 2010
Unit: one billion USD

	2008	2009	2010
Canada	−746.4	−201.8	−282.8
ASEAN	−420.1	−382.2	−373.4
Japan	−726.7	−447.7	−598.0
Mexico	−643.8	−475.4	−663.3
EU of 27 countries	−934.2	−605.4	−797.8
OPEC	−1657.3	−618.5	−956.4
China	−2663.3	−2268.3	−2730.7
Total volume	−8000.1	−5009.4	−6345.9

Data source: USITC Dataweb.

198 The trade statistics working group jointly founded by the Ministry of Commerce, General Administration of Customs, U. S. Department of Commerce and the Office of Trade Representatives have conducted preliminary study on the difference of the statistics of goods trade of America and China. According to its report, the import of America from China shall be lowered from 100.064 billion, 196.699 billion and 287.773 billion USD to 58.609 billion, 146.092 billion and 224.733 billion USD respectively in 2000, 2004 and 2006, with a decline by 41.4%, 25.7% and 21.9%. See in the website of the Ministry of Commerce of China, *Report on the Study of Differences Between Chinese and American Trade Statistics*, October 2009, P12. http://zhs.mofcom.gov.cn/accessory/201004/1271033722404.pdf

3. The Product Mix of the Bilateral Trade of 2009~2010

America's merchandise export to China declined by 2 billion USD in 2009, including a decline of 1.2 billion in machinery and electronics, mainly led by the decline in semiconductor manufacturing equipment and semiconductor and integrated circuit, while the export on agricultural products, iron and steel products and chemical products increased significantly. In 2010, the major growth sectors of America's export to China mainly lay in agricultural products, electronics, chemical products and transportation equipment (see Table 4). According to the U. S. Department of Agriculture, China has surpassed Canada in 2010 and become the largest importer of America's agricultural products. In 2009, China became the largest importer of America's iron and steel scraps. Compared to an increase of 36% in America's export of this category of products to China, the export to other major industrial countries has declined, which mainly resulted from the reducing production in main steel manufacturers and growing steel production in China. American steel mills' demand on scraps dropped by 54% in 2009, leading to a significant price decline.

America's import from China, involving all categories of products, had declined by 42 billion USD in 2009, especially in minerals and metals (9.8 billion USD), miscellaneous manufacturers (9 billion USD) and electronic products (7.2 billion USD). In particular, energy-related products dropped by 85% and transport equipment declined by 21%. America's import of iron and steel products from China fell 67% in 2009, which was related to the sluggish building and manufacturing industry of America and the law suit on the anti-dumping and anti-subsidy of this kind of products in America. The decline of home appliances, including stoves, grills, furniture, tools and baggages, mainly contributed to the decline of miscellaneous manufacturers. It was led by the sluggish residential housing industry of America and the consumption reduction due to economic slowdown.

The changing product mix of the import and export between both parties reveals the status and characteristics of the economic growth of both countries and the changes in enterprise investment and consumption during the crisis. No fundamental change has occurred in the basic product mix. China's export to America still mainly concentrates on processing and trade products and labor-intensive products, while its export from America mainly focuses on capital and technology-intensive products, with a rapid growth in telecommunication facilities, computers and office equipment. America's export to China mainly relies on oil seeds and grains, scraps, semiconductor, elements of electronic products, aircraft and components, resin, synthetic rubber and fibers.

Table 4 America's Merchandise Exports to China, Consumption-Related Import and Balance of Merchandise Exports From 2008 to 2010

Unit: one million USD

Category	2008	2009	2010	Variation Between 2009 and 2010 (%)
America's Export to China (Domestic Goods)				
Agricultural products	12,811	13,762	18,232	32.5%
Forest products	3,518	3,720	5,050	35.8%
Chemical and related products	9,885	10,643	13,344	25.4%
Energy-related products	584	708	1,619	128.7%
Textile products and clothes	940	846	1,083	28.0%
Shoes	35	44	55	25.4%
Mineral products and metals	9,701	8,703	10,791	24.0%
Machinery	6,628	5,424	7,903	45.7%
Transport equipment	9,659	9,193	12,519	36.2%
Electronic products	12,375	11,133	13,494	21.2%
Miscellaneous products	367	362	354	-2.2%
Total amount	67,166	65,124	85,746	31.7%
Import From China (Consumption-related)				
Agricultural products	5,588	4,850	5,653	16.6%
Forest products	7,371	6,281	7,123	13.4%
Chemical and related products	20,918	17,510	21,319	21.8%
Energy-related products	2,025	305	495	62.3%
Textile products and clothes	36,368	35,083	42,095	20.0%
Shoes	14,444	13,415	15,727	17.2%
Mineral products and metals	28,975	19,146	22,208	16.0%
Machinery	29,923	25,996	32,326	24.4%
Transport equipment	10,837	8,553	11,850	38.5%
Electronic products	117,986	110,793	143,716	29.7%
Miscellaneous products	58,917	49,892	57,635	15.5%
Total amount	337,504	295,545	364,047	23.2%
Balance of China-U. S. Merchandise Trade				
Agricultural products	7,223	8,913	12,579	41.1%
Forest products	-3,853	-2,561	-2,073	19.1%
Chemical and related products	-11,033	-6,867	-7,975	-16.1%
Energy-related products	-1,441	403	1,125	178.8%
Textile products and clothes	-35,429	-34,237	-41,013	-19.8%
Shoes	-14,409	-13,371	-15,671	-17.2%
Mineral products and metals	-19,274	-10,443	-11,416	-9.3%
Machinery	-23,295	-20,572	-24,423	-18.7%
Transport equipment	-1,178	640	669	4.5%
Electronic products	-105,611	-99,660	-130,222	-30.7%
Miscellaneous products	-58,550	-49,530	-57,281	-15.6%
Total amount	-270,338	-230,421	-278,301	-20.8%

Note: the import value is estimated based on customs valuation and the export value comes from the calculation based on free alongside ship (FAS) at American ports.

4. The China-U. S. Investment Relations Continue to Develop, with a Rapid Growth in China's Investment in the U. S.

Direct investment is the main body of America's investment in China. The direct investment of America in China had accounted for 29% of total direct investment in China of foreign countries from 2003 to 2009, while China's direct investment in the U. S. only accounted for 1%. In 2008, the number of enterprises founded by America's investment had declined by 32.55%, but the actual invested funds had increased by 12.54%. America's actual investment in China amounted to 2.944, 3.576 and 4.052 billion USD in 2008, 2009 and 2010 respectively, ranking the fifth. America's accumulated investment in China amounted to 45.6 billion USD by 2008, approximately equal to its investment in Brazil and half of its investment in Mexico, and the amount ranked 17th among all countries accepting America's direct investment.

Currently, China only possesses a small direct investment in America. According to statistics from the U. S., China only ranked the 30th among all investors in 2008, but it has seen an extremely rapid growth in recent years. According to the joint statistics from the Minister of Commerce, the Statistics Bureau and the State Administration of Exchange Control of China, China's direct investment in America was approximately 910 million USD in 2009, accounting for 1.6% of the total amount of China's foreign direct investment, having increased by 96.7%. The investment in America ranked 7th, after Hong Kong of China, Cayman Islands, Australia, Luxembourg, British Virgin Islands and Singapore. China's non-financial direct investment in America had reached 605 million USD in the first half of 2010,[199] with a growth of 3.6 times and the accumulated investment is estimated to exceed 1 billion USD for the whole year. By the end of 2009, the direct investment leftover in America by China had reached 3.338 billion USD, ranking 6th behind Hong Kong of China, British Virgin Islands, Cayman Islands, Australia and Singapore and taking up 1.4% of the total direct investment leftover in foreign countries.

41.7% of China's direct investment in America, i.e. 379 million USD, was put into manufacturing in 2009. However, in terms of investment leftover, the total amount of investment on wholesale and retail amounted to 950 million USD, making up 28.5% of the total leftover, while the investment on manufacturing only amounted to 940 million USD, occupying 28.2% (see Table 5) and involving more than 9,300 local employees.

---

199 Ministry of Commerce, State Statistics Bureau and the State administration of Exchange Control, *2009 Statistical Bulletin of China's Outward Foreign Direct Investment*, P 8-22. http://hzs.mofcom.gov.cn/accessory/201009/1284339524515.pdf.

The indirect investment of China in America mainly concentrates on the investment in various American securities, including the long-term national debt of America, institutions supported by the American government, the long-term securities of enterprises, the long-term company bonds and capital stock and short-term securities. As estimated by the U. S. Treasury Department, the total amount of American securities owned by China had reached as high as 1.175 trillion USD in October 2010 and 1.16 trillion USD in December 2010, making China the largest foreign owner of American securities, 277.8 billion USD higher than Japan in the 2nd position and 888 billion USD higher than the UK in 3rd place.[200] Compared to 2002, the total amount of American securities under China's possession had increased by more than 1 trillion USD, raising from the 5th rank to the 1st. American national debt accounts for the most among the American securities held by China. According to the U. S. Treasury Department, China has become the largest owner of American national debt since September 2008.[201]

Table 5 Major Industries for China's Direct Investment in America in 2009
Unit: 10 thousand USD

Industry	Inflow		
Wholesale and retail	12484	1	95265
Manufacturing	37873		94097
Financial industry	14064		48573
Transport/storage and mail industry	396		22323
Scientific research/technology service and geological exploration	12528		22217
Leasing and business service industry	4013		18422
Information transmission/computer service and software industry	2037		11534
Building industry	1047		5141
Real estate industry	1218		4592
Agriculture, forestry, animal husbandry and fishery	1615		3006
Residents service and other service industries	1041		2812
Mining industry	794		2761
Accommodation and catering industry	1598		1717
Other industries	166		1382
Total amount	90874		333842

Data source: Minister of Commerce, Statistics Bureau and the State Administration of Exchange Control of China, *2009 Statistical Bulletin of China's Outward Foreign Direct Investment*, P22.

200 http://www.treasury.gov/resource-center/data-chart-center/tic/Documents/mfh.txt.

201 http://www.treasury.gov/resource-center/data-chart-center/tic/Pages/ticarchives.aspx

II. Upgrading the Product Mix of China's Exports to America

Since the 1990s, China mainly exported labor-intensive products to America, while America mainly exported capital-and-resource intensive products to China, which has been regarded as one of the basic features of China-U. S. goods trade. However, significant changes can be found in the product mix of China's export to America since 1989.

According to relevant statistics, the strong points of China's exports to America in the 1990s mainly lay in the following categories of goods: clothes, not knitted or crocheted, and their accessories; footwear, shin guards and similar products and their accessories; electric motors, electrical equipment and their accessories; nuclear reactors, boilers, machines and mechanical appliances and their components; toys, games, sporting goods and their components and accessories; and leather products, travel articles and suitcases. Among them, the earliest exports to America in large amounts included clothes, footwear, toys and leather products, which occupied a considerable market share of the U. S. and still play an important role in bilateral trade. In particular, toys had a very high and stable market share. Export of mechanical and electrical products (including high-tech products) emerged after the mid 1990s, keeping a stable growth in the market share. America's export to China mainly focused on capital-and-technology intensive products, as well as resource intensive products, with stable export of airplanes, mechanical and electrical products and agricultural products and fluctuant export of other products.

According to HS-4 categorization, traditional labor intensive products such as toys, travel articles and textile products accounted for the most in the top 5 categories of China's export to America in 1989, taking up approximately 50% of China's total export to America, far higher than other categories in both amount and proportion. Export of mechanical and electrical products mainly included products of Category 8527, the products with simple assembly such as radios and recorders. In addition, the export of resource products remained at a certain proportion in the China-U. S. trade structure, similar to the 1970s and 1980s. China's export of crude oil also played an important role in the bilateral trade. The China-U. S. composition of trade in this period was obviously based on the edge of static comparison of both countries, with typical vertical labor division as the job-division scheme and totally complementary bilateral relations. With intra-industry trade as the main body, the exports of the two countries concentrated on completely different categories, so no competition existed between the two countries.

However, the mechanical and electrical products, represented by automatic data processing equipment and its components, and high-tech products reigned supreme in China-U. S. trade, while the products of HS84 and Chapter 85 accounted for 38% in the top 10 categories of export products and reached a proportion of above 44% in total export to America. The products of HS8471, i.e. automatic data processing equipment and its components, magnetic and optical readers etc., ranked below 50$^{th\ place}$ in 1989, 2nd in the export in the 1990s and climbed to the top in 2008, when it surpassed the export amount of toys by about 1/3.[202] According to American official statistics, America imported ATP (Advanced Technology Products) valued at 89.7 billion USD from China in 2009, making up 30.3% in total amount of import, while the imported ATP from China took up 29.8% in total ATP import of America. America's export of ATP to China amounted to 17.2 billion USD in 2009, occupying 24.7% to the total export of America to China and only 7% in the total ATP export of America.

Table 6 Advanced Technology Products (ATP) Trade Between the U. S. and China (Unit: one thousand USD)

Category	America's ATP Export to China by Dec. 2010	America's ATP Import From China by Dec. 2010	America's ATP Export to China by Dec. 2009	America's ATP Import From China by Dec. 2009
Biotechnology	167,910	58,701	123,604	45,340
Life sciences	1,966,809	1,499,918	1,591,488	1,257,731
Photoelectron	463,326	7,551,785	203,597	6,529,862
Information and communications	4,040,826	102,292,181	3,569,690	79,040,037
Electron	6,490,880	2,772,161	5,282,611	1,698,627
Flexible manufacturing	2,286,365	663,640	785,780	459,187
Advanced materials	213,729	165,875	254,255	110,452
Air craft	5,787,326	506,264	5,356,406	410,848
Weapons	715	160,653	894	121,288
Nuclear technology	36,502	893	33,967	1,038
Total amount	21,454,388	115,672,071	17,202,292	89,674,411

Data source: US Census

Therefore, a transition from labor intensive products of low added value and low technology to mechanical and electrical products of higher technology and added value is revealed in China's export to America, according to the data from current trade statistical system. China's export is increasingly relying on high-tech products such as televisions, monitors, computers and semiconductor circuit boards instead of the original clothes, shoes,

202 Data comes from USITC Dataweb.

hats, suitcases and toys.

However, it is not reasonable to reach the conclusion of the upgrading of China's export product mix to America based on the above data. According to statistics, the product mix of China's export to America, or even the whole foreign trade of China after the mid-1990s, has performed in quite a different way with the development level and resources of China, so China's export can be considered "special" to a certain degree. However, the following three factors shall be taken into consideration. Processing trade is the first factor. Accepted by all researchers, the improvement in the technology content of China's export of mechanical and electrical products has little relation with the development of the technical capability of China, since processing trade accounted for the most of China's export, especially in mechanical and electrical products which are developing in a fastest speed and are most representative for the upgrading of product mix. In some scholars' opinions, domestic ingredients in China's exporting products to America account for more than the generally assumed, but it cannot change the conclusion that processing trade dominates China's export to America. America's import from China actually reflects its import from many countries and economies owing to the global production supply chain. Secondly, though some problems lie in the current trade data, it still reveals that China has the most advantages in consumptive electrical products among China's high-tech products export to America, which is mainly reflected in the export product mix. The growth of China's export to America mainly concentrates in a few product categories, which means that China's export to America since the 1990s depended highly on only a few categories of products of the most rapid growth without expanding into new categories. This is a weakness of China's export. Thirdly, the unit prices of China's exporting high-tech products are much lower than America, even for the exactly same category. This is the paradox of the growing trade and the worsening trade conditions emphasized by many Chinese scholars.

The so-called upgrading of China's export product mix is mainly based on the significant growth of export of mechanical and electrical products, since the electronic industry is one of industries of the most elaborate labor division among emerging industries. As indicated in the Trade and Development Report made by the UN Conference on Trade and Development (UNCTAD), the East Asia district is featured with the largest concentration of electronic industry production network. Relying on the sound infrastructure, rich labor resources and policies of opening, China has played an important role in the supply of medium-low level components and assembly in the electronic industry and formed an industrial cluster of components production and assembly of a certain scale.

However, the U. S. is still the forerunner in outsourcing of electronic industry and the supplier and research and development center for the core technology of the industry. The labor division is reflected by the so-called upgrading of China's export product mix to America.

III. Current Major Trade Disputes Between China and America

Under the background of the "Great Recession," President Obama's analysis and understanding of the causes of current economic crisis largely affected his judgment on the status and trend of current China-U. S. trade relations. According to Obama and his economic advisors, the economic crisis mainly resulted from "the economic growth and prosperity relying on the expansion of consumption expenditure for many years," which was led by the "rise of asset price and lax credit criteria." Therefore, the "rebalance" is necessary to overcome the crisis. In the President's Report on Economics in 2011, the Obama administration repeatedly emphasized that the previous economic growth was unbalanced, because the global economic growth was relying too heavily on the consumption of America. As the American economy accounts for approximately 1/4 of the global economy and consumption has taken up about 2/3 of the American economy according to historical average level, the American consumption shall occupy 16% to 17% of global demand, compared to the actual proportion of 22% to 23% from 1996 to 2006. As a consequence, American consumption raised its proportion in American economy to 70%. The personal savings rate became extremely low and the federal government turned from surplus to huge deficit. America had to borrow money from other economies, leading to a trade deficit in current account.

In addition, the export growth of the U. S. was not rapid enough. Owing to the decreasing transport cost and global labor division, a product may go through the product lines of many economies before completion. Its components will be counted in the record of import and export everytime they enter and leave an economy, so the trade value brought by this product may exceed its value in the final sale. Therefore, almost every major economy had experienced an export growth rate faster than its own GDP growth rate in the decade before 2008. The average export growth rate of the top 20 export economies had reached 243%, while the average rate of developed economies was only 143%, compared to 96% of America. The leading superiority of America, who still remained the largest importer and exporter, had been significantly narrowed.

Moreover, the unbalance of major economies was not improved in this economic crisis. Regarding China and Germany, their export and savings have increased, which helps accumulate earnings and provide capital for countries of deficit, but does not provide enough for the world economy's demand. In China, the proportion of the current account surplus in GDP raised from 2% in 2000 to 10% in 2008, while Germany turned a deficit to a surplus in the current account, taking up 7% of GDP. During the financial crisis, the deficit of America dropped below 4% of GDP, and the surplus of China and Germany has reduced, but remained higher than 5% of GDP. Owing to the rapid growth rate of China, its proportion of surplus in the world GDP will continue to develop. [203]

Therefore, the Obama administration positions China as one of its most important partners to solve global economic problems, which means that it requires China to assume the responsibility of economic adjustment. China-U. S. trade relations were the main adjustment objects in the Obama administration's "rebalance" policy on foreign economic relations. Though there was no explicit requirement on the balance of China-U. S. trade relations, increased consumption of China and more savings of America will result in more import of China and more export of America, thus to reduce America's trade deficit with China. Meanwhile, the Obama administration recognized the economic growth mode of China as a cause of America's predicament in China-U. S. trade relations, so it placed more attention on the theory and practices of China's domestic economic policies. In the negotiation and policy implementation of America's trade relations with China, it put forward requirements on market opening for specific products, exchanged rate adjustment and protection of intellectual property, strengthened the trade aid related to China, such as anti-dumping and anti-subsidy and the relief policy, and attached even more importance to the impact of China's domestic policies on America and attempted to link the domestic structure and benefit adjustment of America to China's policies. Therefore, the conventional and new conflicts in China-U. S. trade relations were interweaved together, leading to various disputes in a wider range:

1. Dispute on the Exchange Rate of RMB

The exchange rate of RMB has long been a dispute between China and America. Since the exchange rate reform in July 2005, the exchange rate of RMB to USD rose rapidly, significantly slowing down in the global financial and economic crisis, keeping a stable growth since mid-2009 and revived the rapid growth rate since late 2010.

---

203 *Economic Report of the President: 2011*, United States government printing office, Washington : 2011, pp.81-90.

Many American politicians, labor groups, some medium and small sized enterprises and analysts felt discontented with the speed and range of the value rise of the RMB exchange rate, criticizing China for controlling the exchange rate and required a quicker and more significant value rise. They had different opinions, ranging from 15% to 50%, for the value rise. In their opinions, the low exchange rate of RMB constituted a subsidy to China's export, which greatly damaged America's industrial sectors competing with low cost Chinese finished products and incurred unemployment. They also regarded the exchange rate policy of China as the main reason for their trade deficit with China.

The Chinese government insisted that the RMB exchange rate administration, which ensured the exchange rate stayed within a certain range and remained comparatively stable, aimed not to promote export or inhibit import, but to avoid mass unemployment and maintain the economic and social stability of China. In June 2010, the People's Bank of China announced the start of reform to further promote the exchange rate formation mechanism, and since then, the exchange rate of RMB to USD started to rise again. In 2010, the nominal exchange rate of RMB to USD has increased by more than 3%. As the Obama administration placed the exchange rate of RMB as one of core issues in China-U. S. trade relations and relevant interest groups of America linked this problem with "fair" trade and attacked Chinese economic policies and administration measures, the issue of the exchange rate becomes extremely complicated.

2. Protection of Intellectual Property

The issue of the protection of intellectual property has long existed between China and the U. S. since the 1980s. The U. S. has investigated on the protection of intellectual property in China for a long time and repeatedly threatened and imposed sanctions on China based on the special Clause 301. America recognized the great efforts and achievements made by China in the protection of intellectual property. China has greatly improved the system for the protection of intellectual property, approved several relevant laws, closed many illegal production lines, detained and destroyed large amounts of illegal and pirated audio-visual products, inhibited the export of illegal and infringing products, trained many judges and law enforcers on the protection of intellectual property and expanded the video and audio production permit. However, since the protection of intellectual property is the foundation of American economic competitiveness, America still required further improvement on the system for the protection of intellectual property. Some companies still had a lot of complaints. It is difficult to precisely quantify the loss suffered by American companies due to infringement of intellectual property, because the data provided by these companies is mainly an estimation, which has been demonstrated by the report of the U. S. General Auditing Bureau.

Americans also understands that it is impossible to realize perfect protection of intellectual property in short time owing to the weak public awareness, differences of varying regions and lack of resources and measures for protection. In 2010, the United States Trade Representative (USTR) pointed out in the Special 301 Report that China would still be the focus of America's protection of intellectual property. The Chinese government has been putting forward great efforts to strengthen the protection. On the meeting of China-U. S. Joint Commission on Commerce and Trade in 2010, the Chinese government announced several new measures to improve the protection of intellectual property in China, including promoting government institutions and large-sized state-owned enterprises to purchase legitimate software.

3. Anti-dumping, Anti-subsidy and Abuse of Other Safeguards

China is the object of most anti-dumping and anti-subsidy investigations by America. After China's entry to the World Trade Organization (WTO), America has launched 71 anti-dumping lawsuits involving 83 categories of products, and 86% transactions of these lawsuits were finally imposed with anti-dumping taxes according to the arbitration. Lawsuits on anti-dumping, anti-subsidy or joint investigations even increased in the "Great Recession." In these investigations and lawsuits, the American government did not recognize China's status as market economy, but calculated the dumping and subsidy range based on the subrogate country, putting China at an extreme disadvantage.

In addition, the U. S. also launched the safeguard investigation against China based on Clause 421, i.e. the transitional product-specific safeguard mechanism. During the George W. Bush administration, four out of the six product-specific safeguards were supported by the United States International Trade Commission, (USITC) but not approved by George W. Bush. However, the safeguard application for tires of passenger cars and lightweight trucks obtained support from President Obama in 2009. The safeguard application was proposed by the United Steelworkers of America (USWA), who claimed that the "abnormal grow of the import" of tires from China had incurred great damages to American tire manufacturers from 2004 to 2008, leading to a loss of 5,100 tire-related jobs in America, and a loss of 3,000 job opportunities in 2009. These statements were not supported by American tire producers and sellers. According to some representatives of the tire industry, imposition of extra customs would injure American consumers' benefits, but would not significantly benefit the America tire industry, since most importing products from China belonged to low-end tires, but USITC decided that the import of Chinese tires would shock the American market and suggested to impose extra customs of annual decrease on relevant tire import from China (55% for the 1st year, 45% for the 2nd year and 35% for the 3rd year) and provide trade aid to American companies and workers. In September 2009, President Obama declared to collect additional customs for importing tires from China since then, with a lower tax rate (35% for the 1st year, 30% for the 2nd year and 25% for the 3rd year). The situation in the two years after the enforcement of this policy demonstrated that rejecting Chinese goods from entering America generated no extra production and employment. The Chinese government proceeded against America for this unfair arbitration in WTO.

4. Health and Safety of Some Products Imported From China

Cases related to the safety of Chinese products have once become the hot topics in America in previous years, involving product recall and consumption warning, etc. of Chinese products. Since 2007, the U. S. Food and Drug Administration has adopted product recall, import ban or consumption warning against some Chinese products, including pet food, toothpaste, powdered formulas for babies and dairy products. The U. S. Consumer Product Safety Commission has sent out a large amount of consumption warnings, such as warning on hazardous substances or improper design of Chinese toys.[204] The complaint by American consumers on the quality of gypsum plates made in China had aroused a long-lasting dispute, which has not yet been solved as of now. China and America have signed many agreements on training and communication in terms of health and safety. The Chinese government spared no effort in strengthening the communication and trust, and assisted relevant American institutions in establishing agencies in China. For example, a high-level communication on the safety of consumer goods is conducted between CPSC and the General Administration of Quality Supervision, Inspection and Quarantine of China every two years. The FDA set up offices in three big cities of China in 2008. The CPSC established its office in the U. S. Embassy in China in 2009.

5. Questions on Economic Policies of the Chinese Government

America's misunderstanding on the intent of the Chinese government's relevant policies often arouses this problem, with China's self-renovation policy in 2009 and export

204 Toys made in China has dominated the American market. 90% of American imported toys in 2009 came from China. See CRS Report RL33536, Wayne M. Morrison, *China-U. S. Trade Issues*, Congressional Research Service, December 27, 2010.

quotas of rare earths in 2010 as typical examples. The new policy on self-renovation and the adjustment on the export quotas of rare earths were adopted for the better development of related domestic industries, but not aimed to restrain foreign competitiveness. They were interpreted as measures to prejudice foreign enterprises. The efforts made by the Chinese government clarified the aim of the self-renovation policy. Both countries reaffirmed that the new policy aimed to facilitate the market competition and the opening of the international trade and investment and protect the intellectual property, while the technology transformation, production process and other information conditions related to property rights shall be confirmed by enterprises. In the 2010 meeting of the China-U. S. Joint Commission on Commerce and Trade, China stated that it would be fair to all innovative products made in China without discrimination, no matter produced by foreign enterprises or Chinese-invested enterprises.

6. Government Procurement

China has a large market of government procurement. As estimated by the U. S. Department of Commerce, the annual value of public procurement in China may exceed 85 billion USD. China is undergoing the negotiation on the entry to the Government Procurement Agreement (GPA) of WTO, where the main disagreement lies in China's requirement to open a government procurement market like other developed countries. China also took a stand on the issue of entry into GPA, so this issue is placed as one of the focuses on the bilateral strategic and economic negotiation with America and the China-U. S. Joint Commission on Commerce and Trade.

Fields that China places great significance and care on see slow development. For example, in terms of the benefits of China's investment in America, many proposals of Chinese-invested enterprises investing in America have failed due to non-economic factors, such as Huawei purchasing 3Leaf in 2010. Currently, America makes a commitment to welcoming the investment from China and promises that the Foreign Investment Examination Commission will not discriminate any foreign investment because of its source place. The U. S. and China have signed the Memorandum of Understanding on Promoting Investment in America. Both countries have conduct seven rounds of negotiations on the Bilateral Investment Treaty (BIT) and will continue until a formal document on bilateral legal framework is formed.

Regarding America's control on export to China, America currently has not practical plan to relax the control. Though the reform on the export control system under the national export initiative may loosen the control in some respects, the restraints on China may still remain. For the status of the market economy, America only indicated that it would consider China's status as a market economy and did not expressly admit it.

IV. Recent Prospects of China-U. S. Trade Relations

In 2009, Chinese and American leaders agreed to change the China-U. S. Strategic Economic Dialogue (SED) to China-U. S. Strategic and Economic Dialogue (S&ED), which indicated that both parties became aware of the importance to strengthen bilateral cooperation and policy coordination, jointly cope with global financial and economic crisis and promote the more balanced economic growth of two countries. The U. S. will give a more important play to China in the international economic system in order to turn China to a "responsible stakeholder" in the global economic system. In America's view, China has obtained huge benefits from the global trade system as one of the major economies, so it shall assume the responsibilities necessary to maintain the operation of the system. This may be the reason for some American officials stating that China-U. S. trade relations have come to a historic turn.

In terms of China-U. S. trade and investment relations, since China's special role in the international labor division system, especially in Asian production network, is the most important factor contributing to the current China-U. S. trade structure, it needs to adjust this division system to realize a "rebalance" of bilateral trade. With the given endowment, the adjustment can be realized by the change of global economic structure resulted from the technological progress or other major constitutional innovations, or major changes in the comparative advantages in the labor division system. However, despite the recovery from the economic crisis, no technological or constitutional innovation occurred in the global economic system, while no major change can be found in the comparative advantage of the main producers in Asian production network. Therefore, the China-U. S. trade and investment relations will remain unchanged in a certain period unless America can make achievements in the "rebalance" progress. For the adjustment of China-U. S. trade deficit, the Chinese government promised to insist on the stable growth of foreign trade, adhere to export and import increase and stabilize the international balance of payments in current Chinese items, which means that China will intentionally expand import to balance the international balance of payments. It will facilitate the trade balance between the two countries. However, the U. S. is required to reasonably relax the restraints on export control for balance. As estimated by international organizations such as IMF, the deficit in current items of America will continue to rise under the current trade structure, and America's trade deficit with China is difficult to change in a short time.

Along with the rapid development of the Chinese economy, the original asymmetry between Chinese and American market strength is changing. The Chinese market is playing an increasingly important role in America owing to its rapid economic growth, expanding market, improved living standards and mass group of moderate incomes with strong consuming capacity. The great demand in infrastructure construction and upgrading of industrial structure bring in great needs of foreign products and services. As an important export market, direct investor and debt holder of America, China sees an increasing influence over the U. S., though the change may be a long and uncertain process.

Domestic Politics of the U. S. and the Exchange Rate of RMB

He Xingqiang

Rather than a pure economic issue between China and the U. S., the exchange rate of RMB has been linked to American domestic politics since the very beginning. Although the issue of RMB exchange rate resulted from domestic problems with America, especially the constant decline of the manufacturing industry, and the rapid increase of China's trade surplus to America after China's entry to the World Trade Organization (WTO) in 2001, it was the relevant interest group of manufacturing industry and labors that made this issue a hot topic in China-U. S. relations. Their efforts, including lobbying Congress and presenting a petition to the administration, especially the Treasury Department, enabled American decision-makers to attach more importance to the exchange rate of RMB and gradually made the issue the hot topic about China among public opinions. The exchange rate of RMB finally became one of the main issues in China-U. S. relations.

How did the American interest group interact with Congress and the administration to promote the importance of the exchange rate of RMB in China-U. S. relations? Why did American congressmen accept the idea and promoted the disclosure of bills that required the appreciation of RMB? What were the background and prospects of these bills? How was the relation between the U. S. Congress and administration departments: cooperation, competition or both? What were Chinese government, scholars and media's opinions on this issue? How did the attitude of China affect this issue? This article will comprehensively interpret the domestic political factors affecting the exchange rate of RMB based on the analysis of the above questions.

I. Emergence of the Issue: Beginning of the Politicalization of RMB Exchange Rate

The manufacturing industry of the U. S. has increasingly faced turmoil, along with the economic decline of America, since 2002. The National Association of Manufacturers (NAM), representing the manufacturing industry of America, blamed the difficulties of the industry and workers on the "currency control" of other countries and turned against China, leading to the issue of the exchange rate of RMB. The leaders of NAM established the largest Coalition for A Sound Dollar that represents the interests of the manufacturing industry and agricultural trade groups.[205] In 2003, the Coalition turned its attention to the exchange rate of RMB and placed the issue as the focus of the American government and society after several-months efforts.

In January 2003, the Coalition advised the new U. S. Treasury Secretary John W. Snow to exert pressure upon China, Japan, Taiwan, China and Korea to stop their "currency control" with the aim to facilitate export.[206]

In May, Frank Vargo, the Vice Chairman for international economic affairs of NAM and the Co-Chairman of the Coalition for A Sound Dollar, claimed that the American manufacturing industry encountered a regression and suffered a loss of 2.2 million jobs since March 2001, which mainly resulted from the RMB undervalued by 40%.[207]

In June, the Coalition for A Sound Dollar stated that they were considering a proposal to the Bush Administration to force RMB to appreciate based on "301 Clause."

In August, the Coalition indicated that they were considering requiring the Bush Administration to put the Chinese government's "exchange rate control" on record and conduct formal investigation.

At the beginning of September, the Coalition wrote to John W. Snow and urged him to put a stop of Chinese government's "currency control" as the primary goal in his visit to Asia.

The Coalition had aroused extensive concern by the above behaviors. On September 4th, President Bush issued a statement saying, "I hope our trade partners can be just to our producers, workers, peasants and manufacturers, and they cannot see fair play under the currency control of governments."[208] On September 8th, John W. Snow indicated that America would adopt measures to force Asian countries to stop the so-called "currency

---

205 The Coalition, representing 95% of American exporters, was founded by several dozen of American trade associations, including National Association of Manufacturers (NAM), Association of American Steel Manufacturers (AASM), American Textile Manufacturers Institute (ATMI) and American Institute of Aeronautics (AIA). Number of members developed to 61 by January 2003, 80 by June 2003 and 102 by the end of 2005. http://www.sounddollar.org.

206 Phillips, Micheal M. "U. S. Manufacturers Lobby against Asian Rate Strategies." *The Wall Street Journal*. http://www.sounddollar.org.

207 [US] Report of Bloomberg on May 15 2003. Quote from the website of the Coalition for A Sound Dollar: http://www.sounddollar.org.

208 Ibid.

control."[209]

At the end of September, the American Federation of Labor- Congress of Industrial Organizations (AFL-CIO), as the largest labor organization, had further incited the government to involve itself in the RMB issue. Thea M. Lee, the assistant of the Public Policy Department of AFL-CIO, said that RMB had been undervalued by 40% in the "United States-China Economic and Security Review Commission" of the Congress and the International Relations Commission of the House respectively on September 25th and October 21st. She urged the American government to take every measure, including lodging a complaint to WTO, to give the high sign to Chinese government and show the American government's stand on this issue.[210]

Under the pressures of these interest groups, many congressmen from states of developed manufacturing industries turned their attention to RMB in consideration of the manufacturing industry and unemployment in their states.

On July 31, 2003, 16 members of the Democratic and Republican party, led by Charles Schumer, the New York State Democratic Senator, and Donald Manzullo, the Republican representative of Illinois, wrote to President Bush to urge him to adopt direct actions to facilitate the unrestricted flow of Chinese currency and more effective measures to correct the exchange rate of RMB.[211]

On September 5th, Charles Schumer led the Senate to propose the bill (S.1586) on the exchange rate of RMB and required China to increase the exchange rate of RMB to USD within six months; otherwise 27.5% customs will be collected upon all products exported from the inland of China to America.[212]

On September 9th, Lindsey Graham, the senator from South Carolina and seven other senators jointly released a nonbinding resolution that required the Chinese government to "correct" the undervalue of RMB, which was passed by the Senate on September 26th.[213]

---

209 "Coalition Praises Treasure Secretary for Making Undervalued Currencies a Top Global Issue", 2003. Sep. 8. http://www.sounddollar.org/mnews80.html.

210 Testimony of Thea M. Lee.before the Hearing of Commission on U. S.-China Economic and Security Review," *Federal News Service*, September 25, 2003.

211 "New Bipartisan Congressional Coalition Urges President to Increase Pressure on China to Float its Currency." July 31, 2003. http://www.sounddollar.org/mnews75.html.

212 See the bill content in the Thomas website of the Library of Congress (http://thomas.loc.gov/). The bill was submitted to the Senate Finance Committee after second reading, and no further action was taken. The figure of 27.5% came from the average figure of experts' opinions on the undervalue degree of RMB ranging from 40% to 15%. http://thomas.loc.gov/cgi-bin/query/z?c108:S.1586:

213 "Senate Unanimously Passes Graham Resolution on Chinese Trade Abuses," http://lgraham.senate.gov.

On October 21st, Sue Myrick, a Republican House representative from North Carolina proposed a bill on exchange rate of RMB (H. R. 3364) with same content to Charles Schumer in the House Ways and Means Committee. [214]

On October 30th, Charles B. Rangel and Sander M. Levin, two ranking Democrats, wrote to the President, Treasury Secretary and the trade representative Robert Zoellick to require further actions.[215]

The interest groups representing American manufacturers and labor organizations had lobbied on the exchange rate of RMB around Snow's visit to China in September, including the establishment of the Coalition, the release of study report, convening press conferences, lodging complaints and giving testimony to Congress, in order to create the public opinion that the "undervalue by 40%" of RMB had led to the decline of American manufacturing industry, loss of jobs and trade deficit. The Congress started to utilize the data of these interest groups and approved relevant resolutions, raising Americans' concern on the issue of RMB and exerting more pressures on the appreciation of RMB.

In 2004, the year of the American presidential election, AFL-CIO, as the main voters of the Democratic Party, had obtained the support of many Democratic members, including John Kerry, the Democratic candidate for President. AFL-CIO had become the main force to press on the appreciation of RMB. On September 9th 2004, AFL-CIO, representing the China Currency Coalition founded by 23 industrial and agricultural companies and labor organizations, submitted a 200 page application to the Bush administration to require the government to investigate whether China had controlled the currency and whether sanctions should be adopted according to the 301 Clause of the *1974 U. S. Trade Act.*[216]

Though the United States Trade Representative Office turned down the application in four hours, the application and subsequent statements by the China Currency Coalition had aroused more attention. Under the leadership of Charles Schumer and Sander Levin, 30 members of the Senate and the House established the Congressional China Currency Action Coalition on September 30th, proposed the application of the same content to the China Currency Coalition and continued to urge the administration to take measures on this

214 See the bill content in the Thomas website of the Library of Congress (http://thomas.loc.gov/). No further action was taken. http://thomas.loc.gov/cgi-bin/bdquery/z?d108:H. R.3364:

215 "Opening Statement of the Honorable Sander M. Levin," Oct. 30, 2003. http://waysandmeans.house.gov.

216 "Statement of China Currency Coalition in Response to USTR Rejection of 301 Petition," Sep. 9, 2004. http://www.chinacurrencycoalition.org.

issue.[217] In this way, the public opinion to require appreciation of RMB had been formed in America.

II. Politicalization of RMB Exchange Rate: The Process of Congress of the U. S. to Press on the Appreciation of RMB by Legislation

The U. S. Congress has paid attention to the issue of RMB exchange rate for eight years, since 2003, when Charles Schumer proposed the bill on the RMB exchange rate. However, it was only after 2005 that influential bills have emerged.

1. Pressure from Congress from 2005 to 2007

Most bills on the exchange rate of RMB were proposed in the U. S. Congress in 2005 and 2007, incurring great influence and threats. The Congress passed acts on this issue to exert more pressure and, since then, the exchange rate of RMB has become a political problem.

(1) First Wave of Pressure on Congress in 2005

Interest groups had put more efforts in lobbying Congress in 2005.

On February 1st, NAM issued the NAM Trade Agenda for China 2005 and announced its goal to realize an immediate appreciation of RMB by 40% and make the Treasury Department to list China as the "currency controller."[218]

On February 3rd and 5th, David A. Hartquist, the lawyer of the "China Currency Coalition" and Richard Trumka, the spokesman of the Coalition and the finance executive of AFL-CIO respectively gave testimony at the "United States-China Economic and Security Review Commission" that the undervalue of RMB was an important factor contributing to the huge trade deficit of America between trade with China and was a problem than needed to be solved immediately.

On May 2nd, NAM appealed to and required the American government to push "China to stop the currency control," supported the *Stopping Overseas Subsidies Act* (H. R.1216, S.593) proposed by the Senate and the House, that aimed to impose a retaliatory tariff on

217 The United States Trade Representative Office did not reject the application immediately but one month later, on November 12, to show due respect to congressmen. Refer to the website of the House Ways and Means Committee.

218 "The NAM Trade Agenda for China 2005," http://www.nam.org.

non-market-economy countries,[219] invited enterprises and individuals to join their actions, appealed to their parliament members to fight against unfair trade and promoted parliament members to put more efforts to solve this problem.[220]

As promoted by the interest group, more pressures were exerted on Congress to raise the value of RMB, leading to more proposals on the substantial value rise of RMB.

On February 3rd, Charles Schumer proposed a bill on the exchange rate of RMB (S.295) of the same content as the bill in September 2003, which required China to increase the exchange rate of RMB to USD within six months, otherwise a 27.5% tariff would be imposed upon all products from inland China entering America.

On April 6th, Charles Schumer and Graham proposed the bill S. AMDT.309 in the Senate, as the amendment to the Authorization bill FY2006-2007, State Department, S.600.[221] The Senate launched the vote to set aside the amendment but failed, and the amendment was then officially incorporated in the agenda of the Senate.

On April 7th, the Chinese Currency Act of 2005 (H. R.1498) put forward by congressmen Duncan Hunter, and Tim Ryan had obtained support from 145 congressmen. The Act blamed the Chinese government for its unfair trade practices of "currency control" and pressed the Bush Administration to exert pressures on the Chinese government by creating laws to change China's policy of the fixed exchange rate of RMB in order to turn around the serious unbalance of China-U. S. trade.

Meanwhile, the *Stopping Overseas Subsidies Act* was proposed in both the Senate and the House and was supported by the China Currency Coalition.

On July 21st, the Chinese government announced a 2.1% appreciation of RMB and the implementation of a floating exchange rate system based on a basket of currencies.[222] The "China Currency Coalition" considered these measures nowhere near satisfactory enough and indicated that "China's exchange rate change is inadequate and has no influence on the loss of job opportunities in American manufacturing industry incurred by China's currency

---

219 America has always denied China's status as a country of market economy, so it cannot impose tariff on Chinese products according to relevant laws. Therefore, Phil English and Artur Davis proposed the bill H. R. 1216 in the House one week after the bill on Chinese currency, while Susan Collins and Evan Bayh proposed the bill S.593 in the Senate.

220 *"Chinese Currency Manipulation Must Stop."* in http://www.nam.org.

221 "Schumer-Graham Aim To Level Playing Field On China Trade, Attach Amendment To State Dept. Bill," http://schumer.senate.gov/new_website/record.cfm?id=260959.

222 A composite unit consisting of weighted amounts of the currencies of a group of designated nations. (Translator's note)

control."[223] Within a few months, the "China Currency Coalition" had released several reports to claim that the exchange rate change of China had no impact on the increasing trade deficit and loss of jobs, urged the administration to take immediate actions to push China to abandon the "control of exchange rate" and required Congress to pass the *Chinese Currency Act of 2005.*

On the one hand, NAM felt satisfied about China giving up the fixed exchange rate of RMB to USD and regarded it as the start of more significant appreciation. On the other hand, it presented its discontent with only about a 2.1% value rise.[224] Therefore, NAM issued the *2005 Report to Congress on China's WTO Compliance* a month later, where it claimed that if China failed to raise the value of RMB significantly in a short period and facilitate the market floatation of RMB, the Bush Administration should list China as the currency controller and urge WTO and IMF to take corresponding actions on this issue. This Association also presented their ideas on this issue several days before John W. Snow's visit to China to show their concern on the Chinese currency and urged Congress and administrative departments to press on China based on the U. S. trade law. [225]

On November 28th, the U. S. Treasury Department submitted the semiannual report on the behaviors of major American trade partners, i.e. the *Report to Congress on International Economic and Exchange Rate Policies*, which did not list China as the "currency controller" and was thus fiercely attacked by interest groups. NAM required the American Treasury Department to stand firm against China's "exchange rate control" in IMF. In addition, AFL-CIO indicated that the Treasury Department betrayed the interests of American workers and the manufacturing industry and wrote a letter to the House to urge them to pass the *Chinese Currency Act of 2005* in order to fight against the "illegal currency control."

Despite all this, interest groups lowered their sail owing to several reverses by the end of 2005. For congressmen, they had given enough response to voters and interest groups and felt they should also cope with the pressure from administrative departments. On November 16th, the full Senate unanimously passed a proposal, upon Charles Schumer and Graham's requirements, that agreed to put off the voting date for bill S295 (i.e. Schumer Bill) to March 31, 2006. Schumer stated that the vote on the bill, which should originally be conducted before the end of the first session of the Senate in November, was put off to the

---

223 *"China's Exchange Rate Changes Woefully Inadequate."* July 21, 2005. http://www.chinacurrencycoalition.org/newsarticles/072105.html.

224 Engler, John. *"China's Move on Currency: Potentially of Enormous Importance."* http://www.nam.org.

225 *"Resolution of the NAM Board of Directors: Chinese Currency Manipulation."* http://www.nam.org.

second session, before March 31, 2006, considering President Bush's visit to China where he would consult on the exchange rate of RMB. Then it started a buffer period for the appreciation of RMB.

2006 was the year of mid-term congressional elections. Since congressmen concentrated on the election in this year, the bill was put aside, and the Schumer Bill was not mentioned. On September 28th, Schumer and Graham decided not to officially submit the proposal to the Senate for vote. According to Schumer, the proposal of the import tariff did not aim to establish a law, but to exert pressure on China and arouse America's concern on the exchange rate of RMB. The issue had already become a focus after the proposal was put forward. He believed that the exchange rate of RMB would not rise by 4.6% without this proposal. [226]

(2) Storm on the Exchange Rate of RMB Caused by the U. S. Congress in 2007

America's trade deficit with China maintained a rapid growth in 2006, so the concern on this issue significantly increased after the new Congress came into operation at the beginning of 2007. Congressmen felt more anxious about the trade deficit, and therefore put forward several bills to press on China for the exchange rate of RMB.

In the end of February, the Democratic congressman Ryan, Republican congressman Hunter and the "China Currency Coalition" jointly proposed the "Fair Currency Bill" (H. R. 782), which directly linked the currency misalignment to the trade subsidy, blamed China and some other countries for lowering the currency value for the purpose of subsidy and required American to immediately adopt measures to urge these countries to change their unfair exchange rate policies and otherwise impose anti-subsidy tariff on imported products from those countries.

At the same time, Republican member of the House, English and Democratic member Davis proposed the "Nonmarket Economy Trade Remedy Act of 2007" (H. R. 1229), advocating that the anti-subsidy law was not only applicable for market economy, but also for nonmarket economies such as China, in order to give the U. S. Department of Commerce the right to impose anti-subsidy tariff on all nonmarket economies based on provisions of laws.

The Currency Exchange Rate Oversight Reform Act of 2007 (S.1607), which aimed to

---

226 Yeager, Holly. "US senators drop China imports tariff bill." *Financial times*. 2006. September 29. from FT.com, available at: http://www.ft.com/cms/s/0/421165f8-4f4f-11db-b600-0000779e2340.html#axzz1CiZDG0WF, access on July 17, 2010.

establish a new system for the Treasury Department to respond to any misalignment of other currencies, was jointly proposed by four ranking members, including Max Baucus, the Chairman of Senate Finance Committee, Chuck Grassley, the Chief Republican, Charles Schumer, a Democratic Senator and Lindsey Graham, the Republican Senator.

The Currency Exchange Rate Oversight Reform Act of 2007 was one of bills on the RMB exchange rate in 2007 that had the greatest impact. Charles Schumer spent a long time preparing for the buildup of this bill. In his testimony in the Senate Finance Committee on March 28th, he announced that he would propose a new bill on currency, in line with WTO regulations, to promote the reform of RMB exchange rate. In the same testimonial session, Lindsey Graham placed the exchange rate of RMB as a problem deciding China-U. S. relations. According to Lindsey Graham, Democrats and Republicans had different opinions on most topics, except the exchange rate of RMB. This statement had aroused great concern from all parties. However, China did not make great concessions as they wanted on the exchange rate of RMB and trade unbalance in the China-U. S. Strategic and Economic Dialogue ended in late May. Four congressmen decided to put forward a bill the next month. The U. S. Treasury Department submitted the semiannual report on the international exchange rate on June 13th. The report specified that RMB was undervalued and the Central Bank of China had interfered in the foreign exchange market, but the American government stated that China should not be recognized as a currency controller. On the same day, the four congressmen jointly put forward the Currency Exchange Rate Oversight Reform Act of 2007, which was passed by the Senate Finance Committee by 20 votes to 1 after revision on July 26.

The initial approval of the bill by the Senate Finance Committee had aroused more attention. The clause of the "misalignment of exchange rate" was the most controversial, because it aimed to replace the "currency control" with "misalignment of exchange rate" in order to impose sanctions on other countries, especially China, that utilized the misalignment of exchange rate to provide subsidies to export enterprises. According to the bill, the Treasury Department should report to Congress twice a year on which countries had serious misalignment in the exchange rate, and then the countries would be appointed as the objects of priority actions. In the case that these countries did not take appropriate measures to solve the misalignment of exchange rate in a certain period, the Treasury Department should take further action, including deciding whether the exchange rate undervalued artificially by the country should be counted in America's calculation of dumping. The bill also stated that United States Trade Representative (USTR) should appeal to WTO if the problem was not solved in a year and required the Treasury Secretary to seek advice from the Federal Reserve Board and other central banks to decide whether remedial intervention should be adopted in the currency market.

The bill had stronger operability since it was claimed to be in line with WTO regulations. Unlike many other bills that categorized the misalignment of currency as a subsidy that should be forbidden, it suggested adopting measures largely based on the constitutions of IMF, including anti-dumping investigation and the consequences of WTO actions. The National Retail Federation (NRF) immediately made an objection, because in NRF's opinions, the bill would endanger the interests of many American enterprises if it was established as a law. In the testimonial session of Congress on August 2nd, the officials of the Bush Administration presented their anxiety on the bills striking back on China's policy on exchange rate of RMB. Officials from the U. S. Treasury and Commerce Department further stated their concern regarding the global protectionism that might be incurred by the legislation of these bills. Max Baucus, one initiator of this bill, attempted to relieve the tension. He said that he understood the anxiety of all social circles and believed that this bill would not damage China-U. S. trade relations.

Senator Christopher Dodd and Richard Shelby jointly put forward the Currency Reform and Financial Markets Access Act (S.1677) on August 1st. The bill intended to carry out punitive actions against the mandatory intervention by some countries, China in particular, in the exchange rate market on behalf of the Treasury Department. In mid August, the bill was approved by votes of absolute majority in Senate Committee on Banking, Housing, and Urban Affairs, which produced a great reaction around the country. More than a thousand economists jointly wrote a letter to present their anxiety on the serious impact of the bill on the China-U. S. trade relations and the American economy. Many American enterprises or industrial organizations that had close business relations with China showed concern or objection against this behavior of Congress. Opponents feared that the legislation of the bill would incur the retaliation of China and would cause extensive damages on China-U. S. economic relations.

Under these circumstances, administrative departments employed delay tactics. It was not until December 19th, the last day of the session of Congress, that the U. S. Treasury Department submitted the report on the exchange rate to Congress and refused to list China as the exchange rate controller. Several congressmen strongly opposed this report. Max Baucus accused the Treasury Department of cowardice, while Charles Schumer indicated that Congress had no other choice but to take necessary measures to cope with the issue, since the American administration refused to list China as the exchange rate controller despite the significant sign of exchange rate control of China.

2. Rise and Fall of the Pressure from American Congress from 2008 to 2011

The pressure on the exchange rate of RMB from the American Congress was eased in 2008, mainly because America needed to cooperate with China to get rid of the economic crisis and the upgrading strategic and economic dialogue between American administration and China dominated the economic and trade relations of the two countries. After Obama took office in the White House, the pressure on the exchange rate of RMB raised again under the serious economic situation and increasing protectionism and reached a new peak in the second half of 2010.

(1) Pressure from the Congress was Relieved in 2008, while Strategic and Economic Dialogue Led the Economic and Trade Relations of the Two Countries

The U. S. Congress eased up on the issue of the exchange rate of RMB in 2008, despite an uproar at the beginning of the year. No action was taken on the Currency Exchange Rate Oversight Reform Act, which was proposed by Chales Schumer and Max Baucus and approved by the Senate Finance Committee in the previous year, or any other bills. Congressmen who advocated pressing bills on China in the previous year only briefly mentioned this problem, compared to the intensity and popularity of this issue of the last year. At the beginning of July, four ranking Senators that led the Currency Exchange Rate Oversight Reform Act stated that they would try to formulate a law to ensure China and other American trade partners would abide by the regulations of IMF and WTO in their currency policies, but no more news was heard on this matter. Obama won the presidential election in November of that year. The ranking democratic Senator Christopher Dodd indicated that he would urge the new government to deal with the trade deficit with China and China's exchange rate control more actively, leaving the issue to the next administration.

The administrative departments, including the Treasury Department, had conducted strategic and economic dialogue with China, which led the China-U. S. trade and relations in 2008. Two strategic and economic dialogues between the two countries were respectively initiated at the middle and end of the year had highlighted the bilateral cooperation in energy and environmental protection more and started to discuss the financial cooperation for the first time, compared to the three dialogues before. The two reports on the exchange rate in 2008 still put China aside from the exchange rate controller, but criticized China for slowing down the appreciation of RMB and pointed out the great gap between the real exchange rate of RMB and the balance point and stated that China was still seriously "undervalued." At the beginning of December, Mr. Paulson, the U. S. Treasury Secretary, highly praised China's efforts on the appreciation of RMB in the previous three years, emphasized that China should continue with the process, and still regarded the adjustment of China's economic structure including the reform on exchange rate as the central topic of China-U. S. strategic and economic dialogue.

The reason for the changes in 2008 lay in the more serious financial crisis. The U. S. placed the focus on how to cooperate with China to solve the financial crisis, so the economic and strategic dialogue was more emphasized. As indicated by Roy Stapleton, the former U. S. ambassador to China, in a meeting celebrating the 30th anniversary for the establishment of diplomatic relations between the U. S. and China held by the National Committee on U. S.-China Relations at the end of 2008, the importance of the dialogue consists in the scale and topic, as well as the timeliness. He said, "When the economic and financial crisis swept over America, officials of economic and financial departments, including Paulson and lower ranks, had established the best work relations ever with corresponding officials from China. After the crisis broke out, we realized that China would also be undoubtly affected, owing to its ownership of large amount of bonds in USD. Every move of Paulson could be timely reported to China based on the smooth communication channel."[227] Under these circumstances, it was obviously inappropriate to continue to press on China for appreciation of RMB as in 2007, and the bills of congressmen could not obtain the support from large business groups represented by the American Chamber of Commerce. More importantly, the Bush administration did not agree with the behaviors of Congress. The White House and Treasury Department had repeatedly lobbied Congress and wanted to make them know that it was unnecessary to establish laws on the issue, since the administrative departments could encourage China to adopt the policy of flexible exchange rate by strategic and economic dialogue, the U. S.-China Joint Commission on Commerce and Trade (JCCT) and potential threats to China by lodging a complaint to WTO. In addition, Paulson's several visits to China had played a very positive role in the communication with the Chinese government.

(2) Pressure from the Congress Increased and Peaked in Obama Administration

President Obama moved into the White House in January 2009 and the new Congress began operation. Democrats controlled the Senate and House, as well as the White House.

---

227 Hou Jun, "Paulsen: The Strategic and Economic Dialogue Between China and the U. S. Shall Continue," *China Economic Weekly*, Issue 2 2009.

As a party that has always safeguarded the interests of labor unions and voters from the manufacturing industry, Democrats were more open and willing to adopt measures of protectionism. The global financial crisis continued and the economy and employment conditions were even worse, so Congress turned its attention again to the issue of the exchange rate of RMB. On May 13, 2009, the Democratic congressman Tim Ryan proposed a bill similar to bills from the previous several years, i.e. the Currency Reform for Fair Trade Act, which suggested revising Clause 7 of the Tariff Act established in 1930 so that the Department of Commerce could adopt anti-dumping measures to the misalignment of RMB. 143 congressmen in the House of Representatives supported the bill. On the same day, Senator Debbie Stabenow proposed a bill of the same content before the Senate (S.1027). On June 11th, Schumer again proposed the Currency Exchange Rate Oversight Reform Act of 2009 for the exchange rate of RMB.

In mid 2009, the priority of America was given to the Medicare reform bill promoted by the Obama administration. All congressmen paid their attention to this bill and relevated legislation, including the climate change, financial reform, immigrant bill, etc. The issue of the RMB exchange rate was kept out of sight and no further action was taken on relevant bills.

However, the situation grew tense at the beginning of 2010. The historical Medicare reform bill was approved as a law in March. Congress again turned their attention to the exchange rate of RMB due to the worsening economic and employment conditions in the country. The U. S. Treasury Department submits the report on the exchange rate on April 15 of every year, and President Hu Jintao of the People's Republic of China may attend the nuclear security summit meeting held in Washington D. C. in April, therefore, Congress released many bills that required the Treasury Department to list China as the "currency rate controller" and "take measures to remedy the loss incurred by the U. S. owing to the currency rate control," aiming to press upon the Chinese government and relevant American administrative departments. On March 15, 130 congressmen jointly wrote to the U. S. Treasury Secretary Timothy Geithner and Commerce Secretary Gary Locke, requiring to define China as the "currency rate controller." On March 16, Schumer proposed the Currency Exchange Rate Oversight Reform Act of 2010, with nearly the same content to the bill of 2009. Just before the G-20 Summit, Schumer indicated on June 9th that they would initiate the legislation to penalize Chinese currency policies within two weeks. The U. S. Treasury Secretary Timothy Geithner blamed China for its policy on the exchange rate of RMB in the hearings before Congress on June 10th and indicated that the policy of RMB damaged the global economic balance and inhibited the global economic reform.

On June 19, the People's Bank of China announced plans to restart the form of exchange rate mechanism, but the value of RMB rose slowly. After the parliamentary recess in August, the Congress exerted the pressure on the appreciation of RMB to a new high, along with the approach of the mid-term election in the beginning of November. 93 congressmen, under the leadership of Ryan, jointly wrote a letter on September 13th urging Democrats to take firm actions against Chinese policy on the exchange rate of RMB. On September 15th, the House Ways and Means Committee launched a two-day hearing on the exchange rate of RMB, with the presence of the Treasury Secretary Timothy Geithner, leading to a sharp rise of the pressure on appreciation of RMB. The Currency Reform for Fair Trade Act proposed by Ryan was approved by 348 votes against 79 on September 30, which was the greatest achievement made on the exchange rate of RMB in five years and the bill of highest level currently approved (approved in the House).

The rising concern of American Congress on the exchange rate of RMB since 2009, especially in 2010, mainly resulted from the continued downturn of the American economy in the previous two years. All Americans gave priority to creating jobs and lowering the unemployment rate, and public opinion regarded the undervalue of RMB as a main factor contributing to the unfair trade of China, loss of jobs to China, unemployment of America and the decline of American economy. Under the background, relevant interest groups continued to exert pressures on China. Many congressmen bore greater pressures from voters as the mid-term election was approaching, so more congressmen chose to support the bill aiming to put pressure on China. The increasing number of congressmen that supported the Currency Reform for Fair Trade Act demonstrated it. The Act was supported by 143 congressmen in May 2009 and won 348 votes just before the mid-term election, so the House approved the Act on September 30th.

However, the highest pressure from Congress on the RMB exchange rate did not continue. After the mid-term election, the pressure and people's concern were suddenly relieved. The Republicans regained the control of the House and attached more importance to strike down the Medicare reform bill originally promoted by Democrats. Relevant bills to the Currency Reform for Fair Trade Act had no chance to be proposed in the Senate. This session of Congress came to an end at the close of 2010. Since bills in the Congress would not leave to the new session of Congress without further actions according to the rules of the Congress, the bills on the exchange rate of RMB of this Congress ended in vain. The bill on the appreciation of RMB may be proposed again by the new Congress along with the approach of Hu Jintao's visit to America. The pressure on the exchange rate of

RMB from domestic America will not end until the American economy and employment conditions improve.

III. Essence of the Politicalization of the Exchange Rate of RMB: How to View the Influence of Legislation on the RMB Issue by the U. S. Congress

Generally speaking, it is more possible for Congress to adopt policies of protectionism compared to the President and administrative departments. The Congress tends to restrict the import of other countries' products to the U. S. by legislation in order to protect domestic industrial interests or promote the export of domestic products to other countries. The congressmen do not much consider the influence of foreign trade policies on foreign relations, because the voters are not concerned with these issues. Congressmen are very sensitive to the reactions of interest groups in the electoral district, because they can greatly affect the result of elections by financial aid to campaign advertisement and stirring voters to vote. The Congress mainly adopts legislation as the main way to affect the trade issue and takes various measures according to the Clause 301 of 1974 Trade Act and Super Clause 301 of 1986 Omnibus Trade Act.

Urged by manufacturers represented by NAM and labor unions represented by AFL-CIO, the Congress had proposed a series of bills to require the appreciation of RMB. Schumer and Graham's bill and other bills mainly resulted from the predicament of the manufacturing industry in various states and the loss of jobs in the sector. Schumer explained that the unfair trade from China damaged the manufacturing industry of New York and America, appealed to the federal government to take quick actions to promote the manufacturing industry in northern New York and urged the Senate Finance Committee to call a hearing on "China's currency control" in order to exert more pressures on China.[228] Graham had supported the textile industry of the South Carolina since 2003 and regarded China's currency control as the main reason for the loss of jobs in South Carolina's textile industry. Most other congressmen that proposed or supported the bills also saw difficulties in the manufacturing industry in their own states.

Since 2003, relevant interest groups, Congress and the media has established a leading public opinion that "the serious undervalue of RMB and Chinese government's control of

---

228 *"Schumer Urges President to Convene Summit on China Trade Immediately, Quickly Address Currency Manipulation."* in http://schumer.senate.gov.

exchange rate have greatly damaged the interests of American workers and manufacturing industry, taken away job opportunities in America and led to the trade deficit." China was then faced with the requirements on the appreciation of RMB from America; otherwise it would be imposed with punitive measures. The trade wars were about to break out. From 2005 to 2010, especially in 2005, 2007 and 2010, the Congress asked for the appreciation of RMB, released many bills that blamed China for currency rate control and brought great pressure to the RMB appreciation. However, these pressures never turned into practical actions. The Congress approved no bill on RMB as a law, and bills could seldom get to the vote by the Senate or the House. It needs further analysis on what is the role of the Congress in terms of trade policies, the exchange rate of RMB in particular.

1. Essence of the Legislation of Congress on the Exchange Rate of RMB

(1) Many Issues Concern American Congressmen, and It Is Unnecessary to Directly Control the Trade Policies

The overall goal of congressmen is to maintain and increase their political influence in Washington D. C. and their own states and their ultimate goal is to get re-elected. Therefore, they attach most importance to how voters, the media and the public view their actions in Congress. Most congressmen are concerned with many aspects, including trade. They only need to hold a common stand in trade policies to demonstrate that they are promoting the interests of voters and interest groups in the electoral district. It is not worthwhile or necessary to achieve direct and significant individual influence or reach practical policy results. The practical result on trade policy has nothing related to the three important factors contributing to the re-election of congressmen, "advertisement, standpoint of congressmen and seeking credit from voters and interest groups." For congressmen from states of great pressure on protectionism, such as states with a developed textile industry, they only need to make statements and vote, and they will not be blamed for other congressmen's opposition.

For congressmen in key committees (Senate Finance Committee and the House Ways and Means Committee) who shall pay special attention to trade, it is not the best method for them to improve their own political influence by controlling the practical policies. They do not need to play a role in the result of practical policies, but have better methods that have been tried by others before. Firstly, they can make speech, announce information, call a hearing and visit the capitals of American trade partners. Secondly, they can choose to legislate on less important fields to boast their contributions. And thirdly, they can propose some important bills without expecting them to be established as laws, which are very helpful to promote the congressmen and indicate their standpoints.

Schumer Bill is the most famous among the bills on the exchange rate of RMB. The performance of Schumer from 2003, when he proposed the bill on the exchange rate of RMB in the Senate for the first time, to now can be well explained by the above theory.[229] As the member of the Senate Finance Committee, Schumer needed to improve his political influence by legislating on trade. In 2003, Schumer showed his concern on the exchange rate of RMB for the first time by proposing the relevant bill, wrote to the President jointly with many parliament members and urged the President to take immediate actions and adopt stronger measures to correct the RMB exchange rate. In the same year, the Senate unanimously approved the resolution proposed by Schumer and others, which regulated that China's "act of cheating" in international trade was not binding. In 2004, Schumer and other parliament members required the American government to appeal to WTO according to 301 Clause of Trade Act and to investigate whether China has controlled the currency and apply sanctions. In 2005, Schumer and Graham put forward the well-known Schumer-Graham Bill, which was incorporated in the agenda of the Senate. Schumer successfully presented his concern on the manufacturing industry of America and his own state and achieved results in the change of Chinese system of exchange rate and appreciation of RMB, so he achieved a more significant political influence.

Schumer had maintained concern on this issue since 2006, including visiting Beijing and communicating with Chinese government on the exchange rate of RMB, calling hearings, releasing statements on this issue and some other methods. However, under the lobby of the administrative departments, changing concerns of voters and different situation of America, Schumer aborted any further action of this bill in September 2006, and explained that "the goal of the bill on tariff was to press on China instead of become a law."[230] Based on the increasing trade deficit with China in 2007, Schumer, with other three important members of the Senate, proposed new bill on the sanctions of the exchange rate of RMB that accorded to WTO regulations, which exerted great pressure on China and the China-U. S. strategic and economic dialogue at that time. Schumer continued to propose relevant bills in 2009 and 2010 and presented his concern on the exchange rate of

---

229 See the theory of the behaviors of congressmen on trade in: Deardorff, Alan V and Stern, Robert M., ed. *Constituent Interests and U. S. Trade Policies* (Ann Arbor: The University of Michigan Press), 1998, pp. 97-100.

230 Yeager, Holly. "U. S. senators drop China imports tariff bill." *Financial times*. 2006. September 29.

RMB. Schumer had won great political influence owing to these behaviors and thus became a ranking person in the Democratic Party.

Max Baucus, the Chairman of the Senate Finance Committee, was another ranking parliamentary member that exhibited himself by the exchange rate of RMB. In October 2010, Baucus paid an urgent visit to Beijing after the bill on the exchange rate was approved by the House. Before the visit, he claimed in Washington D. C. that the bill on exchange rate might pass in the Senate if China did not take appropriate measures. However, he never indicated his opinion on the exchange rate again after he met with Chinese leaders, including Xi Jinping, in Beijing, because he had done enough to show his efforts and promote himself and did not need to further promote the bill.

(2) Administrative Departments Attached More Importance to the Control of Trade Policies and the Practical Results Compared to Congress

It seems that the Congress and administrative departments always compete in trade policies. However, administrative departments pay more attention to the results of the control of trade policies. Congressmen are politicians that are concerned with many areas and will not only concentrate on the trade policies. Members of the Senate Finance Committee or House Ways and Means Committee pay equal or even more attention to taxation, social security and medicare than the trade policies.

The Congress is apparently concerned more about the exchange rate of RMB in 2005, 2007 and 2010. The issue was not the hot topic in 2006 and 2008, years of election, when congressmen attached more importance to the election. They did not realize their promises on the exchange rate of RMB, but considered it unnecessary to practically require legislation since they had realized their goal to pressure China and made achievements in the initial legislation. To the contrary, the administrative departments adhered to the baseline of the policy and did not list China as the exchange rate controller by delaying the report on the exchange rate to avoid direct pressure from the Congress, despite the dual pressure from both the Congress and China. Administrative departments even put forth more efforts to maintain the most effective communication with the Chinese government through the strategic and economic dialogue, regardless of the huge pressure from the Congress in 2007 and lobbied the Congress according to the direction of the policy on trade with China supported by President Bush. Therefore, though Congress had announced information related to the legislation on this issue through press conferences, it did not take further actions in practical legislation. The bills were not submitted for vote. Due to the severe economic and unemployment conditions of America and the mid-term election of the Congress, the bill on the exchange rate of RMB was passed by the vote of the House in 2010 for the first time, but it ended up with nothing conclusive, along with the end of this session of Congress, after the mid-term election. Administrative departments, as pressed by the Congress, required the Chinese government to speed up the appreciation of RMB, and meanwhile conducted effective communication with China based on the strategic and economic dialogue and the China-U. S. Joint Commission on Commerce and Trade, which led American government's policies on the exchange rate of RMB.

(3) The Most Effective Way for Congressmen to Affect the Trade Policy Is the Process of Legislation Instead of the Ultimate Results

The most effective way for congressmen to affect the trade policy is to lobby the administrative departments and threaten them with legislation. Though it may not be a real threat, no one can take account of this threat. In this way, congressmen can hit the target country, answer to voters, take credit from voters after the administrative departments take corresponding actions and therefore be awarded with maximum influence.

It is the same with the legislation on the exchange rate of RMB. Congressmen placed pressure on administrative departments and China, based on the weapon of legislation, and responded to voters with their actions to ensure interests of voters, which had become the best method for congressmen, including Schumer, to affect the trade policy. In 2006, Schumer had expressly indicated that legislation was only a tool to urge China to adjust the exchange rate of RMB and it would be unnecessary if the goal were accomplished.[231] After that, Schumer proposed similar bills on the appreciation of RMB to the Senate and pressed on administrative departments with other parliamentary members in 2007, 2009 and 2010 respectively. Only a few people believed that Schumer would attempt to turn the bills into laws after these years, but fewer people could ignore this issue, since congressmen might put the bill to the final legislation when no response was given to the bill. Obviously, administrative departments of the U. S. and China could not accept the situation. Another congressman, Ryan, also started to promote the bills on the exchange rate of RMB since 2005 and finally had his bill approved by the House before the mid-term election in 2010. He had fully presented his efforts to safeguard the interests of voters in his hometown. Actually, the bill had ended up there, too, and few people believed that congressmen would promote the bill in the Senate.

---

231 "Schumer, Graham. *"Withdraw China Tariff Bill as Bush Administration Pushes Long-Term Approach."* from http://info.hktdc.com/alert/us0620a.htm.

(4) The Power Structure Enables the Congress and Administrative Departments to Share the Power on Trade Policies and Enables the Congressmen to Apply the Power Flexibly and Appropriately

According to the U. S. Constitution, the Congress and administration share the power on trade. Under this structure, congressmen have enough room for active measures, while they can stop at any stage, thus to meet their interests. Congressmen can avoid reproach. Administrative officials can flexibly apply their power, respond to the coalition of interest groups established for certain policies according to demand, prevent the approval of regulations on trade barrier by the Congress and control policies in a more flexible way.

This system was perfectly utilized by congressmen on the exchange rate of RMB. They proposed bills to fully present their concerns over this issue, promoted the bills to be approved in the sub-committee, and stopped any further action or turned to other important topics according to circumstances after having obtained initial achievements. Therefore, they showed voters their great efforts on this issue, but the legislation was unnecessary. It was demonstrated by congressmen's performance on the exchange rate of RMB in 2006 and 2008. After the House approved the bill on the exchange rate of RMB at the end of September 2010, the Senate showed no difference, while no congressman attempted to promote the vote of this bill in the Senate. Schumer also put the issue aside without any further action.

(5) Interest Groups, Congress and Administrative Departments Check Each Other and Take What They Want on the Issue of the Exchange Rate of RMB

Compared to the Congress that directly distributes trade benefits to voters, administrative departments make policies that are not favored by voters. However, administrative departments sometimes make a concession with the powerful interest groups, so interest groups will not overthrow this system since they can obtain some benefits. After the Trade Act was approved in 1934, administrative departments have always been biased toward the interests of exporters but opposed the protectionism. Protectionists may also win some protective measures when they are strong enough, though these protective measures may be more flexible than they want.

Some American manufacturers have obtained certain achievements after the moderate appreciation of RMB in 2005. Though they further pressed on the Congress and administrative departments, they exerted less pressure on the Congress along with the constant appreciation of RMB. Congressmen had no action in 2006. Increasing trade deficit in China-U. S. trade in 2007resulted in greater pressure on the exchange rate of RMB. In 2010, the pressure grew again owing to the unfavorable economic and employment conditions and the mid-term election. On one hand, administrative departments adhered to the baseline of policies and prevented drastic measures or the final legislation of the Congress. On the other hand, the Congress adopted a tough stance against China and attacked China for the undervalue of RMB damaging the economy and employment of China to respond to the pressure from the Congress and interest groups. A balance was formed among the interest groups, Congress and the President.

2. Different Roles of the Administrative Departments and the Congress in the Exchange Rate of RMB

American administrative departments lead the formulation of trade policies. The Congress has enhanced its influence over the trade policy since the 1970s. The Congress, particularly the House Ways and Means Committee, plays an important role in the trade affairs, since it is responsible for making laws on taxation. In addition, the Congress also performs its power on trade by formulating and approving laws of so-called "fair trade," including protective clauses, anti-subsidy taxes and anti-dumping taxes. What is the relation between the Congress and administrative departments on the trade policies?

In terms of the power distribution of the U. S. Congress and administrative departments, they have competition in the formulation of trade policies and disagreements on different policies. Meanwhile, as two different departments of the government, they share the same goal to promote American interests, despite different methods to realize the interests. Therefore, their competition effects the trade policies, but they often cooperate in the trade policies to safeguard American interests. They are essentially allies, rather than opponents, in terms of trade policies. The United States Trade Representative Office and key committee of the Congress closely cooperate to cope with existing problems and exert pressure on foreign governments to open their markets. However, the cooperation can attain maximum efficiency upon certain conditions, otherwise their policy orientation may be affected by their different standpoints.

American scholar I. M. Destler listed the four conditions for effective cooperation between the Congress and administrative departments on certain trade policies.[232] The first

232 The four conditions include: firstly the President and the Trade Representative Office give priority to trade expansion and oppose protective measures; secondly, two Parties cooperate; thirdly, the Congress and administrative departments establish sound cooperation in the support to open trade policies; and fourthly, decision makers of trade affairs have obtained benefits from opinions of decision making circles, i.e. to normalize the free and open trade. See in: Deardorff, Alan V and Stern, Robert M., ed. *Constituent Interests and U. S. Trade Policies*. p. 101.

two conditions were respectively the cooperation of two parties and the determination of the administrative departments to promote the trade policies, which acted as a more important part.

Regarding the issue of the exchange rate of RMB, the Congress and the White House were under the control of Republicans in 2005 and 2006, so the two can cooperate in the trade policies. On the other hand, George W. Bush agreed with and promoted the free trade with China and opposed protectionism. Therefore, the Congress and the White House maintained favorable cooperation relations, and exerted great pressure on China in 2005 when China launched the reform of the exchange rate forming system and the value of RMB rose. After the mid-term election in 2006, Democrats regained the control of the Congress. Since 2007, the Bush administration, consisting mostly of Republicans, continued to promote the free trade with China, which caused constant conflicts with the Congress under Democrats' control on the exchange rate of RMB. The Congress and the White House saw greater divergence over this issue. The administrative departments started the strategic and economic dialogue with China, lobbied the Congress to renounce several bills that greatly pressed the appreciation of RMB and adopted delaying tactics, so as to avoid fierce conflict with Congress on this issue.

From January 2009 to the mid-term election in 2010 under the Obama administration, the White House and the Congress, both under the control of Democrats, could establish good cooperation relations. However, Obama did not give priority to trade policies in the first two years. Distinguished from the overall situation under the opposition of the two parties, the two parties cooperated in Congress to press on the appreciation of RMB, while administrative departments could not effectively strike back at the pressure for the pressure was growing larger. Even then, administrative departments still needed to maintain the basic framework for the policy of free trade and safeguard the overall stability of China-U. S. economic and trade relations. Though administrative departments occasionally blamed China for the exchange rate of RMB, it still kept China aside from the list of exchange rate controller. Administrative departments could keep the base line of the policy and maintain normal trade status with China if they wanted, based on its superiority in trade. The White House and the Congress did not effectively cooperate on the issue of the exchange rate of RMB during the Obama administration.

Generally speaking, the Congress and administrative departments have cooperated to some degree on the exchange rate of RMB to urge China to raise the value or RMB from 2005 to now. However, they did not reach an effective cooperation on this issue due to the superiority of administrative departments on the formulation of trade policies and the opposition of two parties, which thus restricted the pressure on the issue.

In addition, different opinions on the exchange rate of RMB also existed in China and the U. S., resulting in the partial relief of the pressure on the appreciation of RMB.

IV. Other Opinions on the Exchange Rate of RMB in China and the U. S.

1. Opinions in the U. S.

America has another opinion on the exchange rate of RMB, which has not been taken seriously owing to inadequate voice and thus lacked influence in the decision making of the government. Firstly, some scholars hold an objective view that the fixed exchange rate of RMB to USD is not the main reason for America's trade deficit with China and the revaluation and appreciation of RMB will not reduce the deficit. Some economists published articles in media to explain the above idea so as to dispel misunderstanding on this issue. Pieter Bottelier, a professor at the Johns Hopkins School of Advanced International Studies (SAIS) and the former representative of the World Bank in China, published an editorial entitled the *Myths About China's Currency*, where he clarified several misunderstandings on China's exchange rate, such as "the revaluation of RMB will favor the U. S.," "the revaluation of the exchange rate of RMB can significantly relieve the global trade unbalance" and "China has controlled its exchange rate for many years."[233] Another American Scholar, Kroeber, published the *Myths About China's Currency* in the *Washington Post*, which also explained the misunderstanding of "the revaluation of RMB is the most important thing for China to reduce its trade surplus."[234]

The American business represented by large commercial companies and organizations, especially the business in China, did not regard the exchange rate of RMB as the most important issue in China-U. S. trade. As indicated by the American Chamber of Commerce in China (AmCham) in the 2010 *White Paper*, "AmCham-China strongly supports progress toward a free floating market valuation of China's currency.... However, while currency is an important issue, AmCham-China is concerned that the U. S. is placing disproportionate emphasis on RMB valuation. The current trade imbalance with China has not significantly affected America's overall trade deficit, but has rather absorbed shrinking deficits with

233 Bottelier, Pieter and Dadush, Uri. "The Myths About China's Currency." *The New York Times*. March 20, 2010. L. H.T. Op-Ed Contributor.

234 Kroeber, Arthur. "5 Myths about China's economic power." *The Washington Post*. Sunday. April 11, 2010. B3.

other Asian countries like South Korea and Japan. Moreover, RMB revaluation would likely result only in a modest decrease in the current trade deficit between the US and China, while focusing on other price distortions, such as factor pricing in China, would possibly result in greater adjustments."[235]

According to the *White Paper*, the exchange rate of RMB to USD has maintained around 6.83 since the summer of 2008, which militated against the profits of American manufacturers. America had grounds for requiring China to continue with the appreciation of RMB after the summer of 2008. Two factors mainly contributed to this opinion. Firstly, in many cases, products can be transferred to Mexico or Vietnam, etc. for production without China, so the revaluation of RMB cannot necessarily bring many jobs to America despite that the employment conditions can be improved a little. Secondly, though the exchange rate of RMB to USD maintained stable during the decline of America, RMB experienced a significant depreciation against other international currencies. Therefore, other countries suffered more from the weak RMB than America.[236]

The question is that the opinion of American business on RMB had no great influence on the public opinions of the exchange rate of RMB. The public opinion that the undervalue of RMB incurred the loss of jobs in American manufacturing industry and America's trade deficit had formed in 2003 and dominated the public and the media along with the proposal of relevant bills in the Congress for years. American decision-makers were also affected by these public opinions. The Treasury Department believed that the policy of RMB hindered the global economic balance, inhibited the global economic reform, required China to promote the reform to establish more flexible system of RMB exchange rate and directly asked for the appreciation of RMB. American business could not create a coalition for lobby as for what they did on the issue of most-favored nation treatment of China and China's entry to WTO because of their divergence on the exchange rate of RMB. As indicated in the *White Paper* of AmCham-China, they paid more attention to the market opening and protection of intellectual property, so they did not strike back the lobby of the other opinion. Only a few organizations such as the United States-China Business Council (USCBC) stated their views in the hearings of the Congress. To the contrary, some economists of interest groups of the manufacturing industry and workers had overwhelming dominance in hearings of the Congress with the opinion that the undervalue of RMB damaged economic and employment conditions of America.

---

235 AmCham-China. *American Business in China: 2010 White Paper*. pp.31-33

236 Ibid.

2. Opinions in China

China has adhered to its own opinion since the emergence of the issue of RMB exchange rate in 2003 and quickly realized the domestic political factors contributing to this issue.

(1) RMB is Not Seriously Undervalued

Domestic economists indicated that RMB was only undervalued to some degree, instead of seriously undervalued, from the perspective of economics. Lin Yifu, the director of the Economic Research Center of Peking University, negated two grounds for the opinion that the exchange rate of RMB had been seriously undervalued and should appreciate by a wide margin. Firstly, Chinese tradable sectors had seen a more rapid growth of labor capacity than non-tradable sectors. The nominal exchange rate has not raised in the recent decade, leading to serious undervalue of the real exchange rate, so a significant rise of nominal exchange rate is necessary to restore the real exchange rate. Secondly, the trade surplus of China was great in recent years, reaching 102 billion USD in 2005 and 170 billion USD in 2006, which demonstrated that the exchange rate of China had been seriously undervalued and significant appreciation was necessary to restore the trade balance.[237] Therefore, RMB was not seriously undervalued since the two main grounds were invalid.

Some foreign professions identified the opinion of domestic economists. Except Fred Bergsten and Morris Goldstein from the Peter G. Peterson Institute for International Economics considered the RMB had been seriously undervalued by 40%, some famous economists such as Robert A. Mundell and Ronald McKinnon believed that RMB was not undervalued and argued against the appreciation of RMB. In conclusion, different economists held different views on whether RMB had been undervalued and the degree of the undervalue. It is a controversial topic.

(2) Appreciation of RMB Will Not Significantly Reduce America's Huge Trade Deficit and Unemployment Rate

Domestic economists, the media and the government hold identical views on this issue:

Firstly, America's trade deficit with China mainly resulted from American domestic

237 Lin Yifu, "Thoughts and Policy Suggestions on the Exchange Rate of RMB," *World Economics*, Issue 3 2007.

consumption exceeding investment and huge government expenditure from the perspective of economics. Therefore, in order to reduce America's trade deficit, the American government needs to reduce expenses, adopt deflationary macro-economic policies and raise the savings rate. Correspondingly, China shall enhance the domestic consumption and reduce the proportion of economic growth driven by the export. But the appreciation of RMB plays a limited role in the reduction of America's huge trade deficit, since America has a much larger economy than China and can more effectively adjust its policies than China.

Secondly, the appreciation of RMB cannot solve the problem of unemployment in America, because China and America have totally complementary economic and trade structures. In recent years, the increasing trade surplus of China has not eaten up the American industry and market. Exports from China to America concentrate on labor-intensive products, mainly including daily necessities, with low flexibiliy in prices. In case of appreciation of RMB, America will continue to import these products in higher prices or import these products from other countries of lower prices. Therefore, the trade deficit of America will rise instead of reducing the significant appreciation of RMB, but will not transfer job opportunities in the manufacturing industry from China to America.

(3) Chinese Government Promotes the Reform of the Exchange Rate Forming System According to its Own Schedule

Most domestic economists of China consider it necessary to transform to a comparatively more flexible exchange rate of RMB. The Chinese government has indicated on many occasions that China has not controlled the exchange rate for unfair competition and has promoted the reform of the exchange rate forming system according to its own conditions and schedule. The exchange rate of RMB has become more flexible.

(4) The Domestic Political Demand of America Urges America to Press on the Issue of the Exchange Rate of RMB

There is no definite answer to whether RMB is undervalued and to what degree. The appreciation of RMB will not significantly reduce America's trade deficit with China and the unemployment rate. The Chinese government declared it would promote the reform on the exchange rate forming system and has realized a flexible exchange rate system to some degree. Then why did the U. S. keep on exerting great pressure on the appreciation of RMB and American and international public opinions propagandize the value rise of RMB?

The answer proposed by Chinese scholars, the media and the government was that the issue was highly politicalized owing to the domestic political demand of America. According to Lin Yifu, America suffered internal and external difficulties, including the burst of the Internet bubble and crash of the Nasdaq Stock Market in March 2001, the September 11th terrorist attacks, the Afghan War, the Iraq War, the increasing deficit of American government, the sluggish economy and growing unemployment rate, so they contributed the difficulties of domestic economy and growth of unemployment rate to China's increasing trade surplus to America, in order to transfer voters' dissatisfaction against the government by blaming China for intentionally undervaluing RMB to export cheap products to America, seizing the market and jobs of America and leading to slow economic growth and increasing unemployment rate.[238]

More scholars have analyzed how America politicalized the issue of the exchange rate of RMB based on the different roles of the Congress and administrative departments in trade policies from the perspectives of the politics of American interest groups and Congress.[239] They believe that this issue started to be politicalized by the operation of American interest groups and Congress. As lobbied by interest groups, American Congress attempted to press on the appreciation of RMB by legislation. American administrative departments answered to the pressure by exerting pressure on the Chinese government, but they needed to handle the issue based on overall balance as the departments responsible for the policies on China and the trade with China. Therefore, administrative departments and the Congress had different opinions on this issue, which were decided by the structure of American government and their different roles. The features of American politics decided the process of the politicalization of the exchange rate of RMB.

3. Influence of Different Opinions on Both Countries in the Exchange Rate of RMB

Different opinions on this issue of both countries relieved the politicalization of this issue to some degree.

(1) Influence of American Opinions

The above opinion from the U. S. was very objective despite the thick atmosphere of politicalization of the issue. The statements in the American media and academic circles

238 Lin Yifu, "Thoughts and Policy Suggestions on the Exchange Rate of RMB," *World Economics*, Issue 3 2007.

239 Ruhe Xingqiang, "American Interest Groups and Pressure on the Appreciation of RMB," *Contemporary Asia-Pacific Studies*, Issue 2 2006; Zhou Yejing, "Interest Groups and American Policies on International Currency," *International Forum*, January 2009, 11(1) etc.

influenced some people's views on this issue, provided certain reference for rational decision making of administrative departments, effected some congressmen's opinions, votes and actions on this issue. Only a group of concerned congressmen promoted the legislation on RMB appreciation, while most congressmen only followed the trend. Congressmen from some agricultural states of large export to China did not concern or support the legislation. They could not stand against these bills under the negative opinions of the entire Congress on RMB or they had to agree with others in vote, but they could explain their opinions to provide rational reference.

The American business circles represented by the Chamber of Commerce of the United States has lower influence on the exchange rate of RMB. After Obama took office, they lobbied the government mainly on the market opening and protection of intellectual rights in order to maintain and inflate their interests in China and did not regard the exchange rate of RMB as an important problem in China-U. S. trade relations. They had made great achievements in lobbying in 2010 and their topics had been given priority during administrative departments' negotiation with China. They were given full play during the strategic and economic dialogue and the mutual visit of leaders in the two countries. They are gradually transferring the central topic of China-U. S. trade relations from RMB exchange rate to market opening, investment, growth of mutual export and protection of intellectual property.

(2) Influence of Chinese Opinions

Influence of Chinese opinions on Chinese government mainly reflects in the communication and negotiation with American administration. The Chinese government, on behalf of China, clarified to the American government that the appreciation of RMB would have nothing to do with the trade deficit and employment problem of America if RMB was not seriously undervalued and pointed out that the high politicalization of this issue in America had affected the rational solution on the issue. Based on these opinions, the American government had to take the position of the Chinese government seriously when it responded to the pressure from Congress or attempted to adopt strong measures against China, and thus made more rational and balanced policies.

V. Conclusion and Prospects

Interest groups, including associations related to American manufacturing industry and labor unions, have promoted the exchange rate of RMB to be the topic of greatest concern since 2003 and created the public opinions that "the undervalued RMB affected the employment, damaged American economy and incurred increasing trade deficit, and the unfair trade shall be corrected." Pushed by interest groups, congressmen were required to issue bills to push for the appreciation of RMB, and administrative departments constantly asked the Chinese government to appreciate RMB. The issue of the exchange rate of RMB had gradually become a highly politicalized topic in America.

The politicalization of the exchange rate of RMB was decided by the congressmen politics in the formulation of American trade policies and the role of the Congress in the trade policies. Congressmen constantly proposed and promoted bills on RMB, aiming to press on the administration and seek credit from voters to improve their political influence and realize re-election, instead of establishing laws. It is not necessary or the best method to directly control the trade policies. Congressmen may possibly make a concession to the administration since they are less concerned with this issue. They may compromise at any time once their goal of improving their political influence is realized. Administrative departments can lead the policy of foreign trade if they pay enough attention. We can have better understanding on the pressure from America on the exchange rate of America based on the recognition of the essence of the issue.

According to the above analysis, we can figure out that the issue of the exchange rate of RMB in China-U. S. relations resulted from the decline of the American manufacturing industry, unbalanced bilateral trade and political operation of this issue by relevant interest groups and Congress. Therefore, America will not stop their concern on this issue until the economic and employment conditions of America improve, the manufacturing industry recovers and China's trade surplus with America stops growing. They will exert pressures at certain time, for instance, the eve of U. S. Treasury Department submitting the report on the exchange rate at mid April and mid October, the eve of strategic and economic dialogues between two countries, eve of annual international economic meetings such as G-8 Summit and G-20 Summit, the eve of the visit of leaders to the other country, or the eve of Presidential election or mid-term election. The American Congress will continue to propose bills to press on the administration to respond to the pressure from interest groups.

According to the analysis on the role of the Congress in trade affairs, China does not need to worry about or shall not disregard fully the legislation of Congress on the exchange rate of RMB. China shall strengthen its interaction with relevant congressmen and invite them to China, because a visit to China is exactly what they want. In addition, China shall control this issue under a certain scope through the communication with American administration and bilateral communication and coordination mechanisms including strategic and economic dialogues and the China-U. S. Joint Commission on Commerce and Trade. The performance of the Bush administration in 2006 and 2008 and Obama's performance in recent two years can prove the above statement.

At the same time, the American government had to consider the Chinese government's attitude in decision making based on the different opinions from both the American and Chinese governments, which can relieve the politicalization of the issue and enhanced the rational solution to the problem. Finally, the issue will be further eased along with the recovery of American economic and employment conditions and gradual appreciation of RMB.

The United States and China-U. S. Relations in Chinese People's Eyes

Research Group of "The United States in Chinese People's Eyes"

The research group of "The United States in Chinese People's Eyes" conducted a random questionnaire survey on the U. S. and China-U. S. relations in eight Chinese cities between June and August 2010. Based on the statistical analysis of the research results, this article attempts to explain the influence of gender, age, educational level, region, profession, income, etc. on interviewees' views.

I. Background for the Survey of "The United States in Chinese People's Eyes"

1. Main Objectives of this Survey

The Chinese economy has maintained a high growth rate in the three decades since the introduction of the reform and opening up policy. Despite the violent impact on major economies due to the financial crisis, the annual growth rate of China has exceeded 9%.[240] The Gross Domestic Product (GDP) of China surpassed Japan in the 2nd quarter of 2010. Since then, China has become the second largest economy of the world. Chinese Prime Minister Wen Jiabao indicated at the Summer Davos Forum in September that "the economic growth of China provides multinational countries with great development opportunities, creates great demand for major economies and surrounding countries and functions as the important engine for the world economic recovery."[241] The rise of China is profoundly affecting the world, as China's international influence increasingly grows.

With the deepening of the reform and opening up policy, the international relations of China have been strengthened, while Chinese people are more concerned with the external

240 According to the State Statistics Bureau, the GDP growth rate of China was 9% in 2008, 9.1% in 2009 and is estimated to be 10.3% in 2010.

241 Wen Jiabao's speech in the 2010 Summer Davos Forum. See the full text in: http://news.xinhuanet.com/politics/2010-09/13/c_12548535_3.htm.

world and Chinese diplomacy. In addition to traditional television, books and magazines, the internet, cultural communication, overseas travel and economic and trade exchange acquaint people with the outside world. The popular view has increasingly become one of factors contributing to the diplomatic decision-making. Le Yucheng, the Director of the Policy Planning Division of the Ministry of Foreign Affairs, indicated in a media interview on September 3, 2010 that decision-making and policy planning on Chinese diplomacy was paying more attention to public opinions and taking information from newspaper and television and netizens' (avid citizens of the internet) opinions into consideration.[242] Under this background, the Chinese Academy of Social Sciences conducted the investigation of the "international outlook of Chinese" for the third time by questionnaire survey, aiming to figure out people's level of concern and focus on international issues.

China-U. S. relations are, without a doubt, one of China's most important bilateral relations. Chinese people show a comparatively greater attention to America and China-U. S. relations, so it is important to understand Chinese people's views on America and China-U. S. relations. Therefore, the "United States in Chinese People's Eyes" was conducted as a sub-item of the "International Outlook of Chinese." Huang Pingzhu, the director of the Institute of American Studies, Chinese Academy of Social Sciences, directed the third round of this questionnaire survey.

This investigations attempted to understand Chinese people's knowledge of America and the China-U. S. relations by the questionnaire survey, study common people's views on China-U. S. relations, conduct in-depth analysis based on the first-hand data, lead the media to provide accurate and comprehensive information according to the investigation results and refer to the results in the decision making related to the foreign relations with America.

2. Background for the Investigation

The international situation surrounding the questionnaire survey, particularly the basic conditions of China-U. S. relations, affected interviewees' opinions, so the basic background for the survey shall be clarified here.

(1) Smooth Transition of China-U. S. Relations

The Democratic U. S. President Barack Obama entered the White House in January

242 Guo Jinchao, Zhongxin Net, September 3, 2010: "Chinese Foreign Ministry Officials: Public Opinions Are Important References to Chinese Diplomatic Decision Making," http://www.chinanews.com/gn/2010/09-04/2511908.shtml.

2009. Since the end of the Cold War, the transitions of China-U. S. relations were often rocky when a new president was sworn in. For example, President Bill Clinton, who took office in 1993, linked China-U. S. relations to the "most-favored nation treatment" and "human rights issue," and President George W. Bush regarded China as the "rival of strategic competition" and claimed to "defend Taiwan" in 2001. However, the China-U. S. relations transmitted smoothly during the first year of Obama's term. In April 2009, leaders of China and the U. S. met in London for the first time, established the new positioning of "working together to build a positive, cooperative and comprehensive China-U. S. relationship for the 21st century," and agreed to begin a negotiation to establish the China-U. S. strategic and economic dialogue mechanism. Obama visited China in November, when leaders of the two countries reached several consensuses and announced the "China-U. S. Joint Statement" that "the two sides reiterated that they are committed to building a positive, cooperative and comprehensive China-U. S. relationship for the 21st century, and will take concrete actions to steadily build a partnership to address common challenges,"[243] making a good start of China-U. S. relations.

(2) Setbacks in China-U. S. Relations

The smooth transition of China-U. S. relations increased both countries' expectation on the bilateral relations, but the setbacks could not be avoided since conflicts and disagreements were not yet solved. America selling weapons to Taiwan and Obama meeting Dalai violently shocked China-U. S. relations. On January 30, 2010, the Obama administration announced that the U. S. would sell "BLACK HAWK" helicopters, "Patriot-3" anti-missile system and minesweepers, reaching a total value of 6.4 billion US dollars (USD) to the Taiwan area. China made quick response to this issue, including stopping the arrangement for the mutual visit of the Chinese and American army, putting off the exchange projects between the Chinese and American army, postponing the negotiation on strategic security, arms control and nonproliferation at the vice-ministerial level, and planning to impose sanctions against American companies involved in the selling of weapons to Taiwan. Immediately following the sales of weapons to Taiwan, President Obama met Dalai in the map room of the White House on February 18, despite China's strong protests, which again damaged the China-U. S. relations.

---

243 "Sino-U. S. Joint Statement," November 17, 2009, Beijing. See the full text in the website of the Ministry of Foreign Affairs: http://www.fmprc.gov.cn/chn/gxh/tyb/zyxw/t627468.htm.

(3) "Cheonan Incident" and U. S.-South Korean Military Exercises

Affairs in Asia-Pacific area either directly or indirectly affect China-U. S. relations without question, while America's policy on the Asia-Pacific area necessarily influences Chinese people's perception of America and China-U. S. relations. On March 26 2010, the "Cheonan" missile destroyer of the South Korean navy sank owing to an explosion accident. South Korea started an investigation and officially declared the results on May 20, which claimed that the "Cheonan" was attacked by a torpedo launched by a small submarine of North Korea. The U. S. exerted pressure on China after the announcement of the results and China called relevant parties to practice restraints. After that, the U. S. and South Korea conducted a series of military exercises to threaten North Korea, including a military exercise involving the "Washington" aircraft carrier located in the Yellow Sea, which China opposed. Domestic media extensively reported on the issue and aroused great concern.

(4) South China Sea and America's Position

China has always opposed foreign military ships conducting any activity that affects Chinese security interests in Chinese coastal waters, and two countries have announced differences on this issue. Regarding the sovereignty disputes on the South Sea, China always adheres to suspending disputes and joint development. Relevant parties have reached the consensus that they shall solve the disputes based on friendly and peaceful negotiation to maintain the stability and development of the South Sea and good-neighborly relations, and shall not make the South Sea an international, multilateral and complicated issue based on the Conduct of Parties in the South China Sea. Chinese Foreign Minister Yang Jiechi and the U. S. Secretary Hillary Clinton attended the meeting of foreign ministers in the 17th ASEAN Regional Forum (ARF) held in Hanoi, Vietnam on July 23 2010. During the meeting, Hillary Clinton made a speech related to the South China Sea, indicating that "the United States, like every nation, has a national interest in freedom of navigation, open access to Asia's maritime commons, and respect for international law in the South China Sea" and America attached great importance to the peaceful solution to the dispute in "South China Sea."[244] Yang Jiechi refuted Clinton's statement.[245]

244 Speech made by the U. S. secretary Hillary Clinton in Hanoi, see full text in http://www.america.gov/st/eap-chinese/2010/July/20100723215323jbnij0.7250788.html.

245 "Foreign Minister Yang Jiechi Refute the False Theory on the South China Sea," July 25, 2010. See http://www.fmprc.gov.cn/chn/pds/wjdt/wjbxw/t719371.htm.

(5) China-U. S. Trade Conflicts Under the Global Financial Crisis

Along with the economic recession and growing unemployment rate in America, the protectionism has gained ground. Democrats have close relations with labor interest groups, and America hopes to expand the Chinese market, so the Obama administration exerted pressure on China on the economic and trade relations, resulting in heightened trade frictions. In 2010, the trade frictions were extended to the financial area. The issue of RMB appreciation was further politicalized owing to the mid-term election of America, and large American enterprises presented their discontent with China fostering industries of self-innovation and considered it to be damaging to their interests. Under these circumstances, large American enterprises in China no longer defended China-U. S. relations in public as they did before.

Generally, several affairs that may affect the investigation results occurred during the questionnaire survey. It will be easier to comprehend the results based the understanding of these affairs.

3. Design Basis and Structure of the Questionnaire

The investigation of the "International Outlook of Chinese" was conducted in a method of questionnaire, so the design of the questionnaire must be rational. After summarizing the experiences learned from the two previous investigations, the research group had repeatedly discussed the questions of the questionnaire and made significant adjustments.

With ordinary people as the respondants, the questions were made clear and simple. The design of the questions and answers for selection fully considered the knowledge of interviewees and attempted to enable interviewees to answer immediately, without looking up materials or consulting others. The abundant choices of answers enabled interviewees to give the most direct answer. Despite the specific goal of the investigation, the questionnaire attempted to avoid any inducing question or answer.

The questionnaire was divided into three parts. The first part mainly referred to the individual information of interviewees, including their nation, gender, age, educational level, profession and income. Some contents, such as income, related to privacy, but interviewees were not required to fill in their names, driving away the interviewees' concerns on privacy. The second part aimed to generally investigate their understanding of international issues, including their understanding of major countries, including America, Russia, Japan and EU, their influence on international affairs, importance of them for China, their attitude on climate change and overall impressions on those countries.

The third part of the questionnaire, composed of 10 questions, was about America and China-U. S. relations, mainly including interviewees' understanding of the basic conditions of the U. S. (Q1 and Q4) and variation of America's influence (Q2 and Q3) as well as the understanding and judgment of America and China-U. S. relations (Q5, Q6, Q7, Q8, Q9 and Q10). The questionnaire also asks for interviewees' comments or suggestions at the end.

4. Issue and Recall of Questionnaires

Due to restrictions of expenses, time and resources, the investigation obtained samples according to simple random sampling, instead of strict probability sampling. Standards were given to the investigated cities and interviewees for this investigation. Based on the principle of regional distribution, questionnaires were distributed in three cities (Beijing, Shanghai and Guangzhou) of coastal areas and five cities (Lanzhou, Kunming, Changchun, Zigong and Changsha) of inland areas, with 350 questionnaires for each city. 1/3 was distributed to college students, 1/3 to enterprise employees and 1/3 to resident community. Certain requirements were also added to this investigation, such as on the proportion of undergraduates and graduate students, proportion of students of arts and students of science, proportion of male and female students; level of community, proportion of male and female residents; proportion of enterprises of different types (state-owned, private and foreign-invested enterprises), level of employees and proportion of male and female employees. A total of 2,800 questionnaires were distributed, while 2,687 were recalled, with a recalling ratio of about 96%.[246]

II. Chinese People's Basic Understanding of the U. S. and China-U. S. Relations

1. Understanding of America

34.9% of interviewees indicated that they "know very well" or "know well" America, 47.4% answered "know something," and 17.6% answered "know a little" or "know nothing." This means that Chinese people have got some degree of understanding of

246 A few interviewees may leave out some questions, so the number of answers to these questions may be not the same. For the convenience of analysis, the research group takes the actual number of people giving answers to questions as the basis for calculation.

America, though they do not know much.

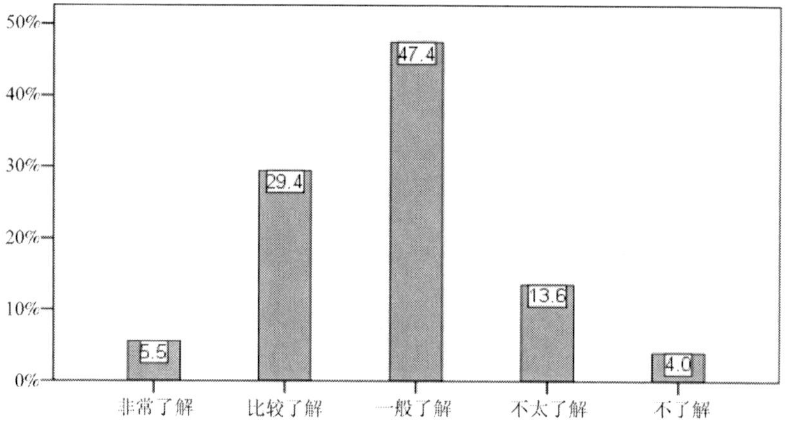

Figure 2-1 How much do you know about America?
In the picture, 非常了解 means "know very well," 比较了解 means "know well," 一般了解 means "know something," 不太了解 means "know a little" and 不了解 means "know nothing."

2. America's Influence on International Affairs

According to the investigation, 92% of interviewees consider America has a "very great influence" or "great influence" on international affairs, comparing to 2.1% people believe that America has a "small influence" or "no influence." This reflects Chinese people's highly uniform opinion on the significance of America on international affairs.

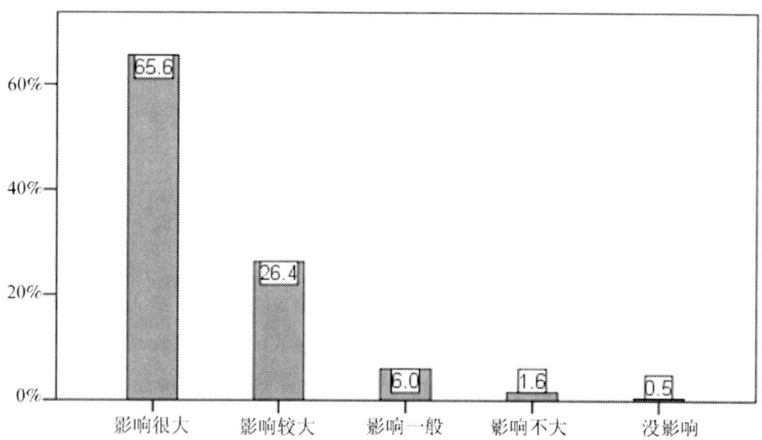

Figure 2-2 How is the influence of America on international affairs?
In the picture, 影响很大 means "very great influence," 影响较大 means "great influence," 影响一般 means "some influence," 影响不大 means "small influence" and 没影响 means "no influence."

3. Importance of China-U. S. Relations

As high as 90.7% of Chinese people think the China-U. S. relations are "very important" or "important," while only 1.3% consider it "not that important" or "not important." This reveals that most Chinese people realize the importance of China-U. S. relations.

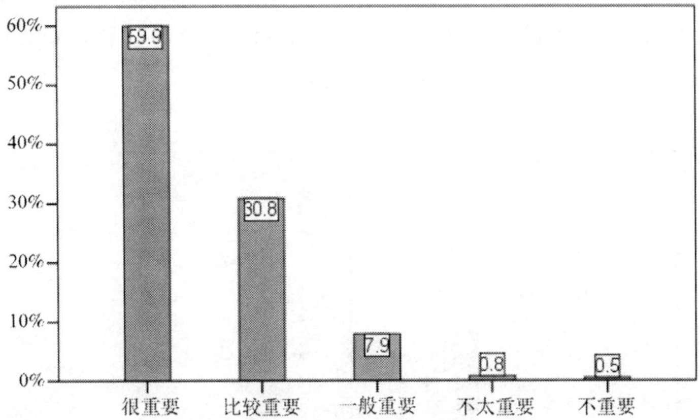

Figure 2-3 How important are the China-U. S. relations for China?
In the picture, 很重要 means "very important," 比较重要 means "important," 一般重要 "a little important," 不太重要 means "not that important" and 不重要 means "not important."

4. America's Stand on the Global Climate Change

Regarding America's stand on the global climate change, 41.3% of interviewees consider

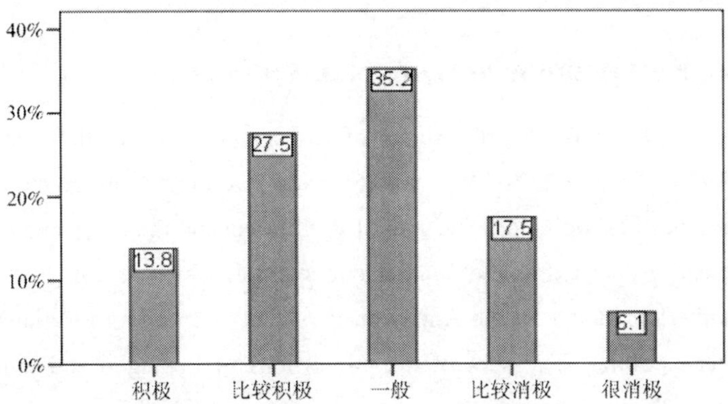

Figure 2-4 What do you think about America's attitude on global climate change?
In the picture, 积极 means "very positive," 比较积极 means "positive," 一般 means "just so-so,"比较消极 means "passive" and 很消极 means "very passive."

it to be "very positive" or "positive," 23.6% regard it as "passive" or "very passive," while 35.2% think America has an "ordinary" attitude on this issue. This reflects that Chinese people have very different opinions on this problem.

5. Overall Impression of the U. S.

According to the investigation, 36.1% of interviewees have a "very good" or "good" overall impression over America, 48.8% have "ordinary" impressions, and 15% have "negative" or "very negative" impressions. These reseults reveal Chinese people's overall impression on the U. S. are not completely negative.

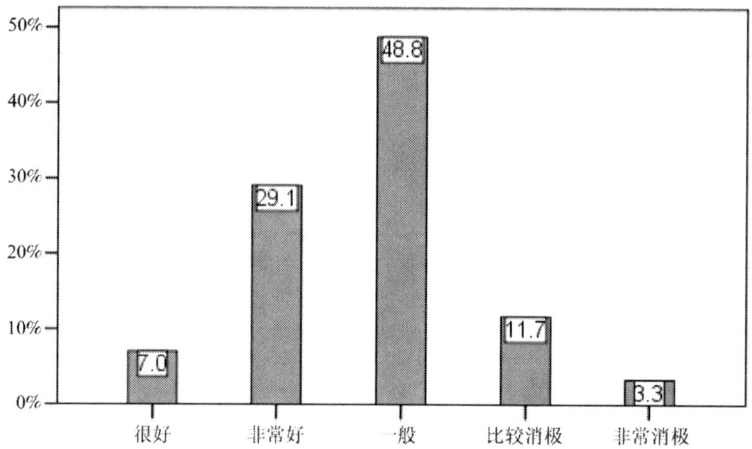

Figure 2-5 What is your overall impression of the U. S.?

In this picture, 很好 means "very good," 非常好 means "good," 一般 means "ordinary,"比较消极 means "negative" and 非常消极 means "very negative."

6. The Most Representative Symbol of America

The White House (26.5%), the Statue of Liberty (20.1%), Wall Street (8.5%), the Pentagon (7.4%) and the USD (6.9%) ranked the top five most representative symbols of America in interviewees' opinions. The sum of Wall Street and the USD amounts to 15.9%. The White House is selected as the number one symbol, which reveals that interviewees have a substantial knowledge of the American President or its administration's significant role in American politics. The sum of the proportions of Pentagon and aircraft carriers reaches 10.4%, reflecting the great power of American political, economic and military strength in Chinese people's eye. In other words, the result reflects Chinese people's focus on America.

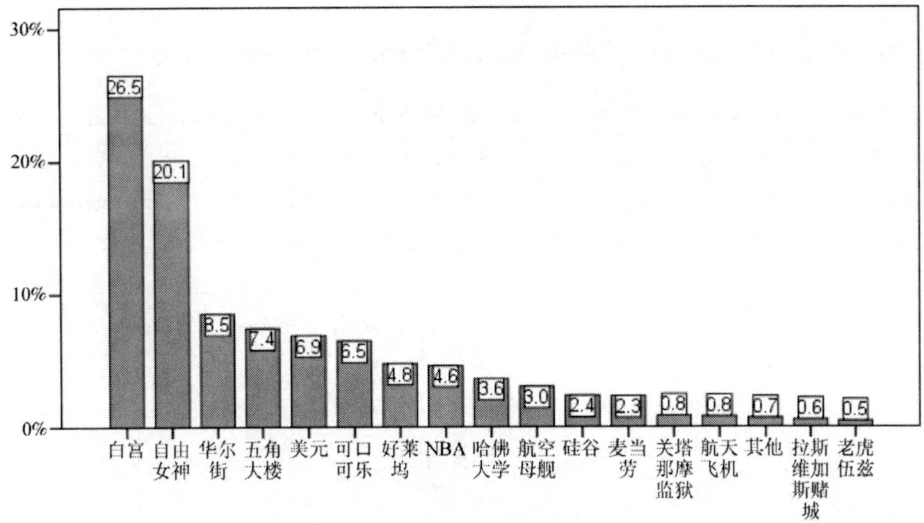

Figure 2-6　What do you think is the most representative symbol of America?

In the picture, 白宫 means the White House, 自由女神 means the Statue of Liberty, 华尔街 means the Wall Street, 五角大楼 means the Pentagon, 美元 means USD, 可口可乐 means Coca-Cola, 好莱坞 means Hollywood, 哈佛大学 means Harvard University, 航空母舰 means the aircraft carriers, 硅谷 means the Silicon Valley, 麦当劳 means McDonald, 关塔那摩监狱 means the Guantánamo Prison, 航天飞机 means the space shuttle, 其它 means others, 拉斯维加斯赌城 means Las Vegas caChinas and 老虎伍兹 means Tiger Woods.

7. Influence of America's Financial Crisis on World Economy

According to the investigation, 93.3% of interviewees think the American economic crisis has a "very great" or "great" impact on world economy, while only 0.7% people consider it as "small" or "very small." This reflects that almost all Chinese people share the same view on the status of American economy in the world economy.

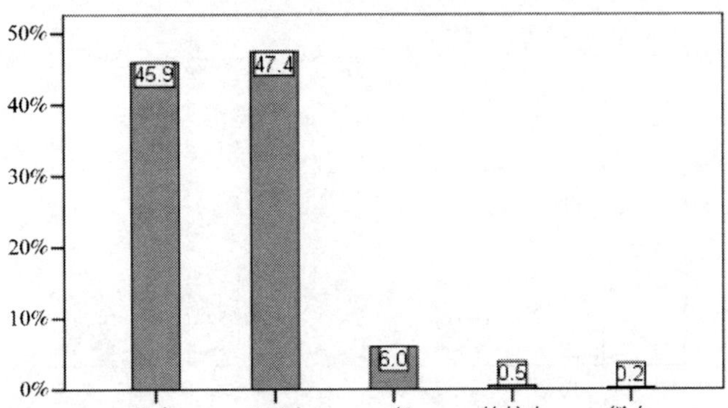

Figure 2-7　What is the impact of the American financial crisis on the world economy?

In this picture, 很大 means "very great," 比较大 means "great," 一般 means "just so-so," 比较小 means "small" and 很小 means "very small."

8. Variation Tendency of American International Influence

20.4% of interviewees consider that America's influence on international affairs will "rapidly grow" or "grow," while 56.3% think it will "remain the same" and 23.4% consider that it will "decline" or "rapidly decline." It can be easily figured out that most interviewees think America will remain or increase its international influence.

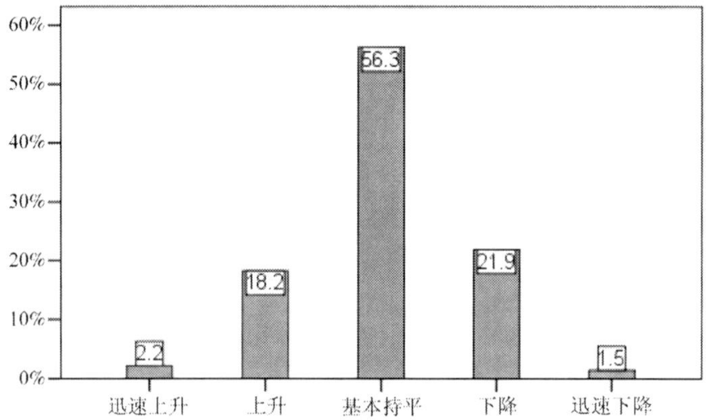

Figure 2-8 How will American international influence change in the future?
In this picture, 迅速上升 means rapidly grow, 上升 means grow, 基本持平 means remain the same, 下降 means decline and 迅速下降 means rapidly decline.

9. Americans' Understanding of China

Regarding how much the interviewees think the common American knows about China,

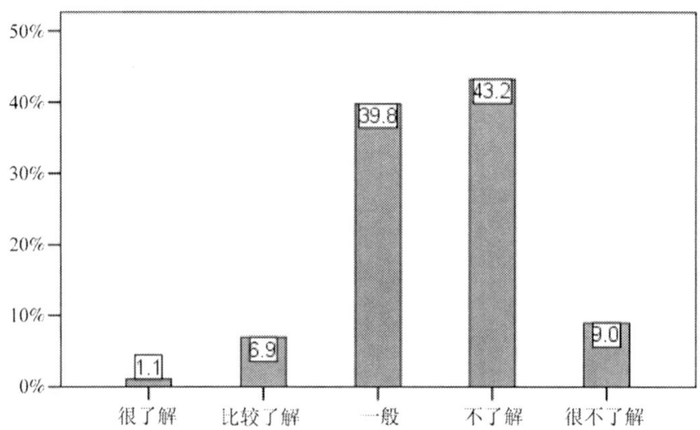

Figure 2-9 How much do you think the average American knows about China?
In this picture, 很了解 means "well understand," 比较了解 means "understand," 一般 means "just so-so," 不了解 means "understand little" and 很不了解 means "don't understand at all."

8% interviewees think they "well understand" or "understand" China, 39.8% of interviews think "just so-so," and 52.2% believe they "understand little" or "don't understand at all." Approximately half of interviewees choose "understand little" or "don't understand at all," which illustrates that many interviewees think common Americans do not have a great understanding of China.

10. Chinese People's Understanding of America

13.2% of interviewees think the average Chinese person "well understand" or "understand" America, 54.5% answer "just so-so," and 32.4% respond with "understand little" or "don't understand at all." More than half interviewees selected "just so-so." This reveals that they think the common Chinese person knows something about America, but do have a great understanding.

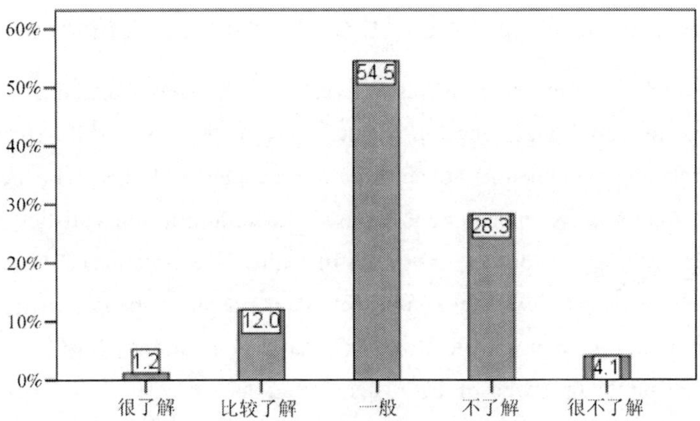

Figure 2-10 How much do you think the average Chinese person knows about the U. S.?
In this picture, 很了解 means "well understand," 比较了解 means "understand," 一般 means "just so-so," 不了解 means "understand little" and 很不了解 means "don't understand at all."

11. General Evaluation of Current China-U. S. Relations

15.8% of interviewees answered with "very good" or "good," 73.5% answer "just so-so," while 10.7% answer "bad" or "very bad." More than 70% of interviewees selected "just so-so," which shows the objective attitude of the common people on recent China-U. S. relations, considering both positive factors and weaknesses in the bilateral relations. The proportion of "good" exceeds the proportion of "bad," and the "very good" surpasses "very bad," illustrating people's general positive attitude towards the current China-U. S. relations.

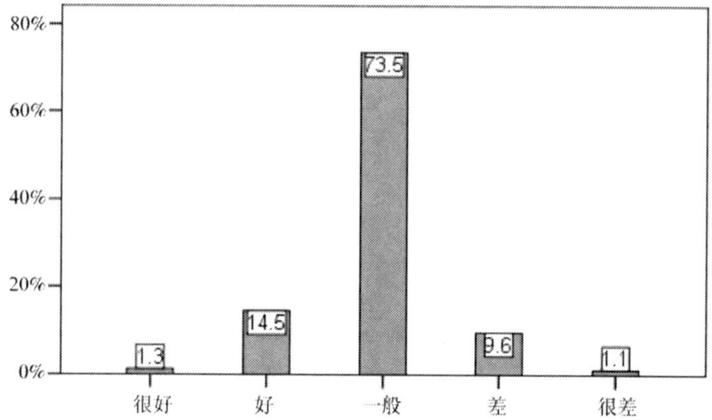

Figure 2-11 How do you view the current China-U. S. relations?
In this picture, 很好 means "very good," 好 means "good," 一般 means "just so-so," 差 means "bad" and 很差 means "very bad."

12. Forecast of the Prospects of the China-U. S. Relations

9.3% and 68.2% of interviewees respectively hold the view that China-U. S. relations will "develop smoothly" and "develop despite twists and turns," while 16.5% think the China-U. S. relations will "neither advance nor retreat," and 4.8% and 1.1% people believe the relations "may regress" and "surely regress." According to the statistics, most people are cautiously optimistic about the prospects of China-U. S. relations. The proportion of 68.2% of "develop despite twists and turns" reveals that Chinese people are getting used to the development despite many difficulties of China-U. S. relations over the years and hold mature opinions on the prospects of the bilateral relations.

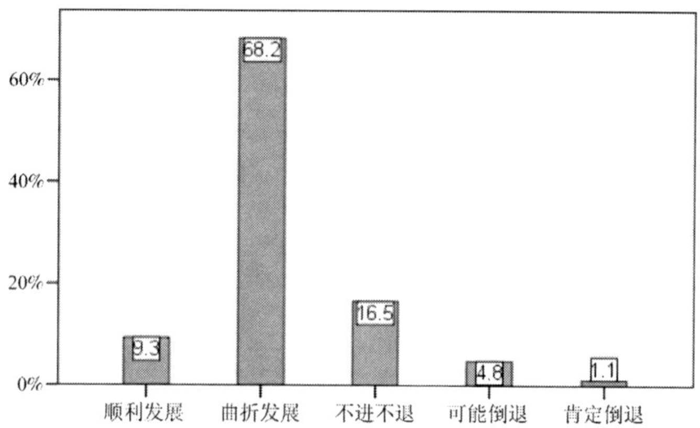

Figure 2-12 What do you think about the prospects of China-U. S. relations?
In this picture, 顺利发展 means "develop smoothly," 曲折发展 means "develop despite twists and turns," 不进不退 means "neither advance nor retreat," 可能倒退 means may regress and 肯定倒退 means "surely regress."

13. The Most Important Issue or Field in the China-U. S. Relations in the Future

In terms of the most important issue or field in future China-U. S. relations, most people consider them the economy and trade, Taiwan and energy issue. 35.8% answered with the economy and trade, 25.7% answered the Taiwan issue and 17.5% selected energy. This illustrates that the "Taiwan issue" is still very important in the China-U. S. relations, while the economy and trade and energy issues become increasingly important. The fact that the proportion of economy and trade even exceeds Taiwan deserves our attention.

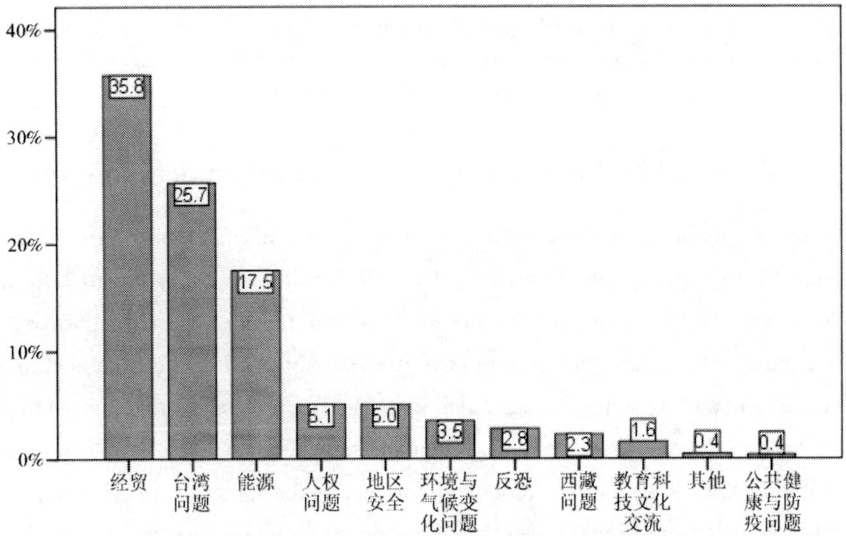

Figure 2-13 What do you think is the most important field or issue in the future China-U. S. relations?
In this picture, 经贸 means "economy and trade," 台湾问题 means "Taiwan issue," 能源 means "energy," 人权问题 means "human rights issue," 地区安全 means "regional safety," 环境与气候变化问题 means "environment and climate change," 反恐 means "anti-terrorism," 西藏问题 means "Tibet issue," 教育科技文化交流 means "exchange of education, science, technology and culture," 其它 means "others" and 公共健康与防疫问题 means "public health and epidemic prevention."

14. Interviewees' Attitude on Handling Relations with America

How should China handle the China-U. S. relations in the future? As shown in the investigation, 45.9% interviews advocate to "adhere to principles more," 12.3% of people think there is "no need to change," and 41.3% suggest to "be more flexible." Obviously, many people actually suggest changing the way to handle the current relations with America, no matter "adhere to principles more" or "be more flexible," while the former man accounts for more than the latter.

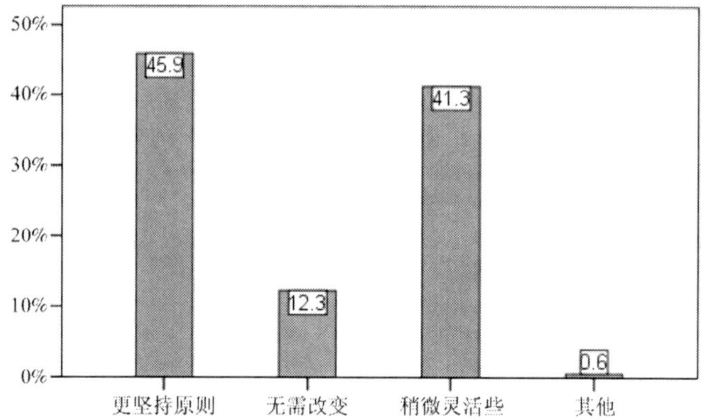

Figure 2-14 How do you think China should handle the relations with the U. S. in the future?
In this picture, 更坚持原则 means "adhere to principles more," 无需改变 means "no need to change," 稍微灵活些 means "be more flexible" and 其它 means "others."

15. Main Channel for Interviewees to Obtain Information on America

As for the main channel for interviewees to obtain information on America, 1,999 people (74.6%) receive information from TV, 1,927 people (72.0%) obtain information from the internet, 1,372 people receive information from newspaper and magazines, while only 84 people receive information from paying a visit abroad. It can be assumed that TV, internet and newspaper and magazines function as important channels for Chinese to obtain information on America, because, along with the rapid development of the internet and television, the media has promoted reports on international affairs and America and become important channels from Chinese people to understand the external world.

Table 2-1 How do you mainly obtain information on America?

	Number of people	Original proportion	Weighted proportion
Newspaper and magazines	1372	51.2%	21.5%
TV	1999	74.6%	31.4%
Broadcast	349	13.0%	5.5%
Internet	1929	72.0%	30.3%
Textbooks	182	6.8%	2.9%
Academic journals	201	7.5%	3.2%
Visit abroad	84	3.1%	1.3%
Relatives, friends and colleagues	234	8.7%	3.7%
Other channels	25	0.9%	0.4%
Total	6375	237.9%	100.0%

III. Some Tendencies and Problems Reflected in the Questionnaire

1. Tendencies of Interviewees on Some Issues

The questionnaire of "International Outlook of Chinese" includes 15 questions on America. Whoever, the 15th question, "How do you mainly obtain information on America?" is a multiple-choice question, where the other 14 are one-choice questions. At least six options are provided for each one-choice question. We believe that the option that more than 50% of people selected can be regarded as the mainstream view and tendency of Chinese people on this issue.

Based on this standard, mainstream views and tendencies are formed in six questions among with the total 14, which are respectively listed as below:

Table 3-1 Views and Tendencies of Interviewees on Some Issues

Question	Opinion of the highest proportion	Proportion of the option in the result
How do you view the current China-U. S. relations?	Just so-so	73.5%
What is the influence of America on international affairs?	Very great influence	65.6%
What do you think about the prospects of China-U. S. relations?	Develop despite twists and turns	68.2%
How important are the China-U. S. relations for China?	Very important	59.9%
How will American international influence change in the future?	Remain the same	56.3%
How much do you think the average Chinese person knows about the U. S.?	Just so-so	54.5%

Obviously, most interviewees have a clear understanding of America's influence on international affairs and the importance of the China-U. S. relations. 92% of people think America has a "very great" or "great" influence on international affairs, which can be regarded as the view of most Chinese people. A total of 90.7% of interviewees think the China-U. S. relations are "very important" or "important." The understandings of most common interviewees reflect that Chinese people fully comprehend the basic international situation and the basic conditions of Chinese diplomacy.

Most interviewees show a "cautious" attitude on the current and future China-U. S. relations. 73.5% of people consider the current China-U. S. relations to be "just so-so." 68.2% of them believe that China-U. S. relations will see a "development despite twists and turns." This demonstrates that most people share increasingly mature and rational views, after having experienced tumultuous bilateral relations for many years, and hold neither too optimistic nor pessimistic views on the current and future China-U. S. relations.

Regarding the variation of America's international influence, most interviewees (56.3%) believe that it will "remain the same." Obviously, most Chinese people think that the s financial crisis, economic recession and Iraq and Afghan War will not seriously damage the international influence of the U. S.

54.5% of interviewees think common Chinese people have just a "so-so" understanding of America, which means that most people think the Chinese do not have a thorough understanding of America. Though many reports of the media relate to America, Chinese people do not think they understand the U. S. well.

2. Interviewees Have Big Divergences on Certain Issues

According to the questionnaire, interviewees have significant differences on some issues, which means that any option out of the six or more options of the question has not reached 45% of interviewees' agreement, or even the two opposite options gain nearly the same number of consenters.

An obvious divergence can be seen among interviewees in terms of the question "How do you think China should handle relations with the U. S. in the future?" 42.6% of interviewees believe that China shall "adhere to principles more," compared to the 38.3% of interviewees supporting to "be more flexible." Only 11.4% think there is "no need to change." It reveals that most people think the strategies shall be altered in handling relations with America, but no mainstream opinion or tendency is formed on this issue. Actually, disputes and divergences on this problem exist in Chinese academic circles, too. The disagreements of common people also reflect the complexity of China-U. S. relations and the difficulty to handle the relations.

Another divergence lies in Chinese people's views on the attitude of America on the global climate change. 13.7 and 27.5% of interviewees respectively hold the view that America has a "very positive" or "positive" attitude on the issue, amounting to a total of 41.2%. 35.2% of interviewees think America has a "just so-so" attitude on this attitude. 17.5% and 6.1%, a total of 23.6%, consider America's attitude on this issue as respectively "passive" and "very passive." This illustrates that Chinese people have a big divergence on this issue. On one hand, it is difficult to define a "positive" attitude from "passive" attitude according to the counter-measures adopted by a country since the global climate change is rather a complicated question. On the other hand, some Chinese people lack the understanding of specific measures adopted by America on this issue. The above two factors contribute to the result.

In addition to the two questions above, interviewees also have a great disagreement on the most representative symbol of America and the most important issue or field in the China-U. S. relations in the future. Regarding the most representative symbol of America, 26.4% choose the "White House," while 20.1% select the "Statue of Liberty," which demonstrates that no mainstream opinion of Chinese people is formed on this issue.

No mainstream view is formed in terms of the most important issue or field in the China-U. S. relations, either. Most people selected the economy and trade (33.8%), the Taiwan issue (24.3%) and energy (16.6%). Since these options (such as "economy and trade," "energy," "anti-terrorism," "environment and climate change," "Taiwan issue" and "Tibet issue" etc.) are all important issues or fields in the future China-U. S. relations, it is rather difficult for interviewees to choose only one. It may be hard to tell which is more important, contributing to the great divergence on this issue.

Moreover, 19 and 13 options are provided for the two questions mentioned above. They distract interviewees' choices since both are one-choice questions, so it is hard to form a mainstream view on this question without revealing different opinions.

3. Several Questions that Interviewees Find Difficult to Understand

The option of "not clear/don't know" is prepared for each question of this survey. Interviewees can choose the option when they do not quite understand the question. According to the analysis, the proportion of the choice of "not clear/don't know" is the highest in the following three questions, which reveals that interviewees found it difficult to understand these questions.

For the question "What do you think about America's attitude on global climate change?" as many as 7.4% of interviewees state that they are "not clear/don't know." As stated above, the global climate change is a complicated issue involving much professional knowledge, and common people lack the necessary understanding on what policies Americans adopt, so many of them cannot evaluate America's attitude on this issue.

6.1% of interviewees chose the option of "not clear/don't know" in terms of the question "What do you think about the prospects of China-U. S. relations?" The China-U. S. relations are important and complicated and have gruelingly developed for many years. It is even difficult for relevant scholars to forecast the prospects of the bilateral relations, not to mention common people.

For the question "How do you think China should handle the relations with the U. S. in the future?" 4.9% of interviewees chose the option of "not clear/don't know." Many internal and external factors shall be taken into consideration for the foreign policy making of a country. It is very difficult for common people to judge how to handle the complicated China-U. S. relations. In addition, the complexity of how to handle China-U. S. relations can be further demonstrated by the great divergence of interviewees on this question.

Generally speaking, questions that interviewees have difficulty understanding are, in fact, fundamentally difficult questions. Even the academic circles have disputes on it, not to mention common people.

IV. Effects of Gender and Age

1. Analysis of the Gender Factor

2,678 people have filled in the gender question among the 2,687 questionnaires recalled, including 1,488 males, accounting for 55.6% and 1,190 females, making up 44.4%.

(1) Understanding of America

Males and females have significant differences in their understanding of America.

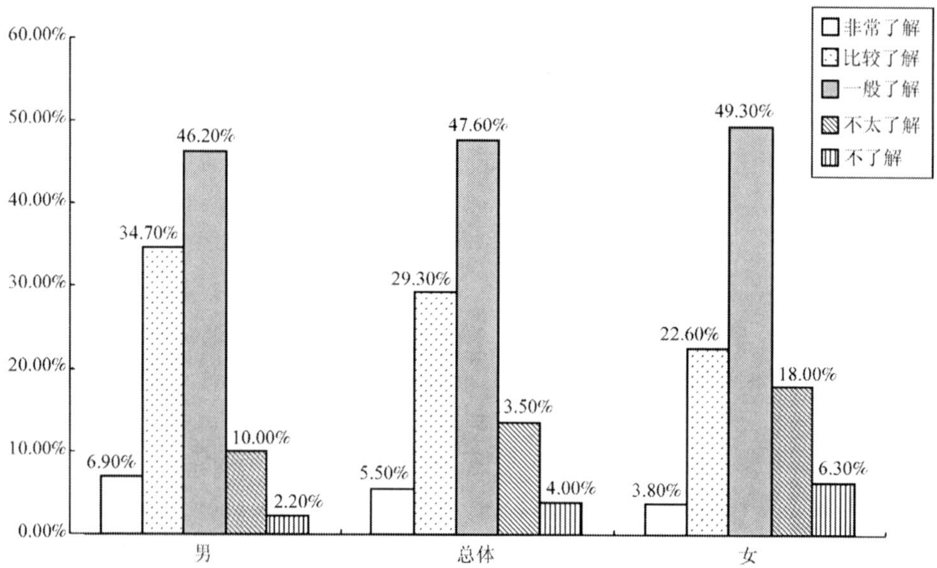

Figure 4-1 How much do you know about America?

In this picture, 很了解 means "well understand," 比较了解 means "understand," 一般 means "just so-so," 不了解 means "understand little" and 很不了解 means "don't understand at all."

男 means "males," 总体 means "overall," and 女 means "females."

Males show more confidence in this respect, as more than 40% males think they "know very well" or "know well" when it came to their knowledge of America, including 7% with the answer "know very well," compared to less than 30% and about 4% for females. This may illustrate that males are more concerned about America and international politics than females.

(2) America's Influence on International Affairs

Interviewed males and females reach an identity of views on this question, with 2/3 of both believe that America has a very great influence on international affairs. The proportion of males choosing "very great influence" was a little higher than females.

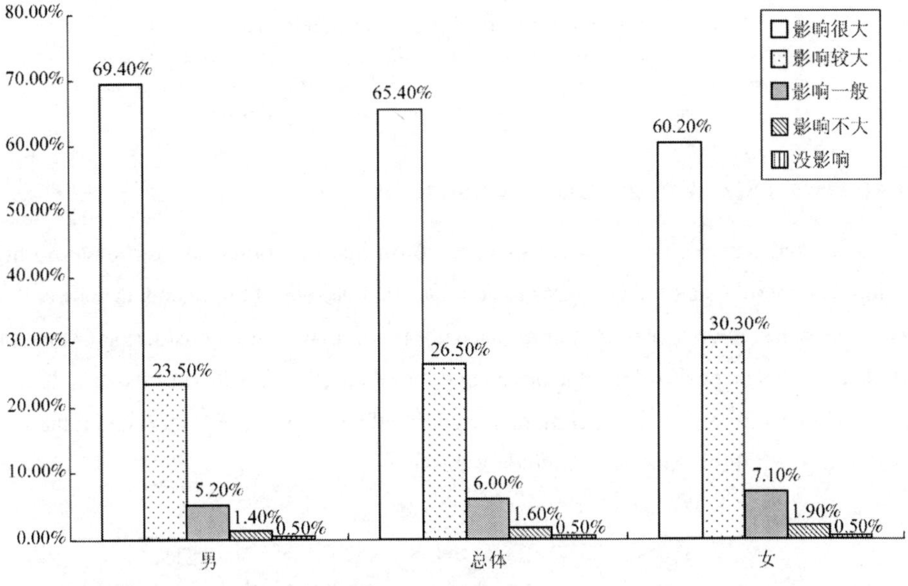

Figure 4-2 What iss the influence of America on international affairs?

In the picture, 影响很大 means "very great influence," 影响较大 means "great influence," 影响一般 means "some influence," 影响不大 means "small influence" and 没影响 means "no influence." 男 means "males," 总体 means "overall," and 女 means "females."

(3) Importance of China-U. S. Relations

Males and females share nearly the same opinion on this question. More than half of both believe the China-U. S. relations are very important, and about 90% think they are very important or important. The proportion of males considering the China-U. S. relations as "very important" are a little higher than females, but there is little difference between the two.

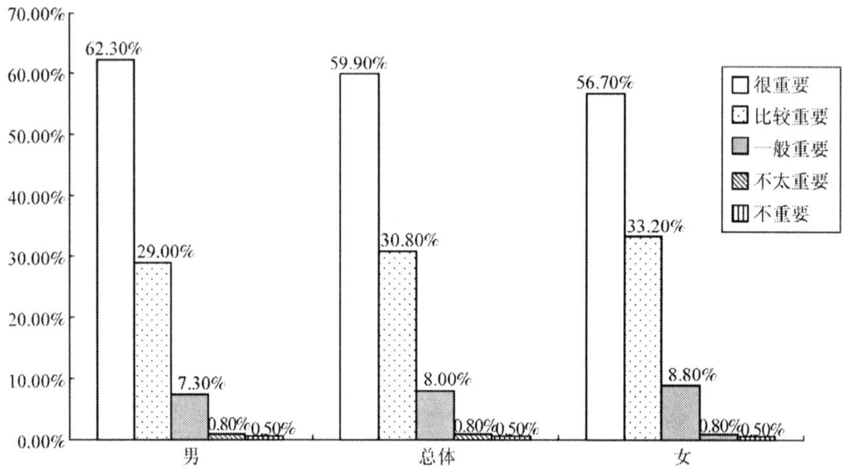

Figure 4-3 How important are the China-U. S. relations for China?
In the picture, 很重要 means "very important," 比较重要 means "important," 一般重要 "a little important," 不太重要 means "not that important" and 不重要 means "not important." 男 means "males," 总体 means "overall," and 女 means "females."

(4) America's Stand on the Global Climate Change

Males and females have a great divergence on this question, but both have no high opinion on America's attitude towards the climate change. 1/3 of both genders answer "just so-so." Females have a better appraisal, with more than 40% considering America's attitude to be "very positive" or "positive" and less than 20% considering its attitude to be passive. Comparatively, males feel more disappointed about America's attitude on the issue and 30% of them think America's attitude is passive.

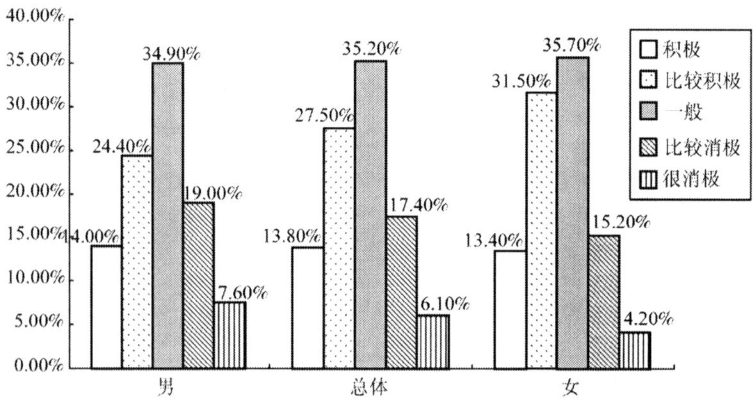

Figure 4-4 What do you think about America's attitude on global climate change?
In the picture, 积极 means "very positive," 比较积极 means "positive," 一般 means "just so-so," 比较消极 means "passive" and 很消极 means "very passive."
男 means "males," 总体 means "overall," and 女 means "females."

(5) Overall Impression of the U. S.

Male and female interviewees show no difference in the overall impression of the America. About half of males and females have a "just so-so" impression of America, about 36% have very good or good impression, and less than 20% have bad impressions.

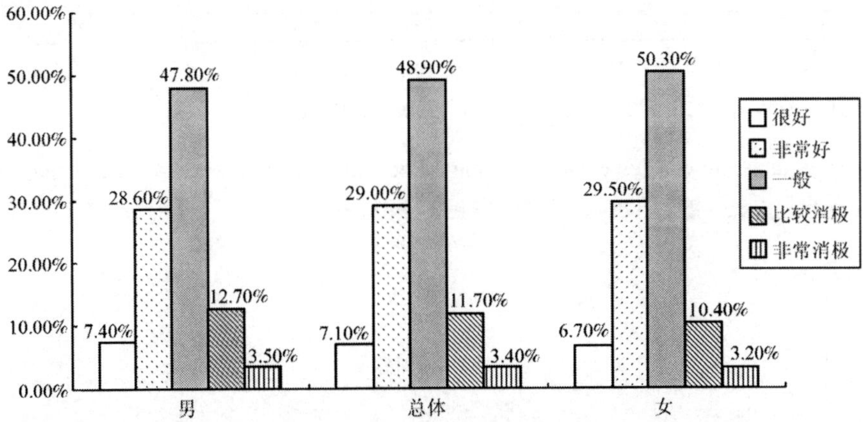

Figure 4-5 What is your overall impression of the U. S.?

In this picture, 很好 means "very good," 非常好 means "good," 一般 means "ordinary," 比较消极 means "negative" and 非常消极 means "very negative."

男 means "males," 总体 means "overall," and 女 means "females."

(6) The Most Representative Symbol of America

Interviewed males and females have the same opinions on the most representative symbol of America, despite a little difference. About 30% males and 30% females choose the White House and 20% selected the Statue of Liberty. The result reflects the influence of American politics.

Table 4-1 What do you think is the most representative symbol of America?

	Male	Female	General
White House	25.4%	27.9%	26.5%
Coca-Cola	6.1%	6.9%	6.5%
Chinatown	8.4%	8.8%	8.6%
Pentagon	8.6%	6.1%	7.5%
Hollywood	3.9%	5.7%	4.7%
Statue of Liberty	17.8%	22.9%	20.1%
Aircraft carriers	4.4%	1.4%	3.0%
Silicon valley	2.2%	2.4%	2.3%
USD	7.6%	6.1%	6.9%
Space shuttle	1.0%	0.5%	0.8%

Continued

	Male	Female	General
McDonald's	2.1%	2.5%	2.3%
NBA	6.3%	2.6%	4.6%
Harvard University	3.2%	4.2%	3.7%
Las Vegas caChinas	0.5%	0.6%	0.6%
Tiger Woods	0.5%	0.3%	0.5%
Guantánamo prison	1.3%	0.3%	0.8%
Others	0.6%	0.8%	0.7%
Total	100.0%	100.0%	100.0%

(7) Influence of America's Financial Crisis on World Economy

Males and females have basically the same opinion on this issue. More than 90% males or females choose "very great" or "great" influence.

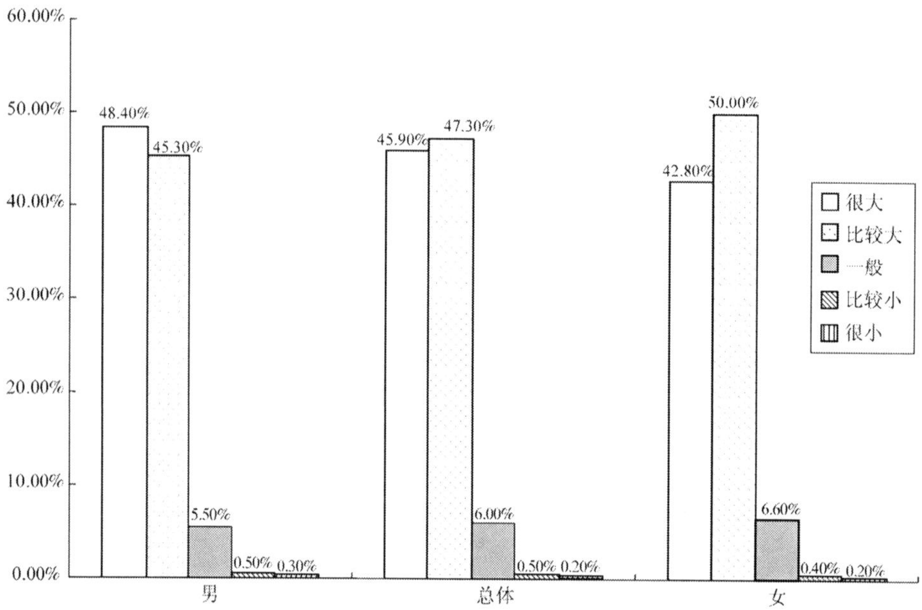

Figure 4-6 What is the impact of the American financial crisis on the world economy?

In this picture, 很大 means "very great," 比较大 means "great," 一般 means "just so-so," 比较小 means "small" and 很小 means "very small."

男 means "males," 总体 means "overall," and 女 means "females."

(8) Variation Tendency of American International Influence

Males and females have similar views on this question. 60% of both think America's international influence will remain the same, while 20% consider it will rise and 20% chose decline.

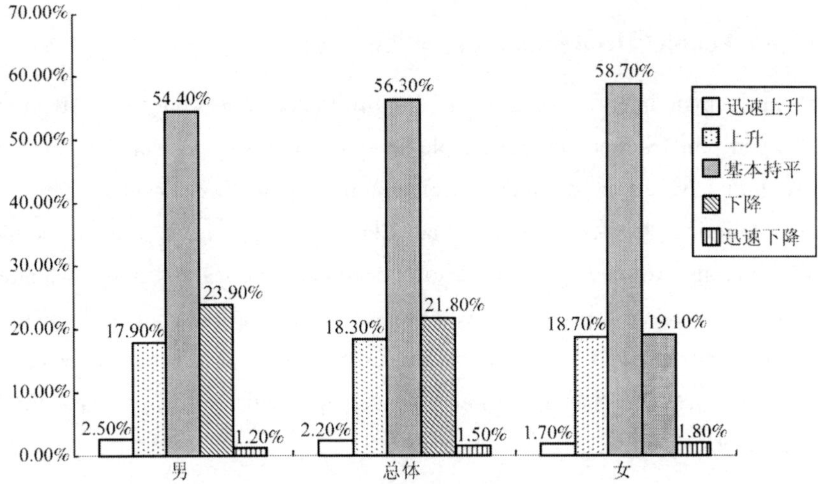

Figure 4-7 How will American international influence change in the future?
In this picture, 迅速上升 means rapidly grow, 上升 means grow, 基本持平 means remain the same, 下降 means decline and 迅速下降 means rapidly decline.
男 means "males," 总体 means "overall," and 女 means "females."

(9) Americans' Understanding of China

Males and females also have similar opinions on this question. Both think that Americans do not know China well. Less than 10% believe that they understand China or understand well, while more than a half of both males and females think they do not understand or do not well understand China.

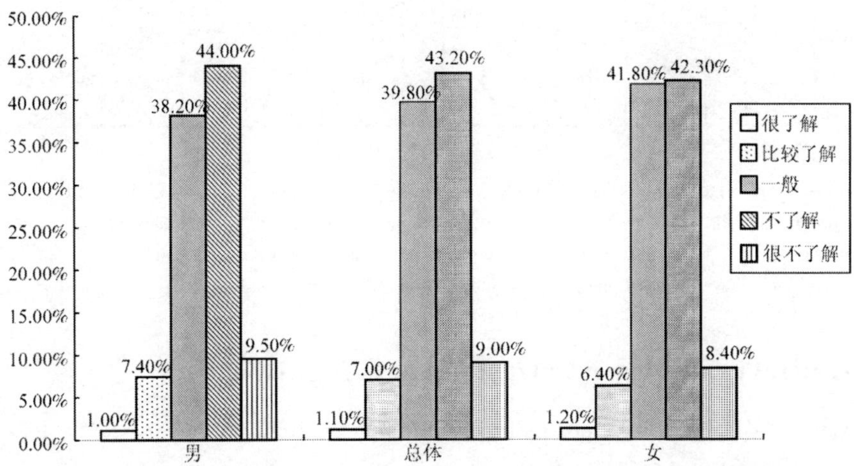

Figure 4-8 How much do you think the average American knows about China?
In this picture, 很了解 means "well understand," 比较了解 means "understand," 一般 means "just so-so," 不了解 means "understand little" and 很不了解 means "don't understand at all."
男 means "males," 总体 means "overall," and 女 means "females."

(10) Chinese People's Understanding of America

Male and female interviewees show no big difference on this question. About 50% of both males and females that Chinese people have a just so-so understanding of America, while 10% think Chinese know America well, and more than 30% consider Chinese do not understand America. It can be found that Chinese people have a good opinion of themselves, and also Chinese are willing to understand America and pay more attention. Interviewees think Chinese people know America better than Americans' knowledge on China. It can be also figured out that interviewees think they have better understanding of America than others. More than 30% of both genders, particularly 40% of males, think they understand America.

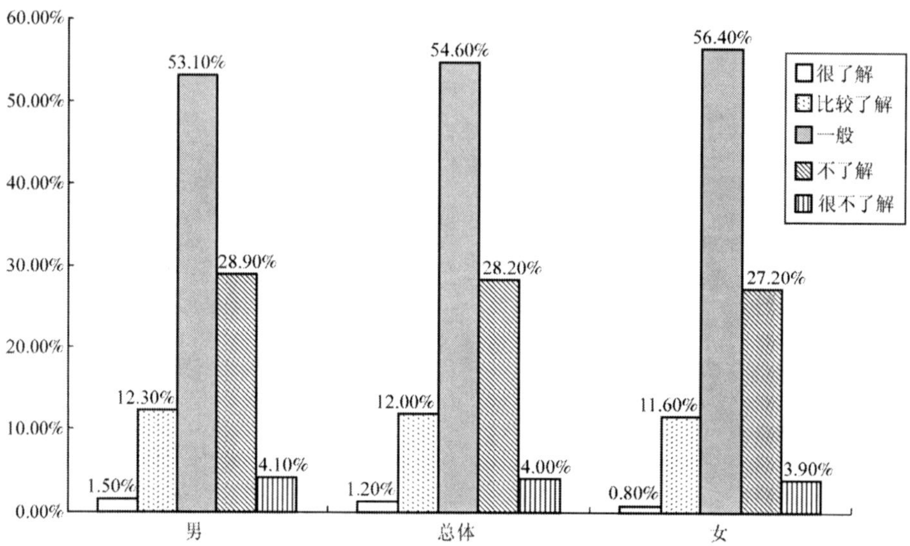

Figure 4-9 How much do you think the average Chinese person knows about the U. S.?
In this picture, 很了解 means "well understand," 比较了解 means "understand," 一般 means "just so-so," 不了解 means "understand little" and 很不了解 means "don't understand at all."
男 means "males," 总体 means "overall," and 女 means "females."

(11) General Evaluation of Current China-U. S. Relations

Males and females have no significant different opinions on this question. More than 70% of both think the China-U. S. relations are "just so-so," only less than 15% consider the relations to be good or very good, and approximately 10% think the relations are bad right now.

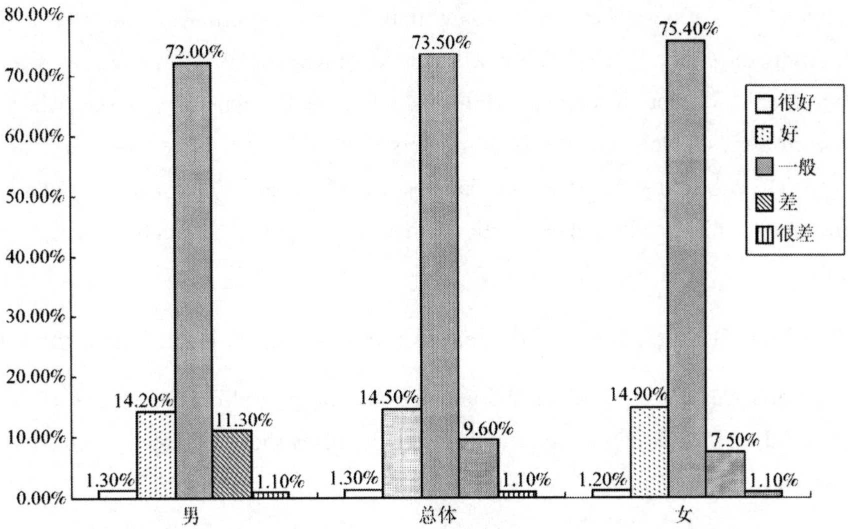

Figure 4-10 How do you view the current China-U. S. relations?
In this picture, 很好 means "very good," 好 means "good," 一般 means "just so-so," 差 means "bad" and 很差 means "very bad." 男 means "males," 总体 means "overall," and 女 means "females."

(12) Forecast of the Prospects of the China-U. S. Relations

Males and females show no significant difference on the forecast of the prospects of

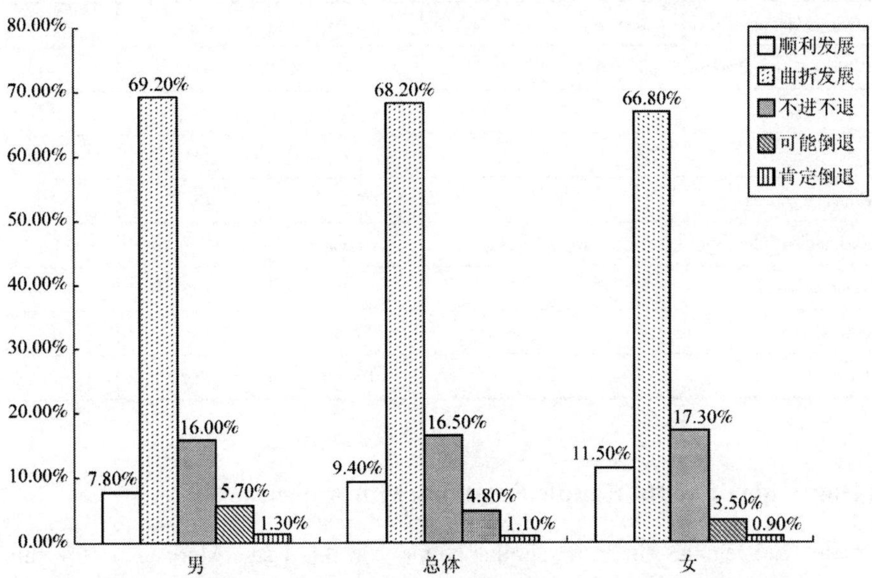

Figure 4-11 What do you think about the prospects of China-U. S. relations?
In this picture, 顺利发展 means "develop smoothly," 曲折发展 means "develop despite twists and turns," 不进不退 means "neither advance nor retreat," 可能倒退 means may regress and 肯定倒退 means "surely regress." 男 means "males," 总体 means "overall," and 女 means "females."

the China-U. S. relations. They are generally optimistic, but cautious. About 80% males or females think the China-U. S. relations will develop, including 70% who believe in a rocky development. More than 20% people think the China-U. S. relations will stay where they are or even regress. Only 10% of both genders think the bilateral relations will develop smoothly. The subtle difference is that females are a little more optimistic, since a higher proportion of females than males believe that the China-U. S. relations will develop smoothly.

(13) The Most Important Issue or Field in the China-U. S. Relations in the Future

Regarding this question, males and females have no great difference. The top three are economy and trade, the Taiwan issue and energy. Females show a greater concern over the economy and trade than males.

Table 4-2 What do you think is the most important field or issue in the future China-U. S. relations?

	Male	Female	general
Trade and economy	34.4%	37.5%	35.7%
Energy	18.0%	16.9%	17.5%
Anti-terrorism	2.9%	2.7%	2.8%
Environment and climate change	3.0%	4.2%	3.5%
Public health and epidemic prevention	0.4%	0.4%	0.4%
Taiwan issue	25.6%	25.9%	25.7%
Tibet issue	1.9%	2.8%	2.3%
Human rights issue	5.2%	4.8%	5.0%
Exchange of education, science, technology and culture	1.8%	1.3%	1.6%
Regional safety	6.5%	3.2%	5.0%
Others	0.4%	0.5%	0.4%
Total	100.0%	100.0%	100.0%

(14) How China Should Handle Relations with America

Males and females share the similar opinion on this issue. More than 10% think it shall remain the same, while approximately same proportion of people suggest to adhere to principles more and to be more flexible. People do not reach a consensus on which is more important, principle or flexibility.

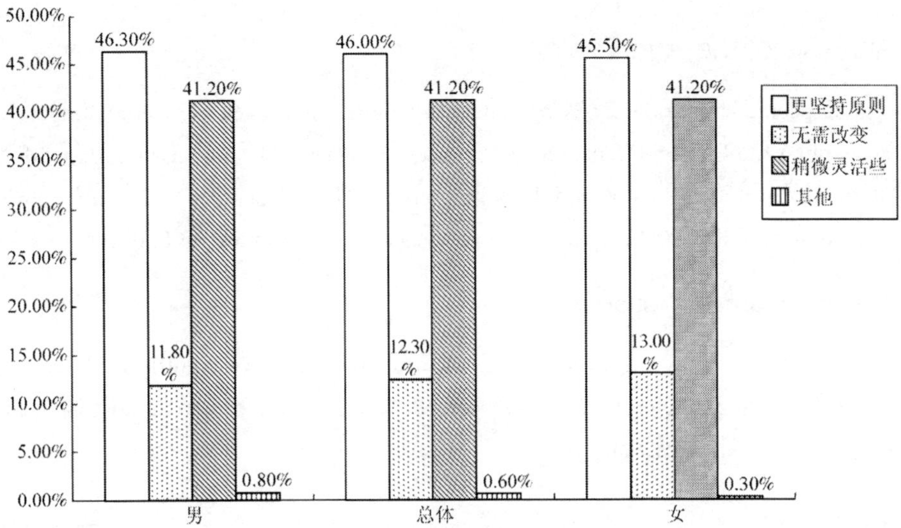

Figure 4-12 How do you think China should handle the relations with the U. S. in the future?

In this picture, 更坚持原则 means "adhere to principles more," 无需改变 means "no need to change," 稍微灵活些 means "be more flexible" and 其它 means "others."

男 means "males," 总体 means "overall," and 女 means "females."

According to the above statistics and analysis, we can come to the following conclusions: 1) Both males and females of interviewees have a certain understanding of America; 2) Males and females have no significant divergence; 3) Most interviewees can identify the complexity of the China-U. S. relations and hold a cautiously optimistic attitude towards the development of the bilateral relations; 4) Males and females have similar views on how China should handle the relations with America, compared to the firmer attitude of males than females in previous investigations. It means that the option of "adhere to principles more" is more acceptable than the previous option of "be firm." A significant rise in the proportion of people choosing "be more flexible" can be seen; 5) Regarding the most influential area for the future China-U. S. relations, most males and females selected economy and trade, followed by the Taiwan issue and energy. It may be because the Taiwan issue has been a long and difficult issue left over by the history despite its importance and the economy and trade issue is urgent and more closely related to Chinese people's live. As the important foundation for economic development and national safety, the energy attracts more attention from Chinese people, especially based on the price rise of oil and gas and power supply shortage; 6) Generally, two mainlines can be found in males and females' understanding of America, the recognition of America's achievements and influence and resentment and vigilance against America's adverse effect on China.

2. Analysis of the Age Factor

2,665 people among the 2,687 respondents supplied their age. 1,137 are younger than 25, accounting for 42.3%; 815 people are between the ages of 26 and 35, taking up 30.3%; 388 are between the ages of 36 and 45, taking up 14.4%; 303 people, 11.3%, are between the ages of 46 and 60; and 22 are older than 60 years old, accounting for 0.8%.

(1) Understanding of America

As shown in the investigation, people of different ages show significant divergence. Though most of all ages chose they "know something," but more people in older ages think they do not know America well.

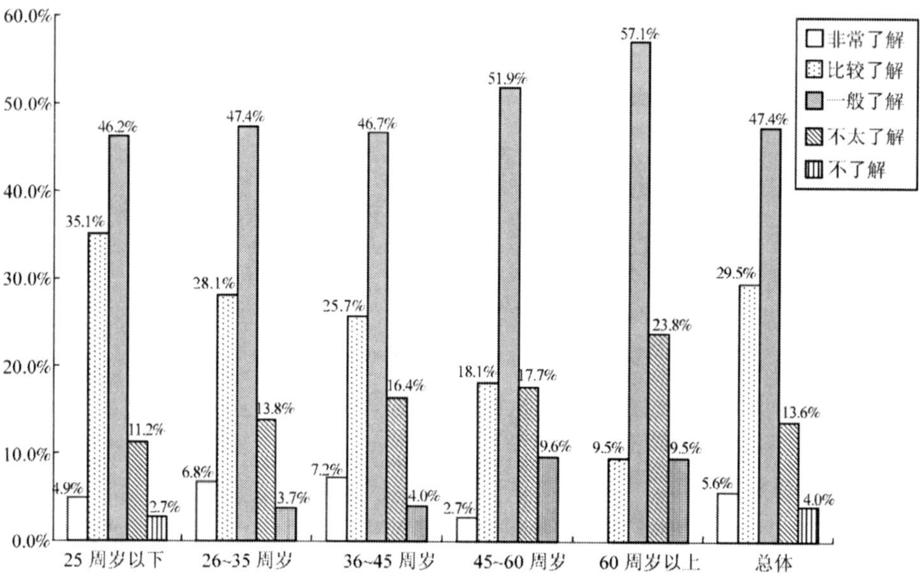

Figure 4-13 How much do you know about America?

In this picture, 很了解 means "well understand," 比较了解 means "understand," 一般 means "just so-so," 不了解 means "understand little" and 很不了解 means "don't understand at all."

25 周岁以下 means "0~25," 26~35 周岁 means "26~35," 36~45 周岁 means "36~45," 45~60 周岁 means "45~60," 60 周岁以上 means "above 60" and 总体 means "general."

(2) America's Influence on International Affairs

Ages bring significant divergence on this problem. The mainstream opinion considers that America has a very great influence on international affairs. However, a larger proportion of younger ages hold this view.

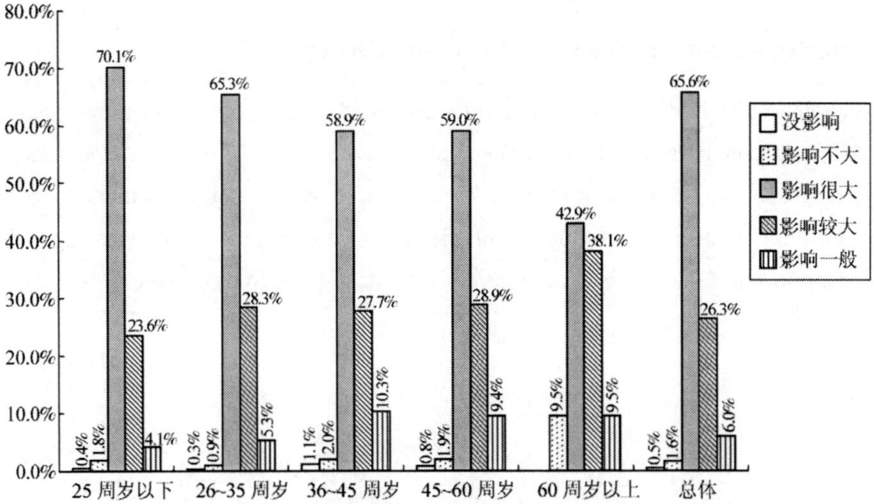

Figure 4-14 America's Influence on International Affairs

In the picture, 影响很大 means "very great influence," 影响较大 means "great influence," 影响一般 means "some influence," 影响不大 means "small influence" and 没影响 means "no influence."

25 周岁以下 means "0~25," 26~35 周岁 means "26~35," 36~45 周岁 means "36~45," 45~60 周岁 means "45~60," 60 周岁以上 means "above 60" and 总体 means "general."

(3) Importance of China-U. S. Relations

No great difference can be seen in different ages. The mainstream opinion is that the China-U. S. relations are very important or important. 90% of all ages believe in this opinion.

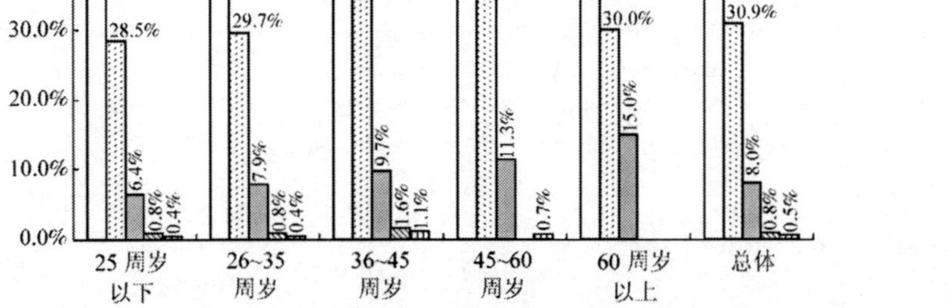

Figure 4-15 How important are the China-U. S. relations for China?

In the picture, 很重要 means "very important," 比较重要 means "important," 一般重要 "a little important," 不太重要 means "not that important" and 不重要 means "not important."

25 周岁以下 means "0~25," 26~35 周岁 means "26~35," 36~45 周岁 means "36~45," 45~60 周岁 means "45~60," 60 周岁以上 means "above 60" and 总体 means "general."

(4) America's Stand on the Global Climate Change

People in different ages hold different views on this issue. The mainstream opinion is that America's stand on the global climate change is just so-so or positive. Comparatively, a smaller proportion of youths under age 25 and people over age 60 think that America has a very positive or positive attitude on this issue than the proportions of other ages, but a larger proportion of these two age groups consider its attitude to be passive.

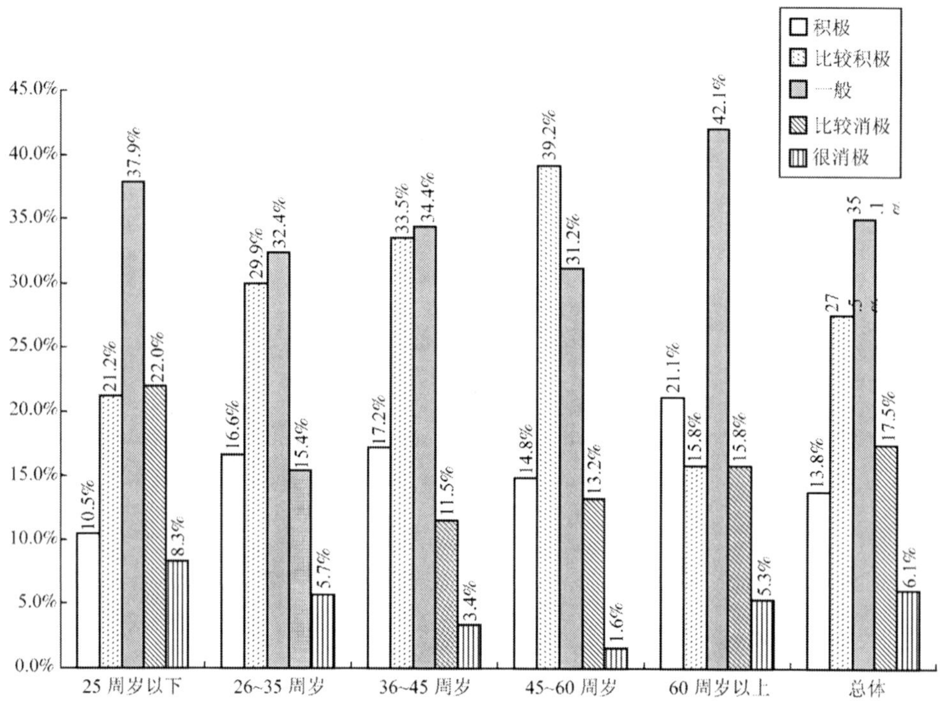

Figure 4-16 America's Stand on the Global Climate Change

In the picture, 积极 means "very positive," 比较积极 means "positive," 一般 means "just so-so," 比较消极 means "passive" and 很消极 means "very passive."

25 周岁以下 means "0 ~ 25," 26~35 周岁 means "26~35," 36~45 周岁 means "36~45," 45~60 周岁 means "45~60," 60 周岁以上 means "above 60" and 总体 means "general."

(5) Overall Impression of the U. S.

Ages have little influence on this issue except for people older than 60. Generally, half of interviewees have a just "so-so" impression of America, 10% have bad impressions and 40% have good or very good impressions, but people older than 60 have significantly worse impressions of the U. S. than other ages.

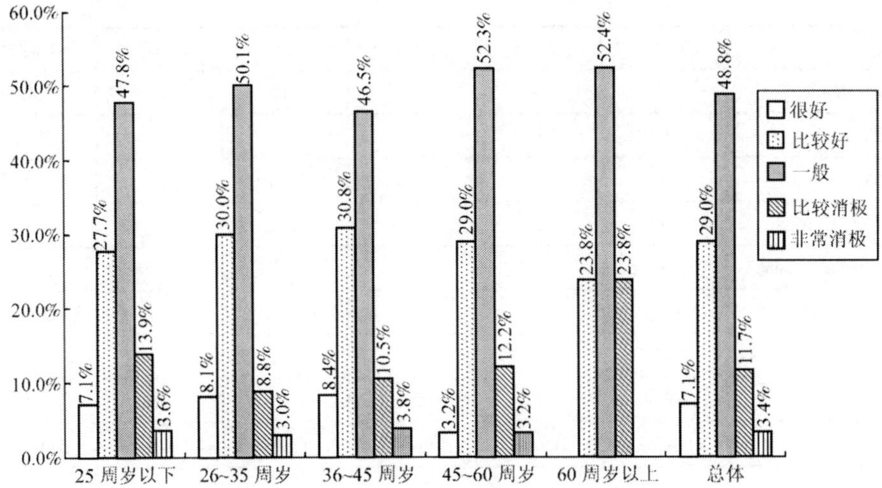

Figure 4-17 Overall Impression of the U. S.

In this picture, 很好 means "very good," 非常好 means "good," 一般 means "ordinary," 比较消极 means "negative" and 非常消极 means "very negative."

25 周岁以下 means "0~25," 26~35 周岁 means "26~35," 36~45 周岁 means "36~45," 45~60 周岁 means "45~60," 60 周岁以上 means "above 60" and 总体 means "general."

(6) The Most Representative Symbol of America

Age has an obvious influence on the answers to this question. Generally, the White House and the Statue of Liberty are the two main representative symbols of America, occupying a much higher proportion than other symbols. The proportions of the choice of the White House and the Statue of Liberty in all ages exceed 20%, while no more than 10% chose the other 15 options (such as USD, McDonald's and Hollywood).

Table 4-3 The Most Representative Symbol of America

	0~25	26~35	36~45	45~60	60 above	General
White House	24.1%	25.2%	29.0%	35.3%	40.0%	26.5%
Coca-Cola	6.4%	7.6%	6.3%	4.2%	5.0%	6.5%
Chinatown	10.4%	8.7%	6.5%	3.8%	5.0%	8.5%
Pentagon	4.9%	9.1%	10.4%	9.0%	5.0%	7.5%
Hollywood	6.2%	3.4%	5.0%	3.5%		4.8%
Statue of Liberty	21.0%	20.4%	19.3%	16.3%	15.0%	20.0%
Aircraft carrier	3.6%	3.1%	2.9%	1.4%		3.1%
Silicon Valley	4.2%	1.2%	0.8%	0.3%		2.3%
USD	5.0%	8.0%	8.1%	9.3%	15.0%	6.9%

Continued

	0~25	26~35	36~45	45~60	60 above	General
Space shuttle	0.4%	1.0%	0.8%	2.1%		0.8%
McDonald's	1.6%	2.1%	3.1%	3.8%	10.0%	2.3%
NBA	5.6%	4.6%	2.9%	3.1%		4.6%
Harvard University	3.6%	3.1%	3.9%	5.5%		3.7%
Las Vegas caChinas	0.8%	0.6%		0.3%		0.6%
Tiger Woods	0.3%	0.6%	0.5%	0.7%		0.5%
Guantánamo prison	1.3%	0.5%		1.0%		0.8%
Others	0.6%	0.9%	0.5%	0.3%	5.0%	0.7%
Total	100.0%	100.0%	100.0%	100.0%	100.0%	100.0%

(7) Influence of America's Financial Crisis on World Economy

Age has little impact on this issue. People of all ages think that the financial crisis of America has a very great impact on world economy, while only 10% think the influence is small.

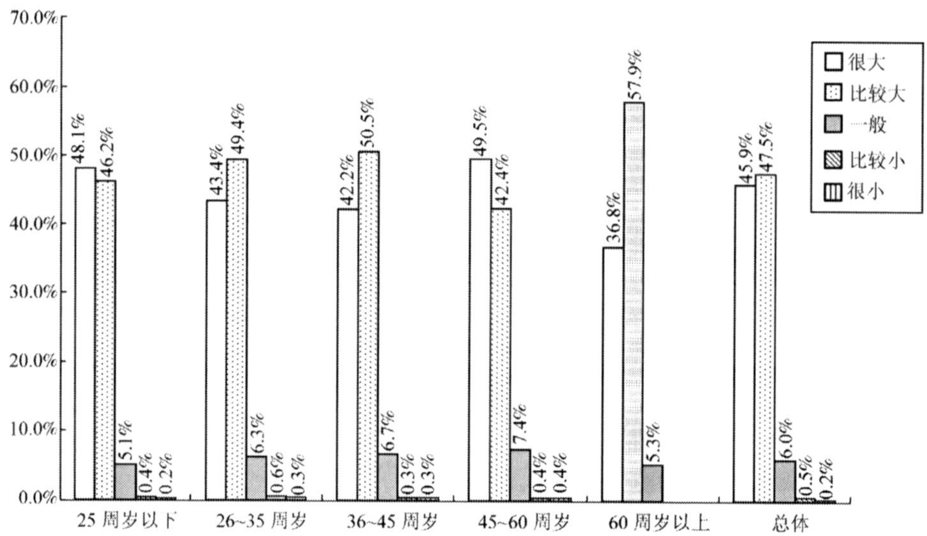

Figure 4-18 Influence of America's Financial Crisis on World Economy

In this picture, 很大 means "very great," 比较大 means "great," 一般 means "just so-so," 比较小 means "small" and 很小 means "very small."

25 周岁以下 means "0~25," 26~35 周岁 means "26~35," 36~45 周岁 means "36~45," 45~60 周岁 means "45~60," 60 周岁以上 means "above 60" and 总体 means "general."

(8) Variation Tendency of American International Influence

Age has certain impact on the answers to this question. Around 60% of interviewees believe that the international influence of America is leaning towards stability. About 20% think its influence is rising, while 20% think it is declining. Most people older than 60 years old think the influence of America remains steady. As shown in the analysis, along with the increase of age, more people think America's influence is rising and less people believe its influence will remain, without change in the proportion of people who think the influence is declining.

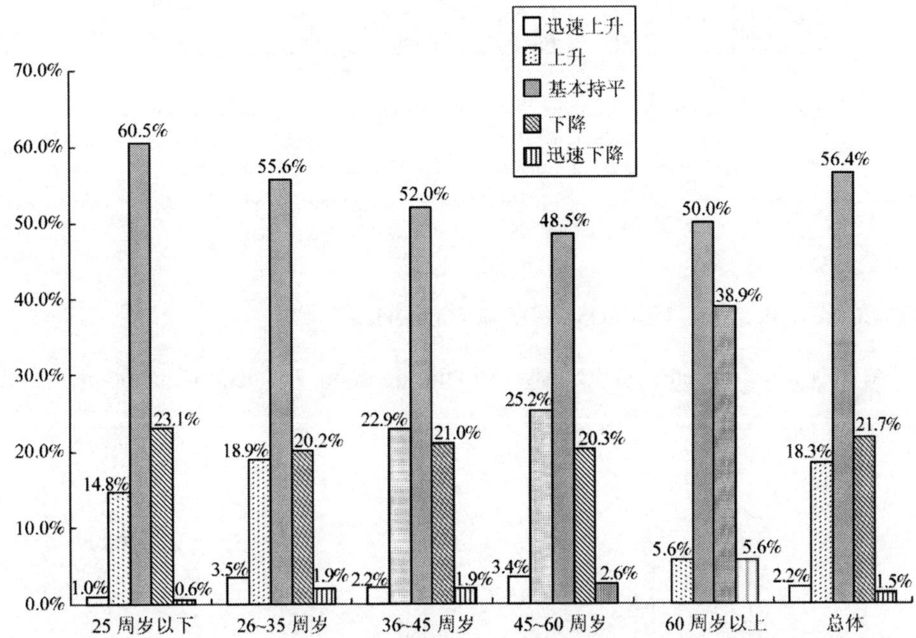

Figure 4-19 Variation Tendency of American International Influence

In this picture, 迅速上升 means rapidly grow, 上升 means grow, 基本持平 means remain the same, 下降 means decline and 迅速下降 means rapidly decline.

25 周岁以下 means "0~25," 26~35 周岁 means "26~35," 36~45 周岁 means "36~45," 45~60 周岁 means "45~60," 60 周岁以上 means "above 60" and 总体 means "general."

(9) Average American's Understanding of China

Age has little influence on this question. The mainstream opinion believes that common Americans do not understand China. Less than 10% of all ages think Americans understand well or don't understand China at all. People age 60 or above tend to believe that Americans do not understand or only understand very little about China.

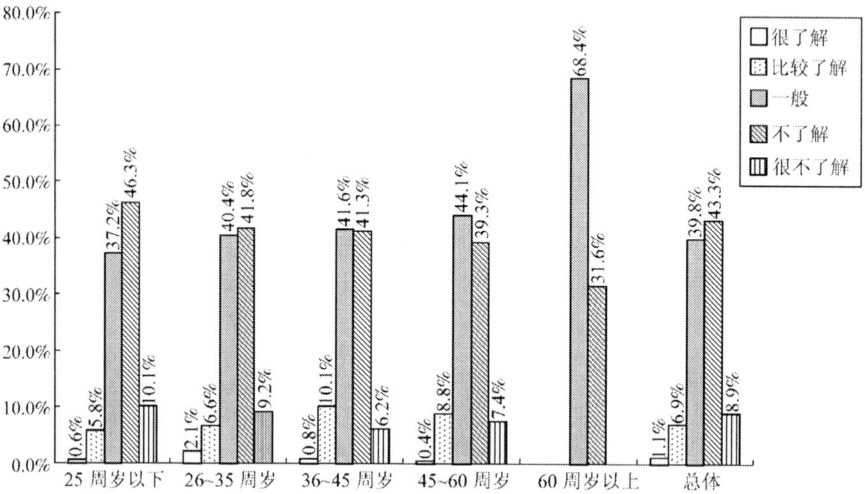

Figure 4-20 How much do you think the average American knows about China?

In this picture, 很了解 means "well understand," 比较了解 means "understand," 一般 means "just so-so," 不了解 means "understand little" and 很不了解 means "don't understand at all."

25 周岁以下 means "0~25," 26~35 周岁 means "26~35," 36~45 周岁 means "36~45," 45~60 周岁 means "45~60," 60 周岁以上 means "above 60" and 总体 means "general."

(10) Chinese People's Understanding of America

Age has some influence on the answers to this question. The mainstream opinion holds

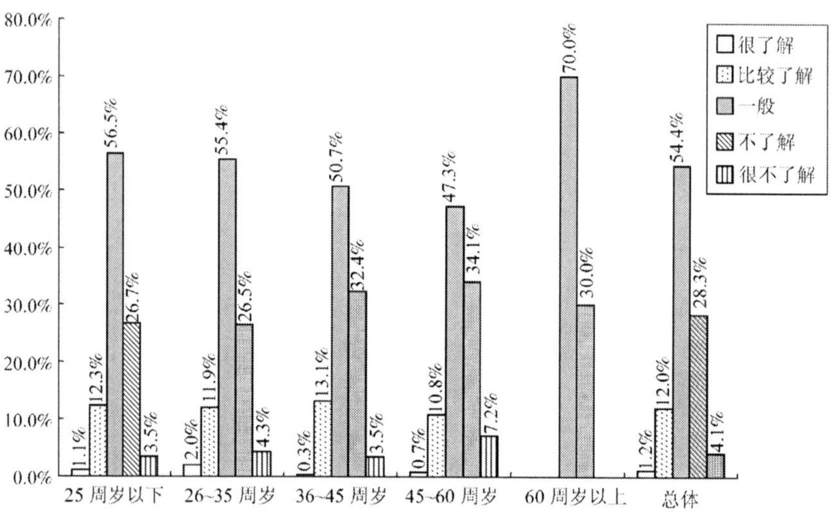

Figure 4-21 How much do you think the average Chinese person knows about the U. S.?

In this picture, 很了解 means "well understand," 比较了解 means "understand," 一般 means "just so-so," 不了解 means "understand little" and 很不了解 means "don't understand at all."

25 周岁以下 means "0~25," 26~35 周岁 means "26~35," 36~45 周岁 means "36~45," 45~60 周岁 means "45~60," 60 周岁以上 means "above 60" and 总体 means "general."

that Chinese do not understand America. Compared to the previous question, the lower proportion of the mainstream opinion demonstrates that Chinese think Americans understand China less than the Chinese people's understanding of America. Only 10% of interviewees think that the Chinese understand America. Along with the increase of ages, more people think that Chinese do not understand America. Distinguished from other ages, people older than 60 mainly choose "just so-so" and "don't understand."

(11) How do you view the current China-U. S. relations?

Age has no impact on this question. The mainstream opinion considers the current China-U. S. relations as just so-so, while about 10% think the relations are bad and about 15% think the relations are good.

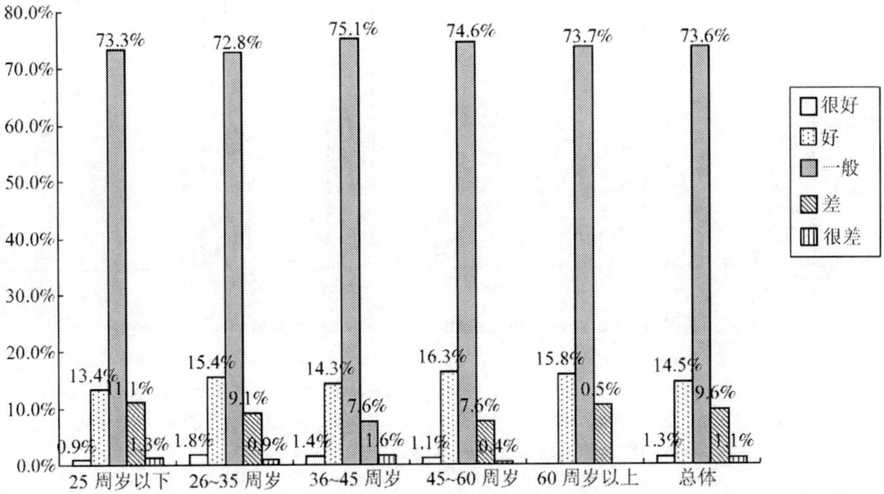

Figure 4-22 How do you view the current China-U. S. relations?

In this picture, 很好 means "very good," 好 means "good," 一般 means "just so-so," 差 means "bad" and 很差 means "very bad."

25 周岁以下 means "0~25," 26~35 周岁 means "26~35," 36~45 周岁 means "36~45," 45~60 周岁 means "45~60," 60 周岁以上 means "above 60" and 总体 means "general."

(12) What do you think about the prospects of China-U. S. relations?

Age has no impact on this question. The mainstream opinion believes that the China-U. S. relations will see a development, including 70% who believe that the China-U. S. relations will develop, despite difficulties and 10% think that the bilateral relations will develop smoothly. About 20% believe that the China-U. S. relations will regress. People older than 60 have more optimistic opinions on the prospects of the China-U. S. relations.

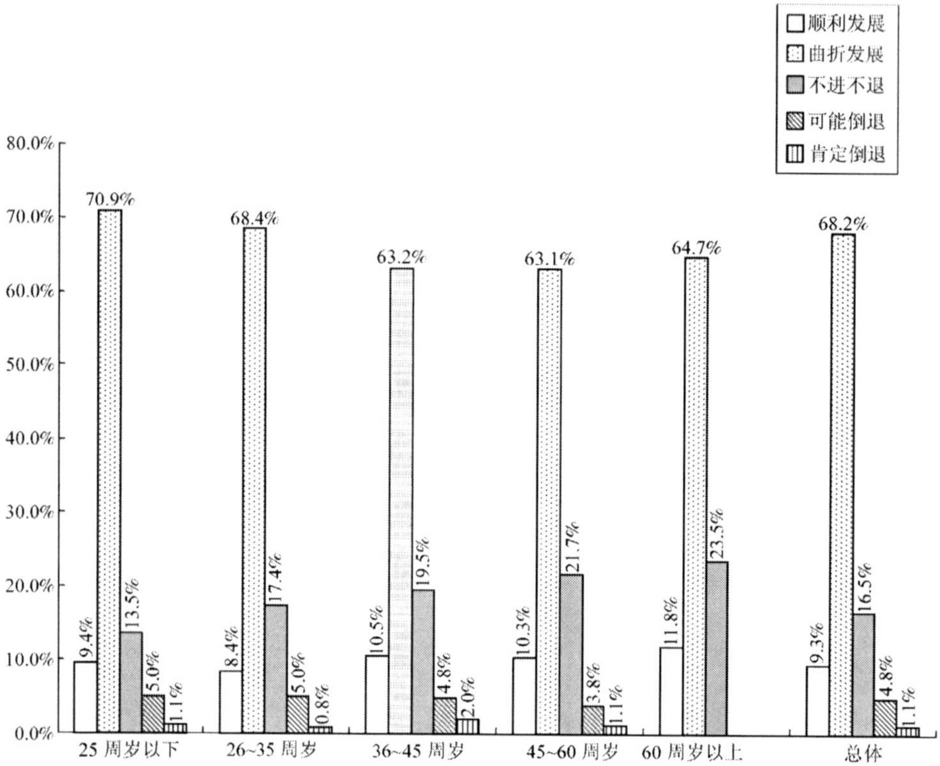

Figure 4-23 What do you think about the prospects of China-U. S. relations?

In this picture, 顺利发展 means "develop smoothly," 曲折发展 means "develop despite twists and turns," 不进不退 means "neither advance nor retreat," 可能倒退 means may regress and 肯定倒退 means "surely regress." 25 周岁以下 means "0~25," 26~35 周岁 means "26~35," 36~45 周岁 means "36~45," 45~60 周岁 means "45~60," 60 周岁以上 means "above 60" and 总体 means "general."

(13) What do you think is the most important field or issue in the future China-U. S. relations?

People of different ages have different answers to this question. Firstly, the top three important fields are selected as the trade and economy, Taiwan issue and energy issue. A total of about 80% of interviewees chose the three options, while only 10% or lower chose other options. For the impact of age on this question, firstly, along with the increase of age, smaller proportion of interviewees regarded the economy and trade as the primary issue. Secondly, people age 60 or older attached more importance to the Taiwan issue, with as high as 50% of them choosing the Taiwan issue as the most important field in the China-U. S. relations. They paid more attention to regional and national security.

Table 4-4 What do you think is the most important field or issue in the future China-U. S. relations?

	0~25	26~35	36~45	45~60	Above 60	General
Economy and trade	38.7%	37.2%	30.9%	25.9%	11.1%	35.6%
Energy	13.5%	19.0%	24.9%	20.2%	11.1%	17.5%
Anti-terrorism	2.0%	3.1%	3.9%	3.8%		2.8%
Environment and climate change	3.1%	3.6%	5.0%	3.0%		3.5%
Public health and epidemic prevention	0.3%	0.3%	1.1%			0.4%
Taiwan issue	29.6%	21.7%	20.7%	27.4%	50.0%	25.8%
Tibet issue	2.1%	2.7%	1.7%	1.9%	11.1%	2.3%
Human rights	3.9%	4.4%	5.2%	11.8%	5.6%	5.1%
Exchange of education, science, technology and culture	2.2%	1.0%	1.4%	0.8%		1.6%
Regional safety	4.1%	6.4%	4.7%	5.3%	11.1%	5.1%
Others	0.5%	0.5%	0.6%			0.4%
Total	100.0%	100.0%	100.0%	100.0%	100.0%	100.0%

(14) How should China handle relations with the U. S. in the future?

The difference of age has no significant influence on this question, but people older than 60 seemed have a stronger attitude, while less of them advocated to handle the relations with the U. S. more flexibly.

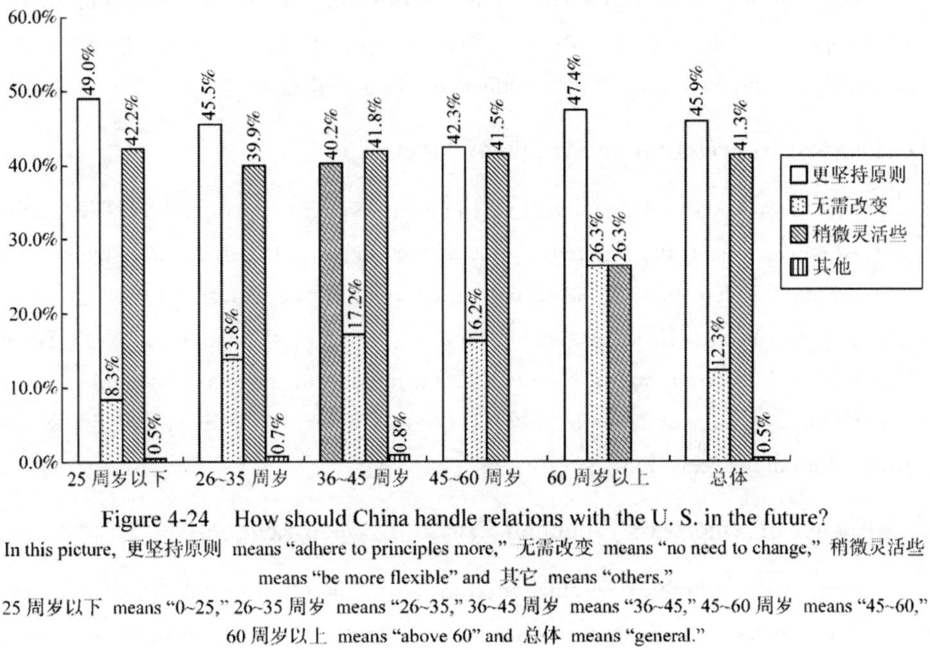

Figure 4-24 How should China handle relations with the U. S. in the future?

In this picture, 更坚持原则 means "adhere to principles more," 无需改变 means "no need to change," 稍微灵活些 means "be more flexible" and 其它 means "others."

25 周岁以下 means "0~25," 26~35 周岁 means "26~35," 36~45 周岁 means "36~45," 45~60 周岁 means "45~60," 60 周岁以上 means "above 60" and 总体 means "general."

We can reach the following conclusions based on the above statistics and analysis: 1) Only a few interviewees of all ages, especially the elderly, chose the extreme answers to questions on America and the China-U. S. relations; 2) Comparedg to the old interviewees, the young and the middle-aged have a more diversified understanding of America and recognize America and its influence more based on the increasing number of channels with which to acquire information on America; 3) The young and the middle-aged are concerned with more issues and have broader views than the elderly, in terms of factors that influence the China-U. S. relations; 4) The elderly have a stronger attitude against America than the young and the middle-aged; 5) Though the elderly have worse impressions of the U. S., they are still optimistic about the prospects of the China-U. S. relations.

V. Effects of Educational Level and Region

1. Effects of the Educational Level

2,684 interviewees supplied an answer for their educational background, including 438 graduate students (16.3%), 1,727 having graduated from university and college (64.3%), 489 students graduated from middle school and technical school (18.2%) and 30 graduated from primary school and other schools (1.2%). With the general higher education as the standard, the interviewees were divided into two groups: college graduates or above (first group) and high school graduates or below (second group). The first group totaled 2,165 people (80.7%) and the second group, taking up 19.3%. The effects of the educational level on their international outlook are discussed as below.

(1) The Most Representative Symbol of America

The two groups showed a comparatively large difference on this question. The top five choices of the first group are respectively the White House, Statue of Liberty, Wall Street, Coca-Cola and the Pentagon. In the second group, the top five representative symbols are respectively the White House, Statue of Liberty, Pentagon, the USD and Wall Street. Differences of the two groups lie in the different ranking of the same "symbol" and the different choices made. For example, the USD does not make the top five of the first group, but ranks third in the second group.

(2) Influence of America's Financial Crisis on World Economy

Though a few of both two groups selected "small" and "very small," the two groups showed a difference on the degree of "just so-so," "great" and "very great." For example, more than 94.2% of the first group thought that the influence of the financial crisis in America had a "great" or "very great" impact on the world, while the figure is 89.3% for the second group. In addition, about 10% of the second group chose "just so-so." Therefore, we can surmise that the first group is more cautious than the second group on judging the influence of the American financial crisis.

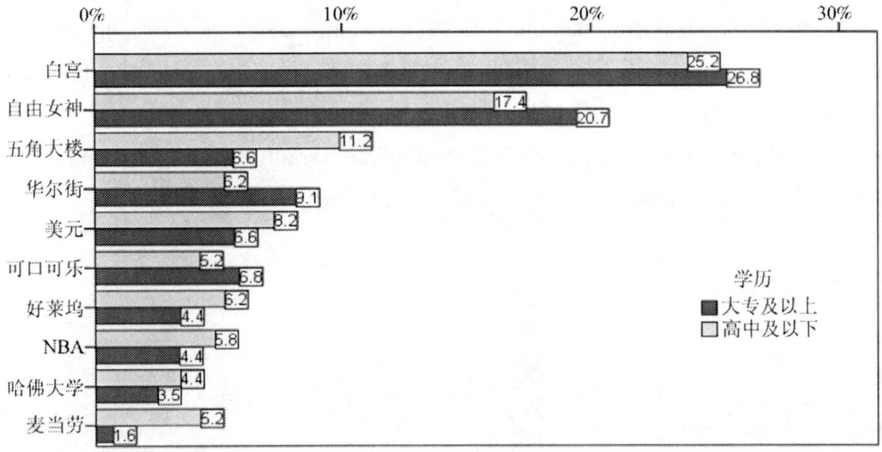

Figure 5-1 What do you think is the most representative symbol of America?

In the picture, 白宫 means the White House, 自由女神 means the Statue of Liberty, 五角大楼 means the Pentagon, 华尔街 means the Wall Street, 美元 means USD, 可口可乐 means Coca-Cola, 好莱坞 means Hollywood, 哈佛大学 means Harvard University and 麦当劳 means McDonald.

学历 means educational background, 大专及以上 means "college graduates or above" and 高中及以下 means "high school graduates or below".

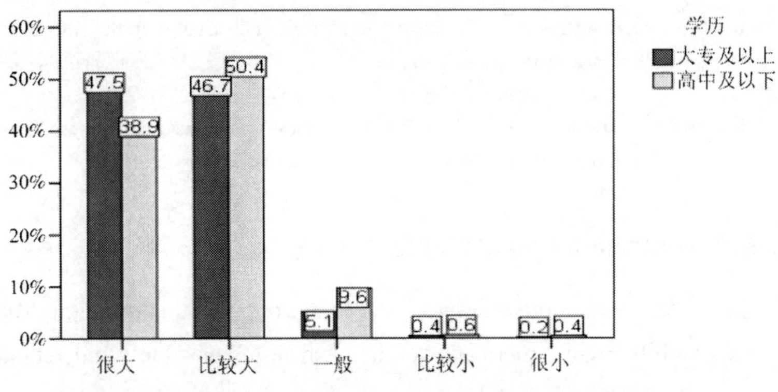

Figure 5-2 What was the impact of the American financial crisis on the world economy?

In this picture, 很大 means "very great," 比较大 means "great," 一般 means "just so-so," 比较小 means "small" and 很小 means "very small."

学历 means educational background, 大专及以上 means "college graduates or above" and 高中及以下 means "high school graduates or below".

(3) Variation Tendency of American International Influence

About 60% of the first group thought America's international influence will remain unchanged. Only 44.3% of the second group held this opinion. This means that the first group tends to believe that America will see no significant variation in its international influence, but the second group tends to believe that its influence is changing. Actually, 22.6% of the first group consider the influence of America to be declining or rapidly declining, compared to 18.6% who believe it is "rising" or "rapidly rising." Comparatively, 27.7% in the second group thought America's influence is "declining" or "rapidly declining," and more than 29% believe it is "rising" or "rapidly rising." Two groups show an obvious difference on the understanding about this question.

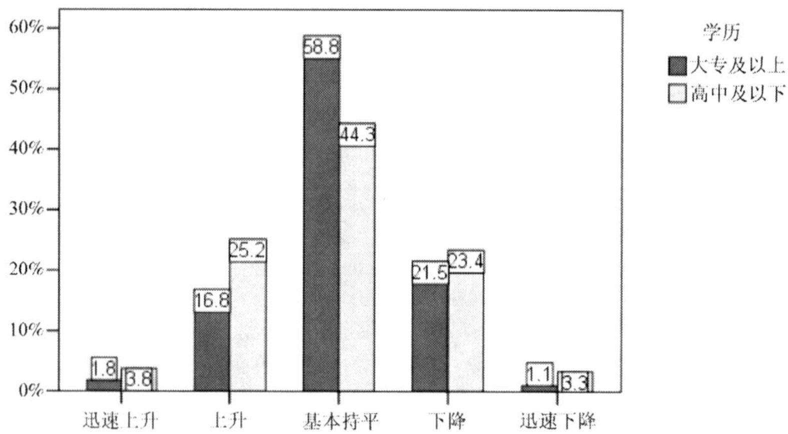

Figure 5-3 How will America's international influence change in the future?

In this picture, 迅速上升 means rapidly grow, 上升 means grow, 基本持平 means remain the same, 下降 means decline and 迅速下降 means rapidly decline.

学历 means educational background, 大专及以上 means "college graduates or above" and 高中及以下 means "high school graduates or below".

(4) American's Understanding of China

A little difference can be found between the two groups on this question. More than a half of the first group thought Americans "understand little" or "don't understand (China) at all," which falls to 46.3% for the second group. A larger proportion of the second group answered "just so-so." In the second group's view, America has a better understanding of China, comparing to the first group. The first group doubted more about whether Americans understand China.

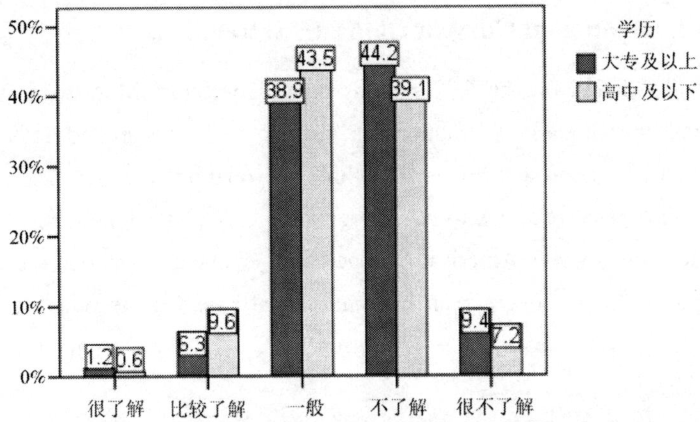

Figure 5-4 How much do you think the average American knows about China?

In this picture, 很了解 means "well understand," 比较了解 means "understand," 一般 means "just so-so," 不了解 means "understand little" and 很不了解 means "don't understand at all."

学历 means educational background, 大专及以上 means "college graduates or above" and 高中及以下 means "high school graduates or below".

(5) Chinese People's Understanding of America

Both groups share similar opinions on this question. More than a half of both groups answered "just so-so," 30% answered "understand little," and 10% answered "understand," with only a few responded with "don't understand at all" and "understand well." According to the survey, it is more common of "understand little" than "understand."

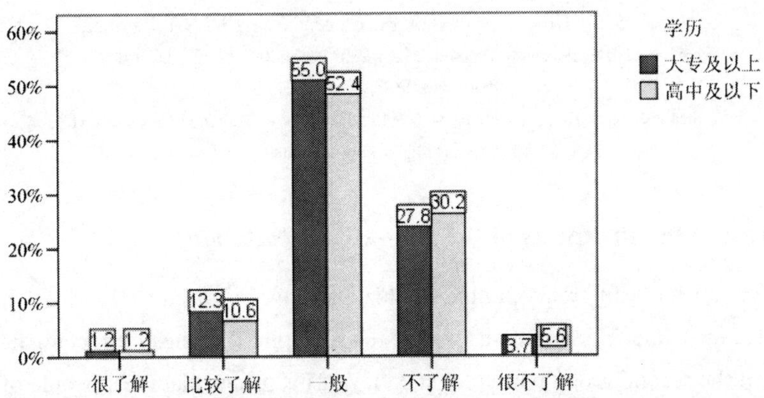

Figure 5-5 How much do you think the average Chinese person knows about the U. S.?

In this picture, 很了解 means "well understand," 比较了解 means "understand," 一般 means "just so-so," 不了解 means "understand little" and 很不了解 means "don't understand at all."

学历 means educational background, 大专及以上 means "college graduates or above" and 高中及以下 means "high school graduates or below".

(6) General Evaluation of Current China-U. S. Relations

Both groups shared the similar opinions on this question. More than 70% of each group evaluated the China-U. S. relations as just "so-so," with around 15% believe the bilateral relations are good and about 10% think the relations are bad. Only a very few consider the China-U. S. relations to be very good or very bad. Chinese people have very complicated feelings towards America. On one hand, China and America see a deepening mutual dependence and cooperate on international affairs. On the other hand, the two countries have obvious divergences and conflicts, while the competition becomes increasingly fierce.

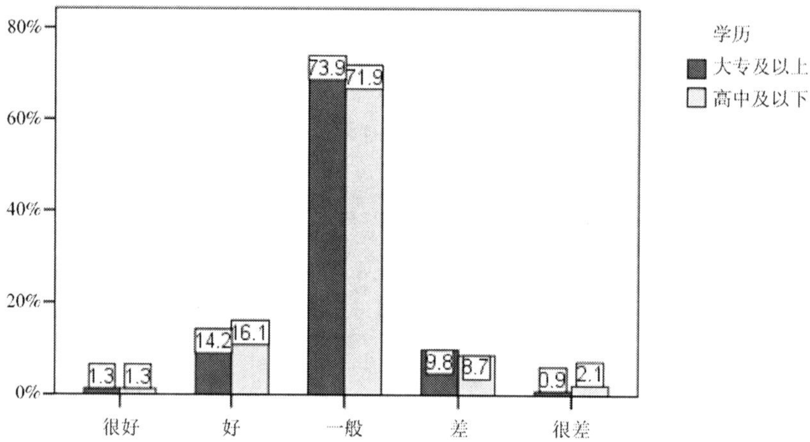

Figure 5-6 How do you view the current China-U. S. relations?

In this picture, 很好 means "very good," 好 means "good," 一般 means "just so-so," 差 means "bad" and 很差 means "very bad."

学历 means educational background, 大专及以上 means "college graduates or above" and 高中及以下 means "high school graduates or below".

(7) Forecast of the Prospects of the China-U. S. Relations

Two groups have different opinions on this question. More than 70% of the first group believed that the China-U. S. relations will develop despite complications, compared to less than 50% of the second group with the same view. This means that most people of the first group did not think the bilateral relations will develop smoothly. However, interviewees in the second group had a very different forecast of the relations, as approximately 30% thought the China-U. S. relations will neither develop nor regress, and 20% believed they will develop smoothly.

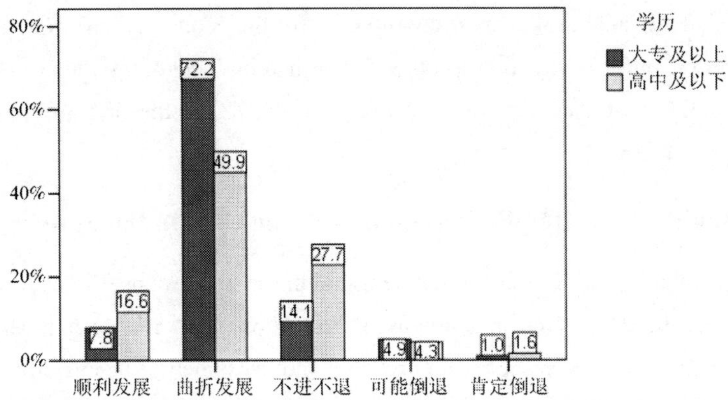

Figure 5-7 What do you think about the prospects of China-U. S. relations?
In this picture, 顺利发展 means "develop smoothly," 曲折发展 means "develop despite twists and turns," 不进不退 means "neither advance nor retreat," 可能倒退 means may regress and 肯定倒退 means "surely regress."
学历 means educational background, 大专及以上 means "college graduates or above" and 高中及以下 means "high school graduates or below".

(8) The Most Important Field or Issue in the Future China-U. S. Relations

Both groups showed a great difference in this question. The first group emphasized more on economy and trade, while the second group focused more on other issues. This means

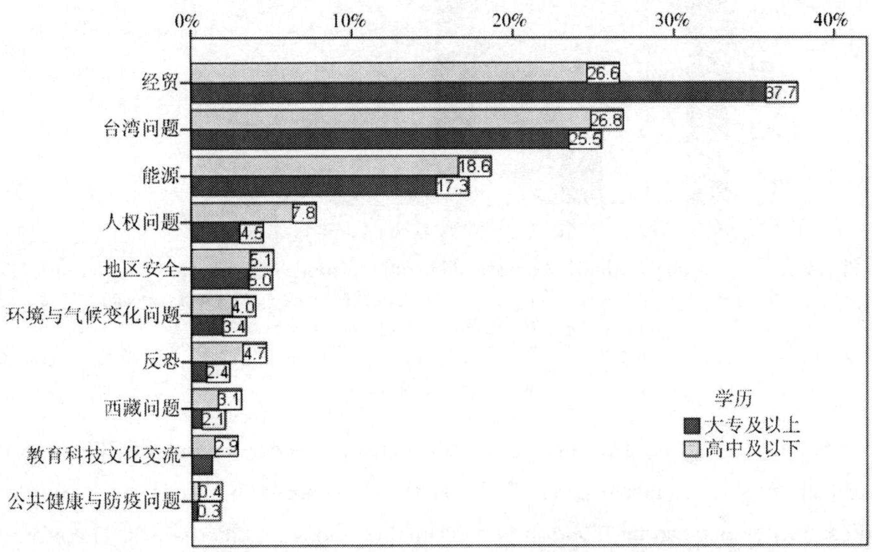

Figure 5-8 What do you think is the most important field or issue in the future China-U. S. relations?
In this picture, 经贸 means "economy and trade," 台湾问题 means "Taiwan issue," 能源 means "energy," 人权问题 means "human rights issue," 地区安全 means "regional safety," 环境与气候变化问题 means "environment and climate change," 反恐 means "anti-terrorism," 西藏问题 means "Tibet issue," 教育科技文化交流 means "exchange of education, science, technology and culture," and 公共健康与防疫问题 means "public health and epidemic prevention."
学历 means educational background, 大专及以上 means "college graduates or above" and 高中及以下 means "high school graduates or below".

that college students and above pay more attention to the economic and trade relations of the two countries, but less attention to other fields than high school graduates or below. A notable situation is that Taiwan issue ranks second (25.5%) in the first group, but first in the second group (26.8%).

(9) How Should China Handle Relations with the U. S. in the Future

Both agreements and differences can be found in the two groups. Firstly, the "bimodal distribution" can be discovered in opinions of both groups, as a large number of people think China shall "adhere to principles more" and another bunch of people advocate to "be more flexbile." However, both groups showed a significant divergence due to different educational levels. Firstly, people from the first group who had acquired higher education were more likely (42.4%) to choose "to be more flexible" than the second group (36.0%). Secondly, the second group showed more support to the current strategy compared to the first group.

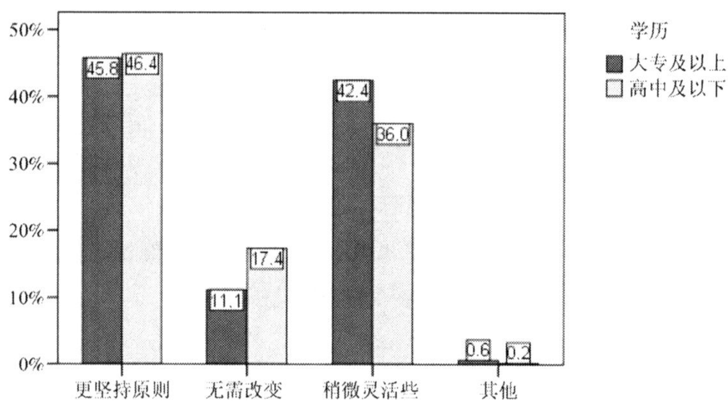

Figure 5-9 How do you think China should handle relations with the U. S. in the future?
In this picture, 更坚持原则 means "adhere to principles more," 无需改变 means "no need to change," 稍微灵活些 means "be more flexible" and 其它 means "others."
学历 means educational background, 大专及以上 means "college graduates or above" and 高中及以下 means "high school graduates or below".

In general, except the two questions of "Americans' understanding of China" and the "general evaluation of current China-U. S. relations" where both groups reach consensus, significant difference can be found in two groups' opinions on other issues. Therefore, the educational level directly affected people's opinions on international issues.

2. Effects of the Regional Factor

The research group divided the interviewees into interviewees in coastal areas and interviewees in inland areas, according to the geographical distribution and different economic conditions of regions. The coastal areas included Shanghai, Guangzhou and Beijing, while the inland areas included Lanzhou, Kunming, Changchun, Zigong and Changsha. Among the 2,687 interviewees, 973 were from coastal areas, accounting for 36.2%; and 1,714 were from inland areas, making up 63.8%.

(1) The Most Representative Symbol of America

Regarding the most representative symbol of America, the top three choices of interviewees in coastal areas were the "White House" (25.4%), "Statue of Liberty" (22.4%) and "Wall Street" (10.7%), while the top three choices for interviewees in inland areas include the "White House" (27.1%), "Statue of Liberty" (18.7%) and "Pentagon" (9.3%). They have similar opinions on this question, as nearly a half of them regard the White House and the Statue of Liberty as the main symbols of America. The difference is that interviewees in coastal areas consider "Wall Street" to be the symbol of America, compared to interviewees in inland areas who consider the "Pentagon" to be the symbol of America.

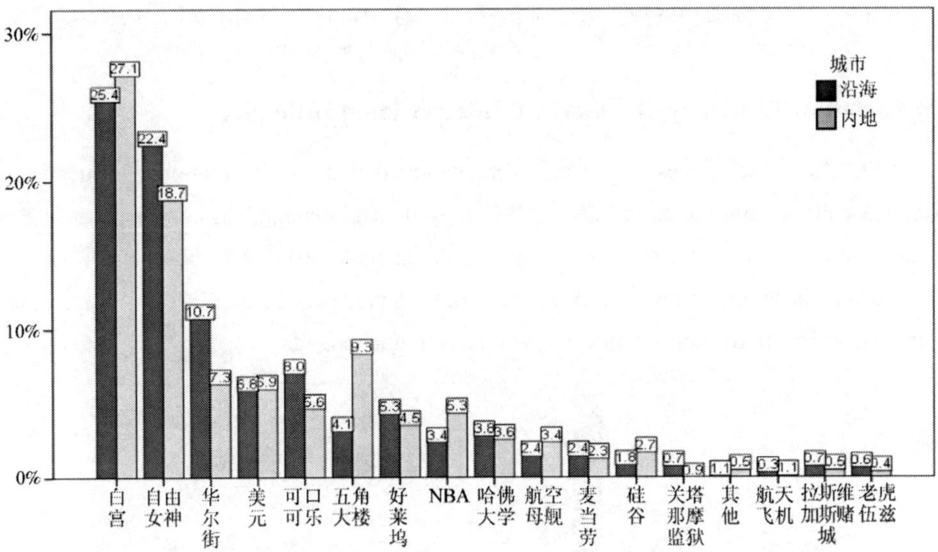

Figure 5-10 What do you think is the most representative symbol of America?

In the picture, 白宫 means the White House, 自由女神 means the Statue of Liberty, 华尔街 means the Wall Street, 美元 means USD, 可口可乐 means Coca-Cola, 五角大楼 means the Pentagon, 好莱坞 means Hollywood, 哈佛大学 means Harvard University, 航空母舰 means the aircraft carriers, 麦当劳 means McDonald, 硅谷 means the Silicon Valley, 关塔那摩监狱 means the Guantánamo Prison, 其它 means others, 航天飞机 means the space shuttle, 拉斯维加斯赌城 means Las Vegas caChinas and 老虎伍兹 means Tiger Woods. 城市 means cities, 沿海 means "in coastal areas" and 内地 means "in inland areas."

(2) Influence of America's Financial Crisis on World Economy

Regarding the influence of the financial crisis in America on world economy, 46.6%

of interviewees in coastal areas answered "very great" and 46.0% answered "great," with 45.9% of interviewees in inland areas who answered "great" and 43.2% answered "very great." We can see that the influence of the financial crisis in America on world economy in coastal-area interviewees' opinions is higher than it in inland-area interviewees' views.

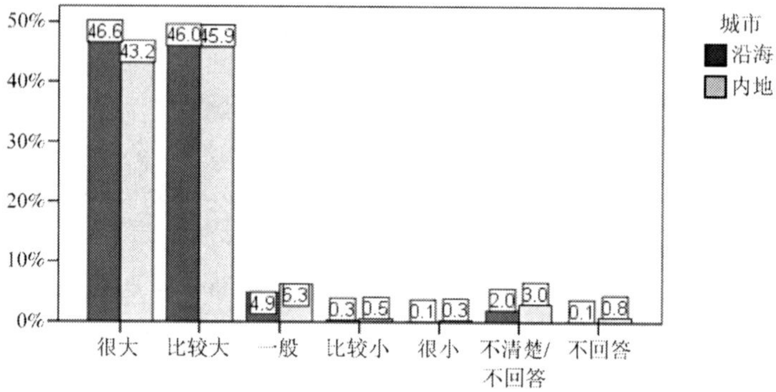

Figure 5-11 What is the impact of American financial crisis on the world economy?
In this picture, 很大 means "very great," 比较大 means "great," 一般 means "just so-so," 比较小 means "small," 很小 means "very small," 不清楚/不回答 means "not clear/don't know" and 不回答 means "no answer." 城市 means cities, 沿海 means "in coastal areas" and 内地 means "in inland areas."

(3) Variation Tendency of American International Influence

56.6% of interviewees in coastal areas believed that the international influence of America will "remain the same" and 21.6% think it will "decline," as compared to 51.3% of interviewees who believed it will "remain the same" and 20.2% of "decline" among interviewees in inland areas. It can be seen that interviewees in both areas share similar opinions, and more than half believed it will remain unchanged.

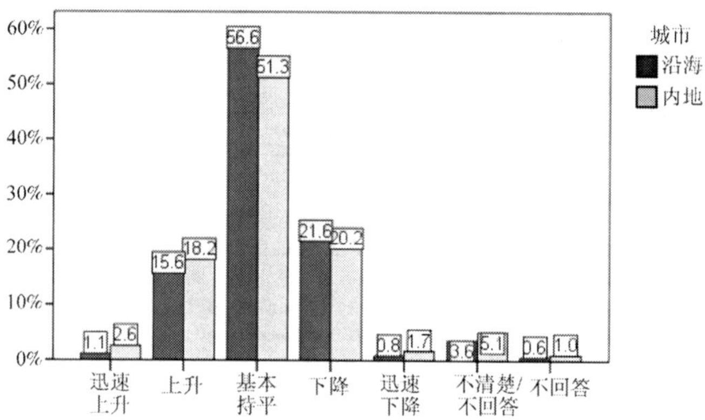

Figure 5-12 How will American international influence change in the future?
In this picture, 迅速上升 means rapidly grow, 上升 means grow, 基本持平 means remain the same, 下降 means decline, 迅速下降 means rapidly decline, 不清楚/不回答 means "not clear/don't know" and 不回答 means "no answer." 城市 means cities, 沿海 means "in coastal areas" and 内地 means "in inland areas."

(4) American's Understanding of China

Regarding American's understanding of China, 42.3% of interviewees in coastal areas thought they "understand little" and 36.7% answered "just so-so," while 40.2% of interviewees in inland areas thought they "understand little" and 38.2% answered "just so-so." Two groups have very similar attitudes, as more than 40% believed that Americans do not understand China.

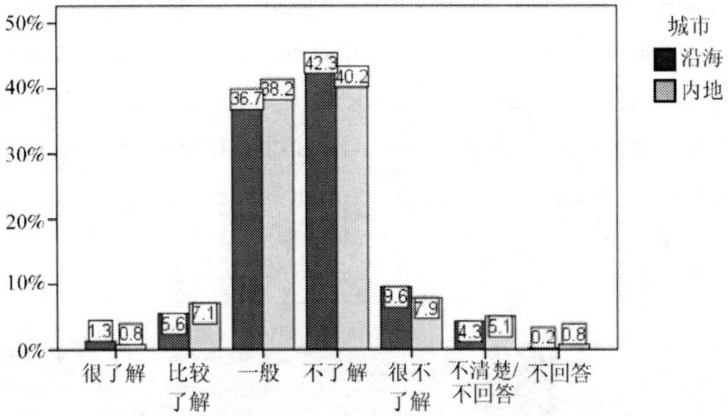

Figure 5-13 How much do you think the average American knows about China?

In this picture, 很了解 means "well understand," 比较了解 means "understand," 一般 means "just so-so," 不了解 means "understand little," 很不了解 means "don't understand at all," 不清楚/不回答 means "not clear/don't know" and 不回答 means "no answer."

城市 means cities, 沿海 means "in coastal areas" and 内地 means "in inland areas."

(5) Chinese People's Understanding of America

52.8% of interviewees in coastal areas thought that common Chinese people have a

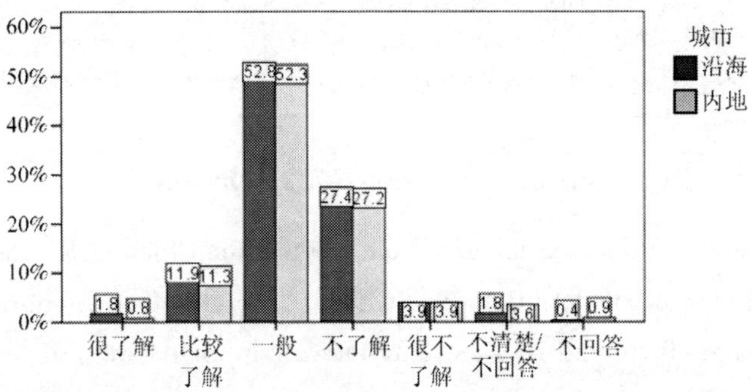

Figure 5-14 How much do you think the average Chinese person knows about the U. S.?

In this picture, 很了解 means "well understand," 比较了解 means "understand," 一般 means "just so-so," 不了解 means "understand little," 很不了解 means "don't understand at all," 不清楚/不回答 means "not clear/don't know" and 不回答 means "no answer."

城市 means cities, 沿海 means "in coastal areas" and 内地 means "in inland areas."

"just so-so" understanding of America and 27.4% answered "understand little," compared to 52.3% and 27.2% of interviewees in inland areas. We can see that interviewees in different areas had very similar opinions on this question, since more than a half believed that common Chinese people have a "just so-so" understanding of America.

(6) General Evaluation of Current China-U. S. Relations

For the evaluation of current China-U. S. relations, 70.5% of interviewees in coastal areas answered "just so-so" and 16.2% answered "good," compared to 68.9% and 12.3% of interviewees in inland areas. We can figure out that interviewees in different areas share the same opinion on the current China-U. S. relations, and more than 70% of them believed that the China-U. S. relations are "just so-so." The little difference lies in that interviewees in coastal areas are more optimistic about the current bilateral relations, demonstrated by a higher proportion of the answer "good."

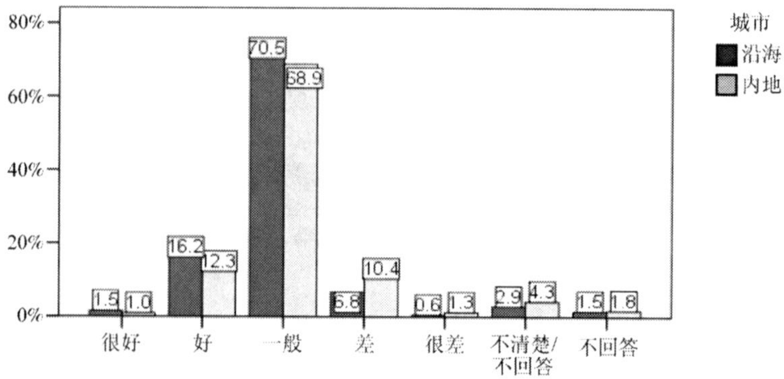

Figure 5-15 How do you view the current China-U. S. relations?

In this picture, 很好 means "very good," 好 means "good," 一般 means "just so-so," 差 means "bad," 很差 means "very bad," 不清楚/不回答 means "not clear/don't know" and 不回答 means "no answer." 城市 means cities, 沿海 means "in coastal areas" and 内地 means "in inland areas."

(7) Forecast of the Prospects of the China-U. S. Relations

66.7% of interviewees in coastal areas believed that the China-U. S. relations will see a development despite probable difficulties, while 12.3% answered "neither advance nor retreat," compared to 60.7% and 16.9% of interviewees in inland areas. It can be seen that two groups of interviewees have similar opinions on the prospects of the China-U. S. relations, and the mainstream opinion is formed as "develop despite twists and turns." However, more inland interviewees think that the China-U. S. relations will remain the current situation, without advance or retreat.

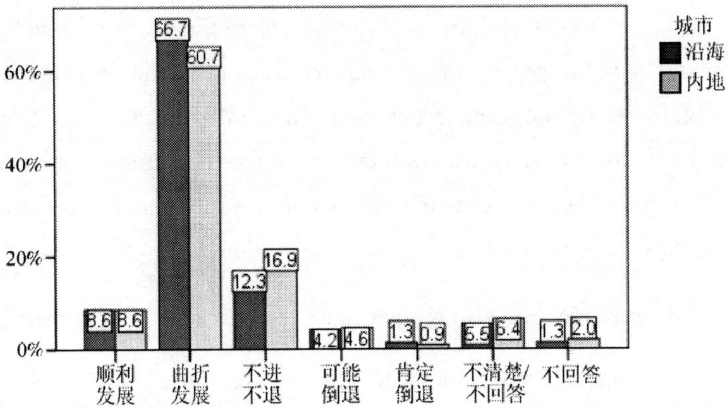

Figure 5-16 What do you think about the prospects of China-U. S. relations?

In this picture, 顺利发展 means "develop smoothly," 曲折发展 means "develop despite twists and turns," 不进不退 means "neither advance nor retreat," 可能倒退 means may regress and 肯定倒退 means "surely regress," 不清楚/不回答 means "not clear/don't know" and 不回答 means "no answer."

城市 means cities, 沿海 means "in coastal areas" and 内地 means "in inland areas."

(8) The Most Important Field or Issue in the Future China-U. S. Relations

In terms of the most important issue in the China-U. S. relations, 44.0% of interviewees

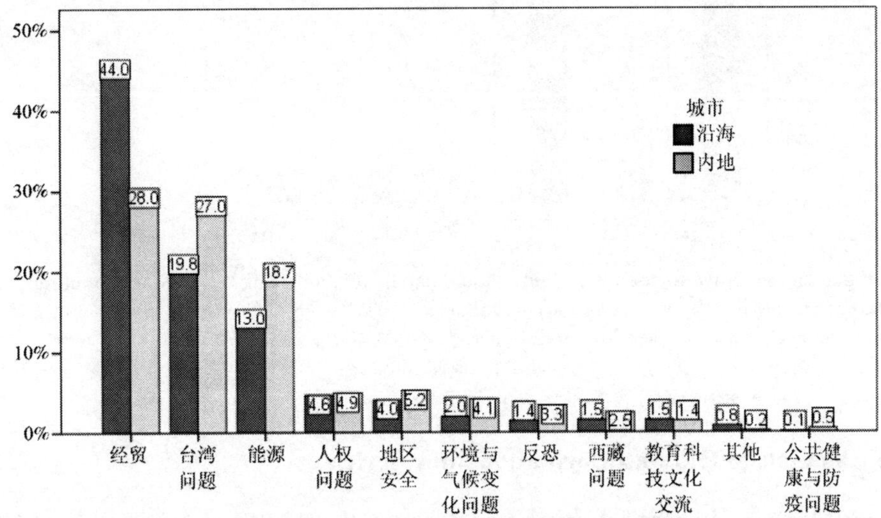

Figure 5-17 What do you think is the most important field or issue in the future China-U. S. relations?

In this picture, 经贸 means "economy and trade," 台湾问题 means "Taiwan issue," 能源 means "energy," 人权问题 means "human rights issue," 地区安全 means "regional safety," 环境与气候变化问题 means "environment and climate change," 反恐 means "anti-terrorism," 西藏问题 means "Tibet issue," 教育科技文化交流 means "exchange of education, science, technology and culture," 其它 means "others" and 公共健康与防疫问题 means "public health and epidemic prevention."

城市 means cities, 沿海 means "in coastal areas" and 内地 means "in inland areas."

in coastal areas chose "economy and trade," 19.8% selected the "Taiwan issue" and 13.0% chose "energy issue," and the proportions for interviewees in inland areas are respectively 28.0%, 27.0% and 18.7% on the same issues. We can see that interviewees from all areas regarded the economy and trade, Taiwan and energy as the most important issues, while a larger proportion of interviewees in coastal areas paid more attention to economy and trade, compared to interviewees in inland areas.

(9) How China Should Handle the Relations with the U. S. in the Future

With regard for how China should handle the relations with U. S., 41.7% of interviewees in coastal areas think China should "adhere to principles more," followed by 39.7% believed China should "be more flexible." 43.2% of interviewees in inland areas thought China should "adhere to principles more," and 37.6% believed China should "be more flexible." It is clear that both groups share the similar opinion on this issue, and more than 40% interviewees hope that China can adhere to principles more in the bilateral relations.

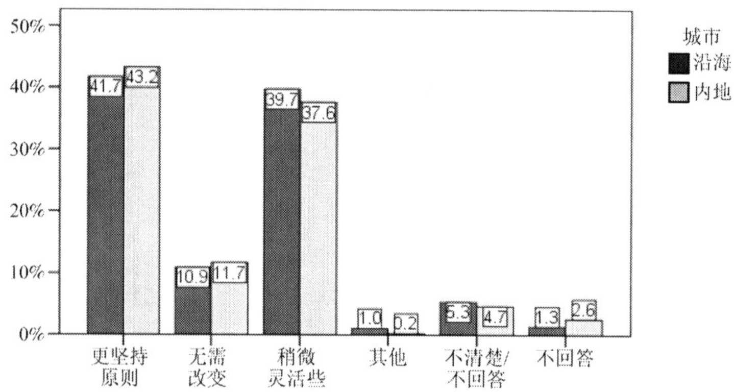

Figure 5-18 How do you think China should handle relations with the U. S. in the future?
In this picture, 更坚持原则 means "adhere to principles more," 无需改变 means "no need to change," 稍微灵活些 means "be more flexible," 其它 means "others," 不清楚/不回答 means "not clear/don't know" and 不回答 means "no answer."
城市 means cities, 沿海 means "in coastal areas" and 内地 means "in inland areas."

(10) Channels to Obtain Information on America

For channels to obtain information on America, the top three among interviewees in coastal areas include the internet (31.4%), television (29.2) and newspaper and magazines (21.0%); but for interviewees in inland areas, top 3 include TV (32.6%), Internet (29.6%) and newspaper and magazines (21.8%). We can see that interviewees in different areas show differences in the channels to obtain information on America, since more interviewees in coastal areas utilized the internet and inland interviewees used television more. This may be a result from the preference of different media by different groups and different infiltration of the internet in different areas. Moreover, interviewees in both coastal and inland areas obtained information averagely from several channels and do not show an over-dependence on any one particular media. Four characteristics can be summarized based on the answers of interviewees in coastal and inland areas: Firstly, no significant divergence can be seen between the two groups; Secondly, interviewees in coastal areas give more concentrative answers compared to interviewees in inland areas. In the eight questions that both groups had the same preference, the proportions of the first choices in six questions of interviewees in coastal areas are higher than interviewees in inland areas. First choices of eight questions for interviewees in coastal areas exceed the proportion of 40%, compared to seven for interviewees in inland areas; Thirdly, the proportion of "don't know/not clear" is higher among inland interviewees. In the nine questions with the answer of "don't know/not clear," the proportion of this option for inland interviewees in seven questions is higher than interviewees in coastal areas. This reflects that inland interviewees may have a less understanding of these questions, or they have other opinions; Fourthly, more interviewees in inland areas choose "no response." In the nine questions with the answer of "no response," two groups shared the same proportion in the "no response" choice in one question, while in the seven out of the other eight questions, the proportion of interviewees selecting "no response" is higher than interviewees in coastal areas.

VI. Effects of Professions and Incomes

1. Influence of the Profession Factor on Interviewees' Opinions

One of the focuses of the investigation was how the profession factor affected interviewees' opinions on America and China-U. S. relations. According to the 2,646 valid questionnaires recalled, the interviewees included (in descending order) students (33.9%), professional technicians (12.7%), workers (10.1%), commercial services personnel (8.4%), others (8.2%), education, science, culture, health and sports personnel (6.5%), enterprise managers (6.5%), civil servants (5.6%), owners of privately or individually-owned business (3.8%), retired personnel (2.2%) and soldiers (1.5%).[247]

---

247 Since the questionnaires were mainly distributed to universities, communities and enterprises of the eight cities, only a few peasants, mainly civilian workers, accounting for only 0.6%, are included in the survey. Since the profession only incorporates a few people and thus cannot be regarded as the representative, it is ignored in the analysis.

Table 6-1 Professions of Interviewees

Profession	Number of people	Proporti-on	Profession	Number of people	Proporti-on
students	897	33.9	enterprise managers	172	6.5
professional technicians	336	12.7	civil servants	149	5.6
workers	268	10.1	owners of privately or individually-owned business	101	3.8
commercial services personnel	221	8.4	retired personnel	57	2.2
Others	218	8.2	soldiers	40	1.5
education, science, culture, health and sports (ESCH) personnel	172	6.5	peasants	15	0.6

(1) The Most Representative Symbol of America

The White House and the Statue of Liberty are selected as the two most representative symbols of America among all professions. Except for owners of privately or individually-owned business, the White House is the first choice for all other professions, followed by the Statue of Liberty, which demonstrates that many people tend to view America in terms of politics and value. The third place is given to USD, Coca-Cola, Wall Street or the Pentagon, reflecting the subtle difference on the perception of America among different professions. Compared with other professions who view America economically, some soldiers, workers and people of other professions tend to view America from the perspective of military.

Table 6-2 What do you think is the most representative symbol of America?

	civil servants	ESCH personnel	Enterpr-ise manag-ers	owners of private busine-ss	Profess-ional technic-ians	students	commercial services person-nel	workers	Peasan-ts	soldiers	retired person-nel	others	overall
White House	32.2	24.7	28.7	15.0	26.8	23.0	23.6	22.7	20.0	37.5	36.5	44.3	26.4%
Statue of Liberty	16.1	21.2	15.8	19.0	21.1	21.4	19.9	21.1	13.3	15.0	13.5	18.4	19.9%
Wall Street	8.1	8.2	8.8	11.0	6.9	10.9	13.0	3.1		7.5	1.9	5.7	8.6%
Pentagon	6.7	2.4	8.8	9.0	6.9	4.5	7.9	18.4	26.7	7.5	11.5	7.1	7.4%
USD	10.7	7.6	7.6	11.0	9.0	5.7	6.5	5.9		2.5	9.6	6.1	7.0%
Coca-Cola	8.7	11.8	9.4	6.0	6.9	6.3	6.5	4.7	6.7	5.0	1.9	2.4	6.5%
Hollywood	3.4	4.7	2.9	7.0	3.3	6.0	6.5	3.9	6.7	2.5	9.6	2.4	4.8%
NBA	2.7	1.2	2.9	6.0	4.5	5.3	4.6	5.9	13.3	2.5	3.8	6.1	4.7%
Harvard University	1.3	7.1	4.1	3.0	2.7	3.6	5.1	2.7		7.5	3.8	2.8	3.6%
Aircraft carrier	4.0	1.2	3.5	1.0	3.9	3.7	0.9	3.5	6.7	2.5		1.9	3.0%
Silicon valley	2.0	1.2	1.2	2.0	0.9	5.1	0.9			2.5		0.5	2.4%
McDonald's	2.0	2.4	2.9	3.0	1.2	1.6	2.8	6.2	6.7	2.5	1.9	1.4	2.4%
Space shuttle		2.9	0.6	3.0	1.5	0.3		0.4		5.0			0.8%
Guantánamo prison			1.2	1.0	2.4	1.1		0.4					0.8%
Others		2.4		2.0	0.9	0.3	0.9				3.8	0.5	0.7%
Las Vegas caChinas	1.3	0.6	1.8	1.0		0.6	0.9	0.4					0.6%
Tiger Woods	0.7	0.6			0.9	0.3		0.8			1.9	0.5	0.5%

(2) Influence of the American Financial Crisis on World Economy

Most interviewees consider the influence of the financial crisis in America on world economy to be "very great" and "great." The sum of the proportion of these two choices of all interviewees are listed as below in a descending order: students (95.3%), civil servants (95.1%), commercial services personnel (94.0%), professional technicians (93.1%), education, science, culture, health and sports personnel (92.8%), workers (90.1%), enterprise managers (89.9%) and owners of privately or individually-owned business (85.1%) (see figure below). This demonstrates that interviewees of all professions believe that America's economy has a great impact on world economy, especially for professional technicians, students, enterprise managers and civil servants. For the four professions, the proportions of the choice "very great" are respectively 9.9%, 4.5%, 3.5% and 3.5% higher than the proportion of the choice "great."

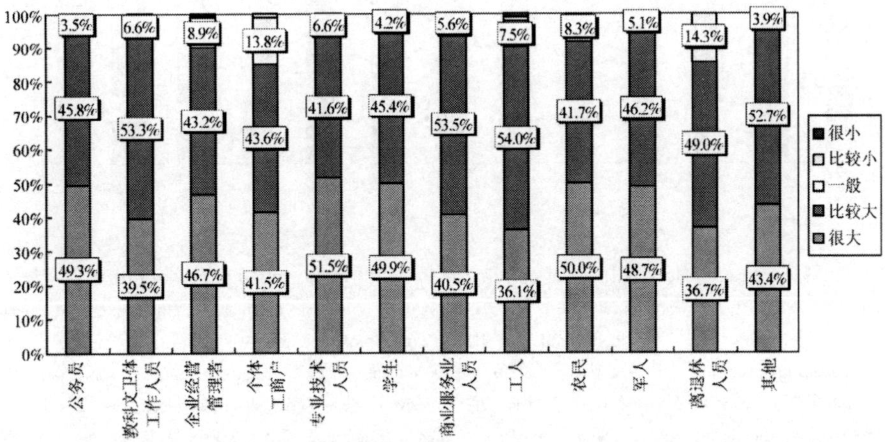

Figure 6-1 What is the impact of the American financial crisis on world economy?

In this picture, 很大 means "very great," 比较大 means "great," 一般 means "just so-so," 比较小 means "small" and 很小 means "very small."

公务员 means "civil servants," 教科文卫体工作人员 means "education, science, culture, health and sports personnel," 企业经营管理者 means "enterprise managers," 个体工商户 means "owners of privately or individually-owned business," 专业技术人员 means "professional technicians," 学生 means "students," 商业服务业人员 means "commercial services personnel," 工人 means "workers," 农民 means "peasants," 军人 means "soldiers," 离退休人员 means "retired personnel" and 其它 means "others."

(3) Variation Tendency of American International Influence

Most interviewees of all professions chose "remain the same," while many others choose "rise" or "decline." Groups that chose "rise" more than "decline" include civil servants (a margin of 12.9%), education, science, culture, health and sports personnel (a margin of 4.2%), professional technicians (a margin of 2.6%) and others (a margin of 6%), while retired personnel, workers, enterprise managers, owners of privately or individually-owned business, students, and commercial services personnel chose "decline" over "rise." Soldiers are divided between "rise" and "decline." It reflects that both a certain consensus and significant divergence exist in the opinions of interviewees of different professions on the variation tendency of American international influence.

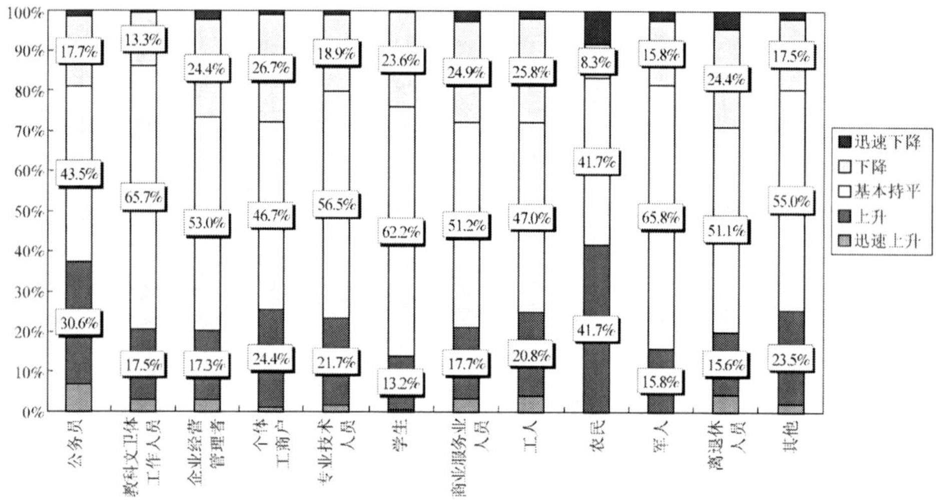

Figure 6-2 How will American international influence change in the future?

In this picture, 迅速上升 means rapidly grow, 上升 means grow, 基本持平 means remain the same, 下降 means decline and 迅速下降 means rapidly decline.

公务员 means "civil servants," 教科文卫体工作人员 means "education, science, culture, health and sports personnel," 企业经营管理者 means "enterprise managers," 个体工商户 means "owners of privately or individually-owned business," 专业技术人员 means "professional technicians," 学生 means "students," 商业服务业人员 means "commercial services personnel," 工人 means "workers," 农民 means "peasants," 军人 means "soldiers," 离退休人员 means "retired personnel" and 其它 means "others."

(4) American's Understanding of China

Most interviewees of all professions chose "just so-so" and "understand little," and the sums of proportions of the two choices for different professions are listed as below indescending order: enterprise managers 78.1%; commercial services personnel 78.4%; civil servants 79.1%; workers 81.5%; students 83.3%; professional technicians 83.8%; owners of privately or individually-owned business 84.0%; education, science, culture, health and sports personnel 85.8%; others 86.1%; retired personnel 89.7%; and soldiers 95%. In particular, 47.4% of professional technicians, 48% of students, 50% soldiers and private business owners think Americans do not understand China.

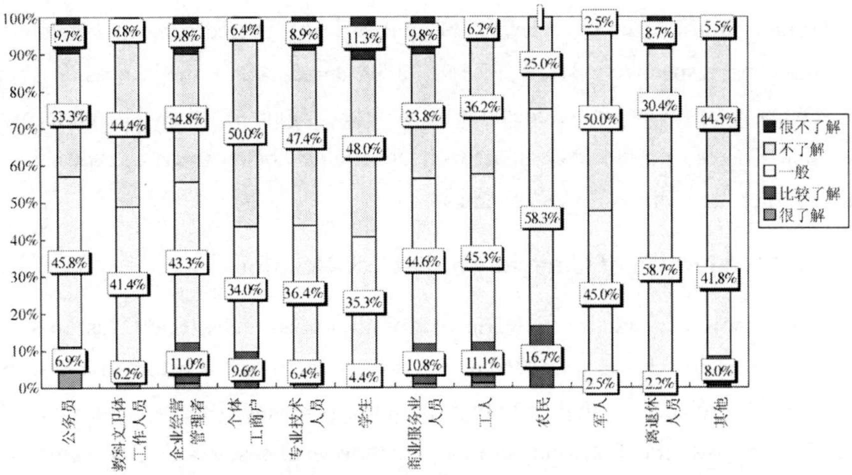

Figure 6-3 How much do you think the average American knows about China?

In this picture, 很了解 means "well understand," 比较了解 means "understand," 一般 means "just so-so," 不了解 means "understand little" and 很不了解 means "don't understand at all."

公务员 means "civil servants," 教科文卫体工作人员 means "education, science, culture, health and sports personnel," 企业经营管理者 means "enterprise managers," 个体工商户 means "owners of privately or individually-owned business," 专业技术人员 means "professional technicians," 学生 means "students," 商业服务业人员 means "commercial services personnel," 工人 means "workers," 农民 means "peasants," 军人 means "soldiers," 离退休人员 means "retired personnel" and 其它 means "others."

(5) Chinese People's Understanding of America

Nearly or more than half of interviewees of all professions selected "just so-so," followed

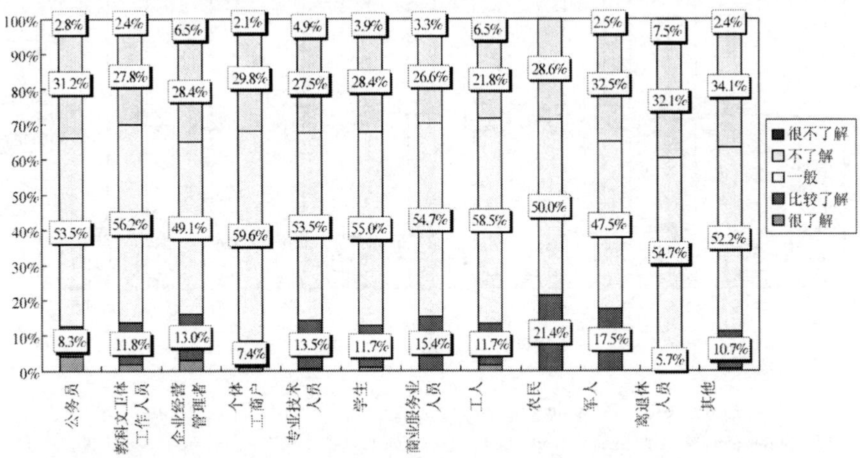

Figure 6-4 How much do you think the average Chinese person knows about the U. S.?

In this picture, 很了解 means "well understand," 比较了解 means "understand," 一般 means "just so-so," 不了解 means "understand little" and 很不了解 means "don't understand at all."

公务员 means "civil servants," 教科文卫体工作人员 means "education, science, culture, health and sports personnel," 企业经营管理者 means "enterprise managers," 个体工商户 means "owners of privately or individually-owned business," 专业技术人员 means "professional technicians," 学生 means "students," 商业服务业人员 means "commercial services personnel," 工人 means "workers," 农民 means "peasants," 军人 means "soldiers," 离退休人员 means "retired personnel" and 其它 means "others."

by "understand little." More interviewees of civil servants, retired personnel, soldiers and other professions, respectively 31.2%, 32.1%, 32.5% and 34.1% of the professions, believe that the common Chinese person does not know much about America. Therefore, we can surmise that Chinese people have limited understanding about America, especially civil servants, soldiers and retired personnel and so on.

(6) General Evaluation of Current China-U. S. Relations

Nearly or more than a half of interviewees of all professions selected "just so-so," and the proportions of this choice for different professions are listed as below in a descending order: education, science, culture, health and sports personnel (81.1%); others (76.9%); students (75.5%); owners of privately or individually-owned business (74.7%); professional technicians (73.8%); workers (73.5%); soldiers (71.8%); civil servants (71.7%); retired personnel (70.8%); enterprise managers (69.5%) and commercial services personnel (66.2%). The choices of "good" or "bad" were placed as the second and third place, respectively, while more people chose "good." Only a small proportion of all professions selected "very good" or "very bad." This reflects that most interviewees hold a "so-so" evaluation of the current China-U. S. relations.

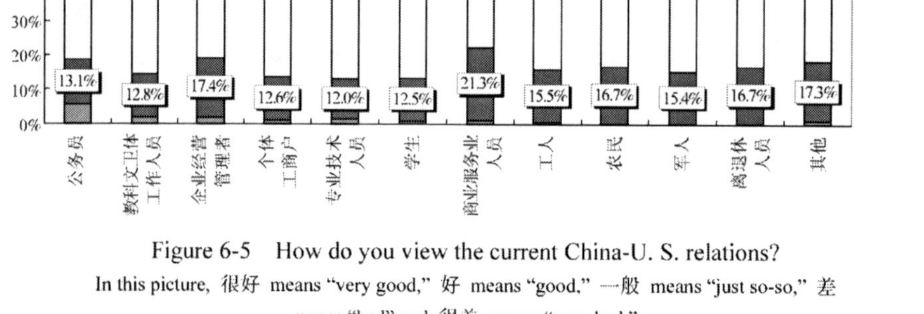

Figure 6-5 How do you view the current China-U. S. relations?

In this picture, 很好 means "very good," 好 means "good," 一般 means "just so-so," 差 means "bad" and 很差 means "very bad."

公务员 means "civil servants," 教科文卫体工作人员 means "education, science, culture, health and sports personnel," 企业经营管理者 means "enterprise managers," 个体工商户 means "owners of privately or individually-owned business," 专业技术人员 means "professional technicians," 学生 means "students," 商业服务业人员 means "commercial services personnel," 工人 means "workers," 农民 means "peasants," 军人 means "soldiers," 离退休人员 means "retired personnel" and 其它 means "others."

(7) Forecast of the Prospects of the China-U. S. Relations

Most interviewees in all professions chose "develop despite twists and turns." More interviewees of education, science, culture, health and sports personnel, students and soldiers, respectively, 71.5%, 74.6% and 76.3% of the professions, selected the "develop despite twists and turns." It means that interviewees of all professions are cautiously optimistic about the prospects of the China-U. S. relations.

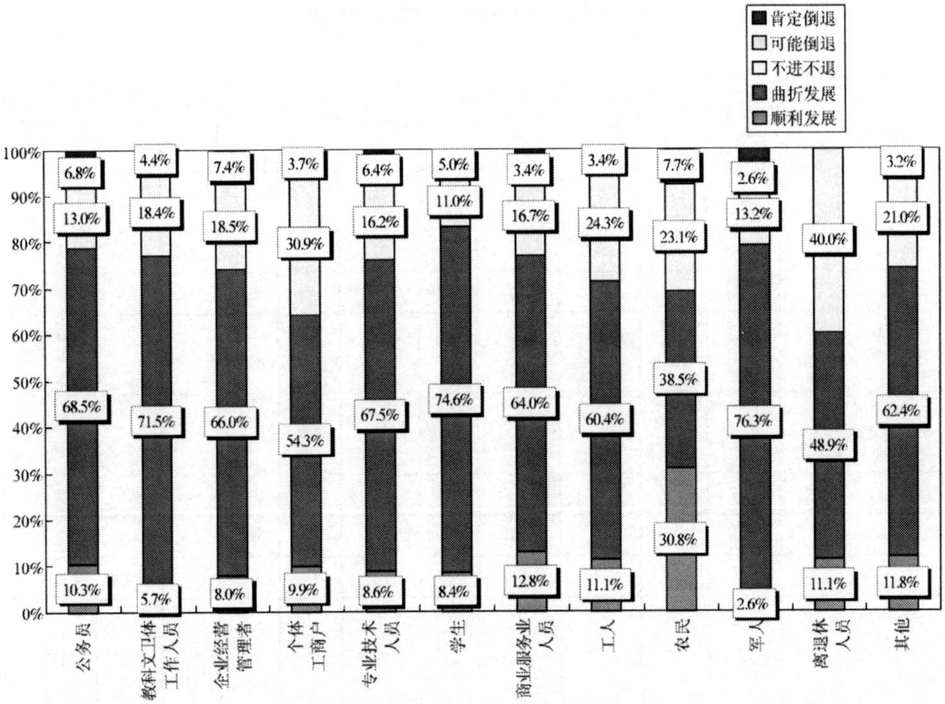

Figure 6-6 What do you think about the prospects of China-U. S. relations?

In this picture, 顺利发展 means "develop smoothly," 曲折发展 means "develop despite twists and turns," 不进不退 means "neither advance nor retreat," 可能倒退 means may regress and 肯定倒退 means "surely regress." 公务员 means "civil servants," 教科文卫体工作人员 means "education, science, culture, health and sports personnel," 企业经营管理者 means "enterprise managers," 个体工商户 means "owners of privately or individually-owned business," 专业技术人员 means "professional technicians," 学生 means "students," 商业服务业人员 means "commercial services personnel," 工人 means "workers," 农民 means "peasants," 军人 means "soldiers," 离退休人员 means "retired personnel" and 其它 means "others."

(8) The Most Important Issue or Field in the China-U. S. Relations in the Future

Out of the eleven options, interviewees of all professions selected the economy and trade, energy and the Taiwan issue as the most important issues in the China-U. S. relations.

Most soldiers and retired personnel chose the Taiwan issue (respectively in 33.3% and 31.7%), while the first choices of other professions are all "economy and trade." Energy was selected as the second most important issue by civil servants and the education, science, culture, health and sports personnel, compared to the Taiwan issue as the second place in other professions. It can be surmised that interviewees in different professions have significantly different opinions on this question.

Table 6-3 What do you think is the most important field or issue in the future China-U. S. relations?

Professions / Most important issue or field	civil servants	education, science, culture, health and sports personnel	enterprise managers	owners of privately or individually -owned business	Professional technicians	students	commercial services personnel	Workers	Peasants	Soldiers	retired personnel	Others	Total
Economy and trade	35.1	40.5	28.7	28.2	36.0	40.7	40.1	25.5	13.3	28.2	22.0	33.0	35.7%
Energy	20.3	22.1	18.3	23.5	19.3	13.4	21.7	16.5	13.3	17.9	14.6	21.8	17.6%
Anti-terrorism	5.4	0.6	5.5	3.5	4.0	1.5	1.9	3.3	6.7	2.6	9.8	2.0	2.8%
Environment and climate change	4.7	2.5	3.0	7.1	2.5	2.6	3.4	4.1		2.6		8.1	3.5%
Public health and epidemic prevention	1.4		1.2			0.4	0.5	0.4					0.4%
Taiwan issue	18.2	21.5	26.2	24.7	20.8	29.8	23.7	24.7	53.3	33.3	31.7	22.8	25.6%
Tibet issue	4.1	1.2	1.2	2.4	2.5	1.4	1.4	4.5	6.7	2.6	4.9	3.6	2.3%
Human rights	5.4	3.7	7.3	7.1	6.5	3.6	2.9	9.5			12.2	4.1	5.1%
Exchange of education, science, technology and culture		1.2	1.2		1.2	2.4	1.4	1.6	6.7	2.6		1.0	1.6%
Regional safety	4.7	6.7	6.7	3.5	6.5	3.9	1.9	9.9		10.3	4.9	2.5	5.1%
Others	0.7		0.6		0.6	0.4	1.0					1.0	0.4%

(9) How China Should Handle Relations with America

In terms of how China should handle the relations with America, the first two places were given to "adhere to principles more" and "be more flexible," for all professions, while both choices far exceeded the "no need to change." More civil servants and education, science, culture, health and sports personnel hope China will "be more flexible" (the proportions of "be more flexible" of the two professions are respectively 2.1% and 22.2%

higher than the proportions of "adhere to principles more"), but for other professions, more people chose "adhere to principles more" than "be more flexible." This suggests that interviewees of all professions tend to change the current policies somehow, but different professions have different attitude on the direction of change. The education, science, culture, health and sports personnel prefer a more flexible method, and "others" and soldiers tend to be more firm.

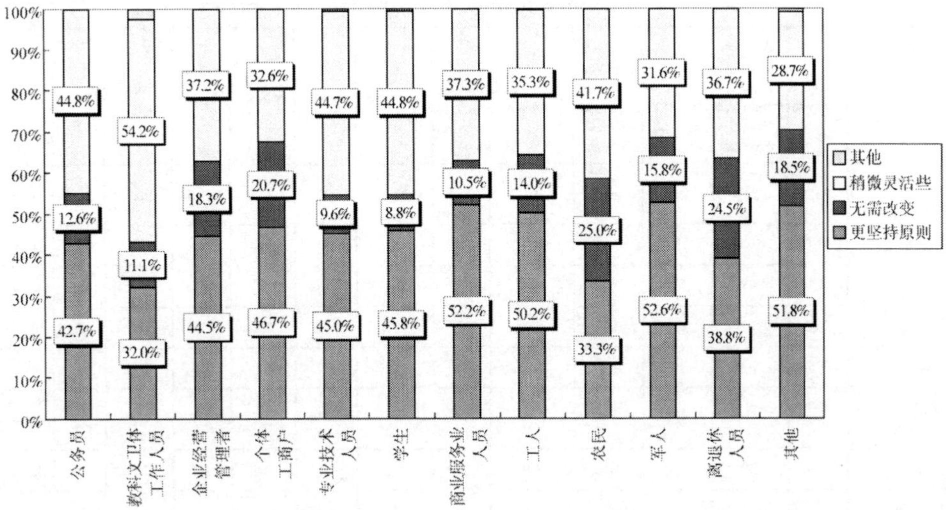

Figure 6-7 How do you think China should handle relations with the U. S. in the future?

In this picture, 更坚持原则 means "adhere to principles more," 无需改变 means "no need to change," 稍微灵活些 means "be more flexible" and 其它 means "others."

公务员 means "civil servants," 教科文卫体工作人员 means "education, science, culture, health and sports personnel," 企业经营管理者 means "enterprise managers," 个体工商户 means "owners of privately or individually-owned business," 专业技术人员 means "professional technicians," 学生 means "students," 商业服务业人员 means "commercial services personnel," 工人 means "workers," 农民 means "peasants," 军人 means "soldiers," 离退休人员 means "retired personnel" and 其它 means "others."

(10) Channels to Obtain Information on America

With the exception of retired personnel (13.3% of them choose "broadcast," compared to 11.7% choice of "internet"), other professions mostly gave answers of "TV," "internet" and "newspaper and magazines." "Internet" was the first choice for education, science, culture, health and sports personnel, professional technicians, students and soldiers, followed by "TV" as the second choice, while "TV" was the first choice of civil servants, enterprise managers, owners of privately or individually-owned business, commercial services personnel, workers, retired personnel and other professions. The third position was given to newspaper and magazines for all professions except the retired personnel (their second choice was "newspaper and magazines"). We can see that TV, internet and newspaper and magazines are the main channels for all professions to obtain information on America, but differences still exist between the different professions. Education, science, culture, health and sports personnel, professional technicians, students and soldiers tend to obtain information on America via the internet.

Table 6-4 Channels to obtain information on America

Professions / Channel	civil servants	education, science, culture, health and sports personnel	enterprise managers	owners of privately or individually-owned business	Professional technicians	students	commercial services personnel	Workers	Peasants	Soldiers	retired personnel	Others	Total
Newspaper and magazines	23.0	20.9	18.4	20.9	19.7	22.1	18.1	22.5	27.3	25.5	26.7	24.4	21.6%
TV	31.5	29.5	32.1	35.1	30.6	27.2	35.3	38.9	36.4	28.6	39.2	34.4	31.3%
Broadcast	5.7	5.8	7.0	9.8	6.7	2.4	6.2	8.6	12.1	4.1	13.3	6.5	5.5%
Internet	29.2	30.9	29.8	25.3	32.2	34.4	28.9	23.2	9.1	34.7	11.7	27.3	30.3%
Textbooks	2.6	3.2	0.7	3.1	1.5	4.8	2.8	1.4	6.1	1.0	0.0	1.1	2.9%
Academic journals	3.4	3.7	2.6	2.2	2.5	5.2	1.2	0.7	3.0	2.0	1.7	1.3	3.2%
Visit abroad	1.0	1.9	4.4	0.9	1.9	0.8	1.2	0.7	0.0	1.0	1.7	0.8	1.3%
Relatives, friends and colleagues	3.4	3.7	5.1	2.7	4.2	2.7	6.0	3.8	0.0	3.1	5.8	3.4	3.6%
Other channels	0.3	0.5	0.0	0.0	0.6	0.4	0.2	0.2	6.1	0.0	0.0	0.8	0.4%
Total	100%	100%	100%	100%	100%	100%	100%	100%	100%	100%	100%	100%	100.0%

Three features can be summarized from the perspective of professions: Firstly, interviewees of different professions reached a consensus on the macro opinion on America and China-U. S. relations, but also have divergences in specific questions. However, these divergences are reflected as divergences under consensuses; Secondly, professions can affect interviewees' perspectives on certain issues. They believe America's influence is rising from the perspectives of politics and culture, but consider its influence to decline in the economic perspective; Thirdly, civil servants and education, science, culture, health and sports personnel share similar opinions on the influence of America, the most important field or issue in China-U. S. relations and how to handle the relations with America. Some of the interviewees of the two professions think that America's international influence will rise, the energy issue will play a more important role than Taiwan issue in the future

China-U. S. relations and advocate for more flexible method to handle the relations with America.

2. Analysis of the Income Factor

The research group divided the incomes of interviewees in 2009 (including wages, bonuses, revenue incomes and investment incomes) into seven levels: 1) no income; 2) below 12,000; 3) 12,000~36,000; 4) 36,000~60,000; 5) 60,000~120,000; 6: above 120,000, in order to study the similarities and differences of interviews of the same income level. (All incomes mentioned in this chapter refer to an annual income in a unit of RMB yuan) 2,374 interviewees filled in their income status in 2009. 27.2% fill in no income, matching the 1/3 of students of interviewees. Interviewees with an annual income below 12,000 accounted for 11.7%, 12,000~36,000 (21.3%), 36,000~60,000 (14.7%), 60,000~120,000 (10.2%), and interviewees with an annual income account for only 3.3%.

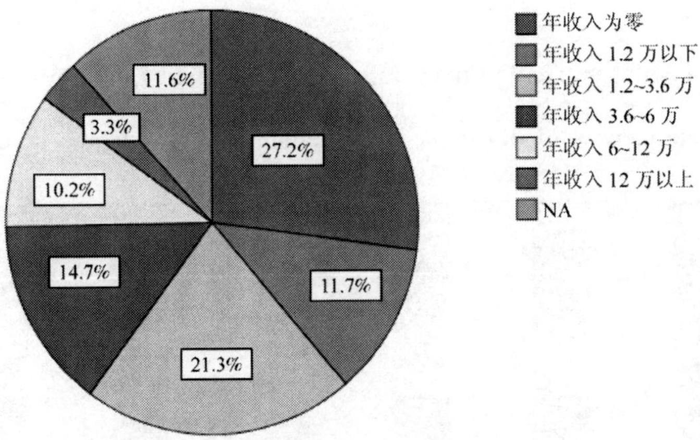

Figure 6-8 Income Levels of Interviewees

年收入为零 means "no income," 年收入 1.2 万以下 means "below 12,000," 年收入 1.2~3.6 万 means "12,000~36,000," 年收入 3.6~6 万 means "36,000~60,000," 年收入 6 万~12 万 means "60,000 ~ 120,000," and 年收入 12 以上 means "above 120,000."

(1) Most Representitive Symbol of America

Income has a significant effect on the answers to the "most representitive symbol of America" question. The proportions of the White House, Hollywood and Silicon Valley chosen by the interviewees with an annual income below 12,000 yuan were higher than the average level, which shows a significant difference with interviewees with an annual income above 12,000 yuan. More interviewees with an annual income between 12,000 and 60,000 selected the White House and USD more than other interviewees. For interviewees with an annual income between 60,000 and 120,000, they tended to choose space shuttle, Las Vegas caChinas, Coca-Cola and USD. This demonstrates that interviewees with different income levels have different opinions on the most representative symbol of America.

Table 6-5 What do you think is the most representative symbol of America? (%)

Symbol \ Income	Annual income below 12,000	Annual income from 12,000~36,000	Annual income from 36,000~ 60,000	Annual income from 60,000~120,000	Annual income above 120,000	Total
White House	28.5	28.8	30.5	24.5	24.4	27.0
Hollywood	5.3	4.4	4.4	4.1	1.1	4.5
Silicon Valley	3.0	0.9	0.5	1.5	1.1	2.3
Space shuttle	0.3	0.2	1.3	2.2	1.1	0.8
Las Vegas caChinas		0.2	1.3	1.1	1.1	0.5
Coca-Cola	5.0	4.6	7.2	7.8	6.7	6.3
USD	4.6	7.3	9.3	7.8	7.8	7.1

(2) Influence of America's Financial Crisis on World Economy

Most interviewees of all income levels thought it has "very great influence" or "great

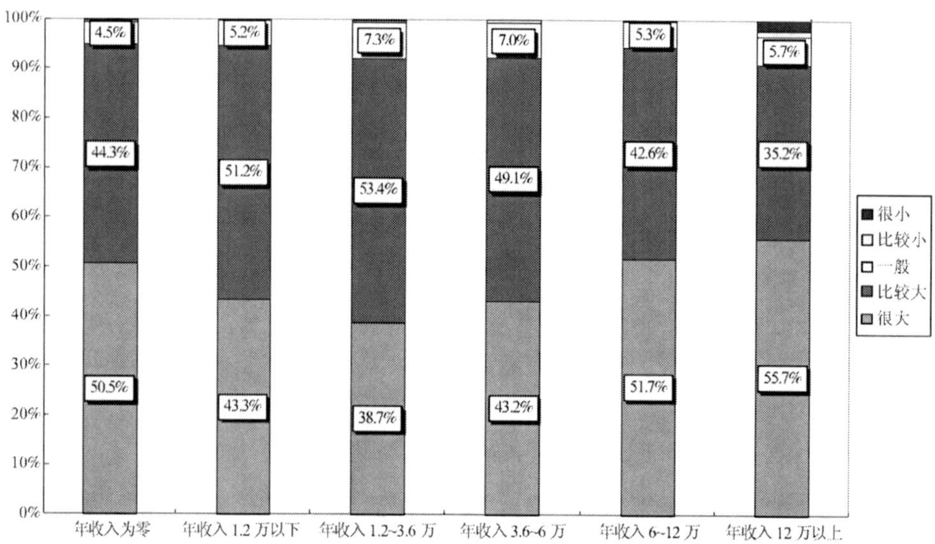

Figure 6-9 What is the impact of American financial crisis on the world economy?

In this picture, 很大 means "very great," 比较大 means "great," 一般 means "just so-so," 比较小 means "small" and 很小 means "very small."

年收入为零 means "no income," 年收入 1.2 万以下 means "below 12,000," 年收入 1.2~3.6 万 means "12,000~36,000," 年收入 3.6~6 万 means "36,000~60,000," 年收入 6 万~12 万 means "60,000 ~ 120,000," and 年收入 12 以上 means "above 120,000."

influence." More than half of the interviewees with no income, an annual income between 60,000 and 120,000 and above 120,000 chose "great influence," while 38.7% of interviewees with an annual income between 12,000 and 36,000 answered "very great influence" and 53.4% of them answered "great influence." Generally, it is widely accepted by interviewees of all income levels that "America's financial influence has a great impact on world economy."

(3) Variation Tendency of America's International Influence

Most interviewees at every income level believed that America's international influence will "remain the same," and the choice exceeded 50% of answers to this question at all levels. More than 60% of interviewees with no income selected "remain the same" for the question. The proportions of the choice of "rise" or "decline" were similar in all groups, without significant polarization. Extremely few people of every income level, less than 5% of every group, chose "rapidly rise" or "rapidly decline." It suggests that most interviewees share the same opinion that America's international influence will remain the same.

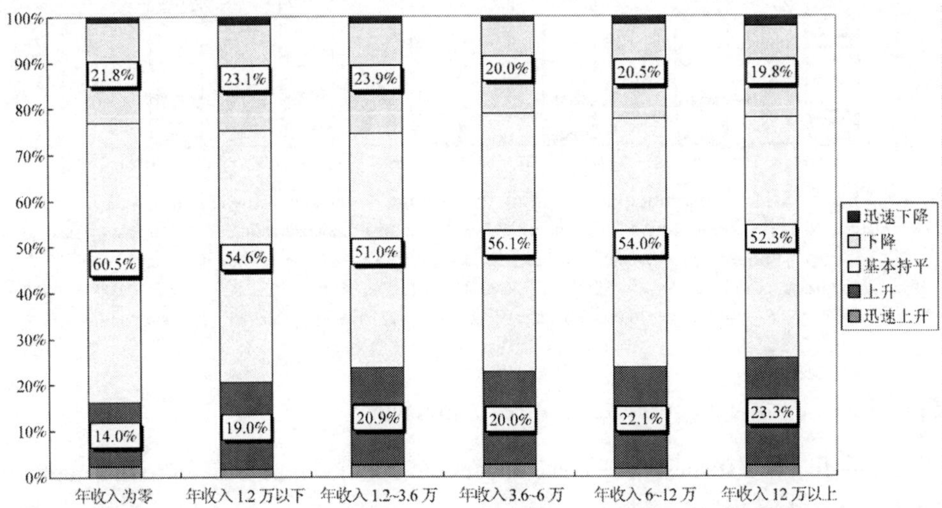

Figure 6-10 How will American international influence change in the future?

In this picture, 迅速上升 means rapidly grow, 上升 means grow, 基本持平 means remain the same, 下降 means decline and 迅速下降 means rapidly decline.

年收入为零 means "no income," 年收入 1.2 万以下 means "below 12,000," 年收入 1.2~3.6 万 means "12,000~36,000," 年收入 3.6~6 万 means "36,000~60,000," 年收入 6 万~12 万 means "60,000~120,000," and 年收入 12 以上 means "above 120,000."

(4) American's Understanding of China

Most interviewees answered "just so-so" and "understand little" when asked this question, which are the same with all income levels. The proportions for the option of "understand little" for different income levels range from 37 to 48% and "just so-so" from 35% to 47%. Only a few of interviewees at every income level think Americans "understand well" and "don't understand at all."

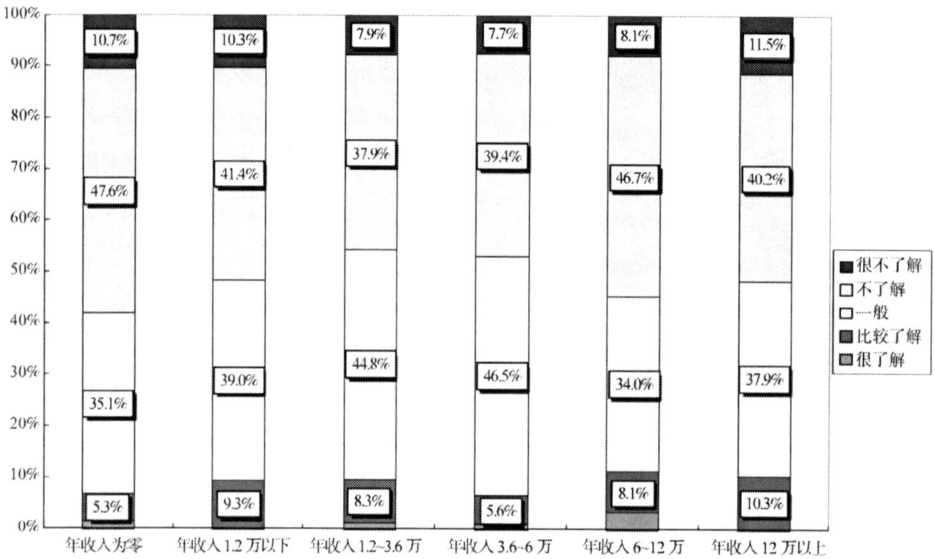

Figure 6-11 How much do you think the average American knows about China?
In this picture, 很不了解 means "don't understand at all."不了解 means "understand little" 一般 means "just so-so," 比较了解 means "understand,"一般 means "just so-so," 很了解 means "well understand," 年收入为零 means "no income," 年收入 1.2 万以下 means "below 12,000," 年收入 1.2~3.6 万 means "12,000~36,000," 年收入 3.6~6 万 means "36,000~60,000," 年收入 6 万~12 万 means "60,000 – 120,000," and 年收入 12 以上 means "above 120,000."

(5) Chinese People's Understanding of America

According to statistics, the income factor does not affect the answers to this question significantly. Most interviewees at every income level, ranging from 46% to 56%, thought that Chinese people have a "just so-so" understanding of America, 24% to 33% interviewees thought Chinese people understand little about America and more than 10% of interviewees at each income level select "understand." Compared to the previous question, we can surmise that interviewees believe Chinese people have a better understanding of America than American's understanding of China.

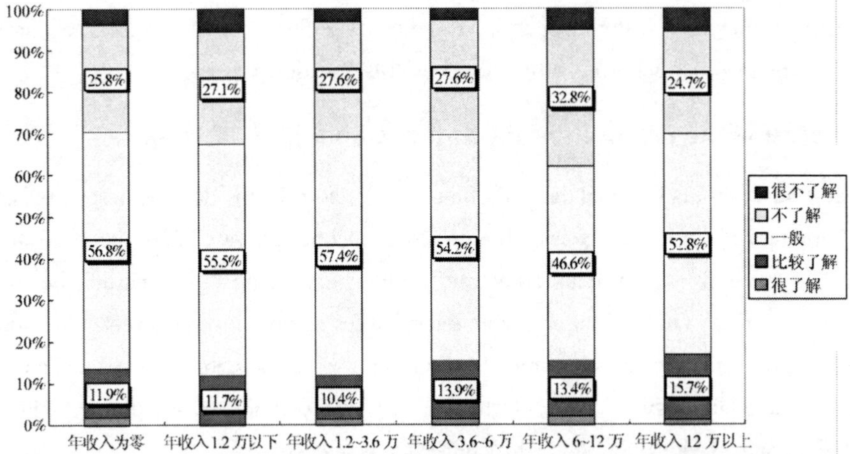

Figure 6-12 How much do you think the average Chinese person knows about the U. S.?

In this picture, 很了解 means "well understand," 比较了解 means "understand," 一般 means "just so-so," 不了解 means "understand little" and 很不了解 means "don't understand at all."

年收入为零 means "no income," 年收入 1.2 万以下 means "below 12,000," 年收入 1.2~3.6 万 means "12,000~36,000," 年收入 3.6~6 万 means "36,000~60,000," 年收入 6 万~12 万 means "60,000~ 120,000," and 年收入 12 以上 means "above 120,000."

(6) General Evaluation of Current China-U. S. Relations

Most interviewees at every level selected "just so-so" to describe the current China-U. S. relations. More than 70% of interviewees with an annual income from 0 to 120,000 yuan chose "just so-so." More interviewees of all income levels choose "good" rather than "bad." Only very few interviewees chose "very bad" or "very good." This

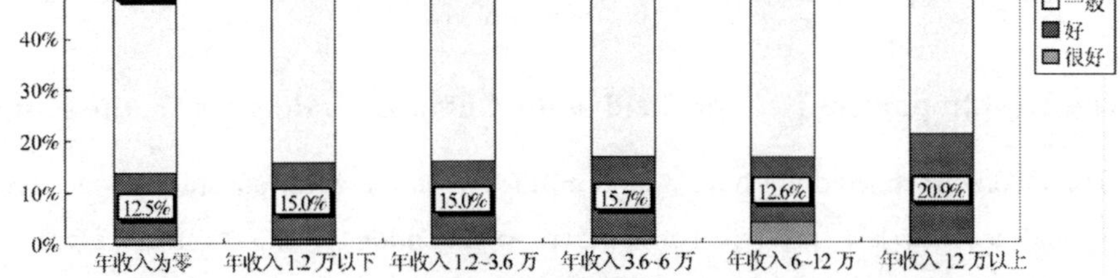

Figure 6-13 How do you view the current China-U. S. relations?

In this picture, 很好 means "very good," 好 means "good," 一般 means "just so-so," 差 means "bad" and 很差 means "very bad."

年收入为零 means "no income," 年收入 1.2 万以下 means "below 12,000," 年收入 1.2~3.6 万 means "12,000~36,000," 年收入 3.6~6 万 means "36,000~60,000," 年收入 6 万~12 万 means "60,000~120,000," and 年收入 12 以上 means "above 120,000."

demonstrates that most interviewees have a neutral opinion on the current China-U. S. relations. The income factor has little impact on this question.

(7) Forecast of the Prospects of the Future China-U. S. Relations

Most interviewees believed that the China-U. S. relations will "develop despite twists and turns." About 9.1% of interviewees with an annual income above 120,000 believed that the China-U. S. relations will develop smoothly, a little higher than the proportion of "neither advance nor retreat." On the contrary, more interviewees in other income levels chose "neither advance nor retreat" than "develop smoothly." Generally speaking, interviewees had a rational attitude towards the development of the China-U. S. relations in the future, with both expectations and consideration of the difficulties and challenges.

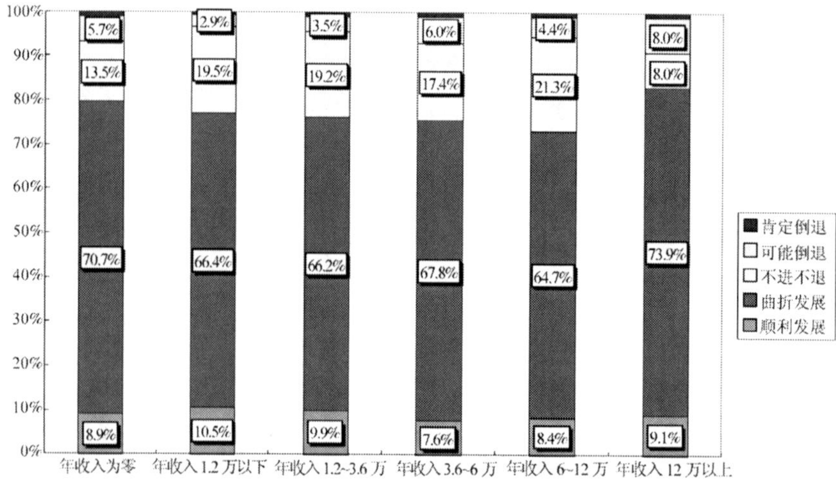

Figure 6-14 What do you think about the prospects of China-U. S. relations?

In this picture, 顺利发展 means "develop smoothly," 曲折发展 means "develop despite twists and turns," 不进不退 means "neither advance nor retreat," 可能倒退 means may regress and 肯定倒退 means "surely regress." 年收入为零 means "no income," 年收入 1.2 万以下 means "below 12,000," 年收入 1.2~3.6 万 means "12,000~36,000," 年收入 3.6~6 万 means "36,000~60,000," 年收入 6 万~12 万 means "60,000~120,000," and 年收入 12 以上 means "above 120,000."

(8) The Most Important Issue or Field in the China-U. S. Relations in the Future

The income factor did not have a large influence on the question. Interviewees with a low annual income less than 12,000 paid more attention to the "Taiwan issue" and "exchange of education, science and culture" in the China-U. S. relations, while interviewees with an annual income between 12,000 and 120,000 attachd more importance to the "energy issue" and "anti-terrorism," and interviewees with an annual income over 120,000 show more concerns to energy. The Taiwan issue was very important for interviewees at every income level, but along with the increase of income, interviewees paid more attention to energy and anti-terrorism.

Table 6-6 What do you think is the most important field or issue in the future China-U. S. relations?

	Annual income below 12,000	Annual income from 12,000~36,000	Annual income from 36,000~60,000	Annual income from 60,000~120,000	Annual income above 120,000	Total	Annual income below 12,000
Taiwan issue	29.8	25.2	23.1	22.1	24.4	14.9	25.1
Exchange of education, science, technology and culture	1.9	3.5	1.1	0.8	0.4	1.1	1.5
Energy	11.4	17.0	20.4	21.1	22.1	19.5	17.5
Anti-terrorism	1.9	2.8	3.2	4.3	3.4	1.1	2.9

(9) HowChina Should Handle the Relations with America

When asked this question, the top three choices for interviewees of every income level were the same: "adhere to principles more," "be more flexible" and "no need to change." Among the interviewees with an annual income over 120,000, the proportion of "adhere to principles more" was 14.7% higher than "be more flexible." This was the most obvious difference among all income groups. However, generally speaking, most interviewees think China shall adhere to principles more in the future China-U. S. relations.

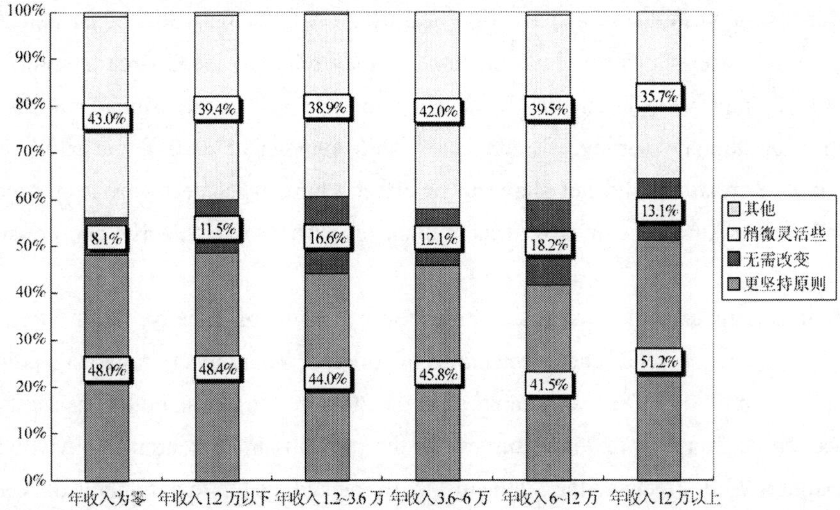

Figure 6-15 How do you think China should handle the relations with the U. S. in the future?
In this picture, 更坚持原则 means "adhere to principles more," 无需改变 means "no need to change," 稍微灵活些 means "be more flexible" and 其它 means "others."
年收入为零 means "no income," 年收入 1.2 万以下 means "below 12,000," 年收入 1.2~3.6 万 means "12,000~36,000," 年收入 3.6~6 万 means "36,000~60,000," 年收入 6 万~12 万 means "60,000~120,000," and 年收入 12 以上 means "above 120,000."

VII. Conclusion

The following conclusions can be reached based on the analysis of the data obtained from the questionnaire.

Chinese fully understand America's international status and influence. As high as 90% of interviewees realized America's influence on international affairs. Correspondingly, more than 90% of Chinese people believed that America's financial crisis has "very great" or "great" impact on world economy, which indicates that Chinese people have highly uniform views on the important status of American economy on the world economy. After all, common people have felt the effect of the global financial storm. Despite the economic recession of America, more than half interviewees believed that America will remain at its current international influence, and even more than 20% people believed America will see a rapid rise or rise in its influence on international affairs.

Though conflicts between China and the U. S. have increased in the previous year, Chinese people's overall impressions of America have not turned negative. According to the investigation, about a half of interviewees have a "just so-so" impression about America, which reflects that Chinese people's impressions about America largely depend on America's behaviors. The result was similar with the previous two investigations. However, the good impressions have significantly grown, reaching 36.1%, far better than the results of the previous two investigations. It may relate to the Obama administration attempting to improve its international image and the relatively steady China-U. S. relations. Since the questionnaire survey was conducted in the summer of 2010, the negative factors in China-U. S. relations did not show up or effect Chinese people's views on America, especially when America emphasized its military presence in West Pacific and pressed on China.

In interviewees' opinions, the White House, Statue of Liberty, Wall Street and Pentagon are the most representative symbols of America. This reflects America's political, economic and military influence. Compared to the 2008 investigation, both consistency and changes can be found in this new survey. In the previous investigation, Hollywood, the White House, Wall Street and the Statue of Liberty ranked the top four symbols of America, and more than half (54.9%) of interviewees selected Hollywood as the most representative symbol. However, only 4.8% interviewees answered Hollywood for this survey, which only ranksranks.

Generally speaking, the Chinese have rational and objective opinions about

China-U. S. relations without any extreme views. About 90% of interviewees realized the importance of China-U. S. relations and most of interviewees had a cautious view on the current China-U. S. relations. A high proportion of 69.5% interviewees evaluated the current China-U. S. relations as "just so-so." 62.7% of interviewees believed that the China-U. S. relations will develop despite difficulties, which reflected the Chinese people's objective attitude towards the current bilateral relations, considering both positive factors and problems in relations. Generally, interviewees had a cautiously optimistic attitude towards the future of the China-U. S. relations. Only 6% of interviewees held the view that the China-U. S. relations "may regress" and "surely regress." Economy and trade, the Taiwan issue and energy were regarded as the most important issues or fields in the future China-U. S. relations, which were similar to the result of the previous investigation, except that the economy and trade issue had exceeded the importance of Taiwan issue in interviewees' opinions. This may relate to the global financial crisis and increasingly fierce conflicts in China-U. S. economic and trade relations, as well as the relatively stable situation of situation across the Taiwan Straits. When asked about how to handle the relations with America, Chinese people showed a divergence in this respect. A large number of people advocated to change the current way in which to deal with the relations with America, with some suggesting "adhere to principles more" (45.9%) and some asking to "be more flexible" (41.3%). Only 12% advocated "no need to change." This reveals that interviewees were not so satisfied with China's policies on America and hoped for changes.

As demonstrated by the investigation, the three channels for Chinese people to obtain information on America were television, internet and newspaper and magazines. The result was similar to the previous two investigations. However, along with the development of the internet, it has shown a momentum of catching up with and even surpassing TV. This means that more and more people get to know the world and America via the internet, as the internet is spreading in China.

Regarding gender, male and female interviewees have no significant difference on the opinions of these questions and even show great similarities. Previously, males had a firmer stand, while females were more flexible in the question of how to handle the relations with America.

Interviewees of different ages did not show a great divergence on most questions. Majority interviewees were optimistic about the prospects of China-U. S. relations, while the elderly had worsening impressions of America and held a stronger stand. The young and middle-aged had a more diversified understanding of America and increasingly recognized America and its influence based on more channels to know and get in touch with America. This subtle difference was also presented in the previous survey result.

People in inland and coastal areas have similar opinions, despite a little difference. Interviewees in the two areas shared similar opinions on most questions. More interviewees in coastal areas regarded Wall Street as the symbol of America, while more interviewees in inland areas considered the Pentagon to be the symbol, which revealed that people in coastal areas attached more importance to economy, while people in inland areas paid more attention to American military. Correspondingly, more interviewees in coastal areas regarded economy and trade as the most important issue or field in the China-U. S. relations, while interviewees in inland areas held different views and most answered "don't know/not clear" or "no response." This reflects that interviewees in inland areas may have less knowledge about America and the China-U. S. relations, or they have other opinions.

The education background directly affects people's views on international issues. According to the analysis of the investigation, college graduates or above and high school graduates or below showed no significant difference. However, college graduates or above had comparatively more consistent opinions with higher consensus, while high school graduates or below had more dispersive views, because people having acquired a higher education have better understanding of the external world and think deeply. This was similar to the result of the last investigation.

Common people of different professions or income levels shared some similar opinions on questions related to America and China-U. S. relations, despite some small differences in specific questions. This is the difference under consensus. For example, professions will affect interviewees' point of view on America and China-U. S. relations, and thus bring differences to their opinions. Comparatively, the education background had a more significant influence on people's opinions than professions and incomes.

To be more precise, factors including age, gender, education background, professions, incomes and areas jointly formed a cross-impact on interviewees' opinions on America and the China-U. S. relations. Therefore, it is difficult to figure out which factor is the most influential.

This book is the result of a co-publication agreement between Social Sciences Academic Press (China) and Paths International Ltd (UK).

China - America Relations: Review and Analysis (Volume 1)
Editor-in-Chief: Ni Feng

ISBN: 978-1-84464-110-9

Lightning Source UK Ltd.
Milton Keynes UK
UKOW010854050412

190214UK00004B/5/P

9 781844 641109